READINGS IN INFANCY

Also Available from Bloomsbury

Jean-Francois Lyotard: The Interviews and Debates, Jean-Francois Lyotard, ed. Kiff Bamford
Libidinal Economy, Jean-Francois Lyotard, trans. Iain Hamilton Grant
Lyotard and Critical Practice, ed. Kiff Bamford and Margret Grebowicz
Sharing Common Ground: A Space for Ethics, Robert Harvey

READINGS IN INFANCY

Jean-François Lyotard

Edited by Robert Harvey and Kiff Bamford

BLOOMSBURY ACADEMIC
LONDON • NEW YORK • OXFORD • NEW DELHI • SYDNEY

BLOOMSBURY ACADEMIC
Bloomsbury Publishing Plc
50 Bedford Square, London, WC1B 3DP, UK
1385 Broadway, New York, NY 10018, USA
29 Earlsfort Terrace, Dublin 2, Ireland

BLOOMSBURY, BLOOMSBURY ACADEMIC and the Diana logo are trademarks of Bloomsbury Publishing Plc

First published in 1991 in France as *Lectures d'enfance* by Éditions Galilée
© Dolorès Lyotard

First published in Great Britain 2023

Copyright © Robert Harvey and Kiff Bamford, 2023

Robert Harvey and Kiff Bamford have asserted their right under the Copyright, Designs and Patents Act, 1988, to be identified as Editors of this work.

For legal purposes the Acknowledgements on p. xiii constitute an extension of this copyright page.

All rights reserved. No part of this publication may be reproduced or transmitted in any form or by any means, electronic or mechanical, including photocopying, recording, or any information storage or retrieval system, without prior permission in writing from the publishers.

Bloomsbury Publishing Plc does not have any control over, or responsibility for, any third-party websites referred to or in this book. All internet addresses given in this book were correct at the time of going to press. The author and publisher regret any inconvenience caused if addresses have changed or sites have ceased to exist, but can accept no responsibility for any such changes.

A catalogue record for this book is available from the British Library.

A catalog record for this book is available from the Library of Congress.

ISBN: HB: 978-1-3501-6735-3
PB: 978-1-3501-6734-6
ePDF: 978-1-3501-6736-0
eBook: 978-1-3501-6737-7

Typeset by Deanta Global Publishing Services, Chennai, India
Printed and bound in Great Britain

To find out more about our authors and books visit www.bloomsbury.com and sign up for our newsletters.

CONTENTS

Foreword by Robert Harvey   vi
Acknowledgments   xiii

Infans   1

Return: Joyce   3

Prescription: Kafka   21

Survivor: Arendt   39

Words: Sartre   61

Disorder: Valéry   75

Voices: Freud   89

Afterword by Kiff Bamford   107

Notes   119
Bibliography   135
Index   159

FOREWORD

Readings in infancy. Here we have them, all together, finally, in one volume, as Lyotard meant them to be. His *Lectures d'enfance*.

What Lyotard readings these are, the straightforwardness of the table of contents is already your preview. Of course, *your* reading of these readings will only deepen that knowledge. We did, however, feel it necessary for one of us to say something at the outset, before you begin, about the words we've chosen to translate a deceptively simple book title.

Infancy, then. Why not childhood? Childhood is, after all, a perfectly valid English equivalent for *enfance*. It was ostensibly to children—actual children—that Lyotard set out to explain the postmodern in 1986.[1] But as the inaugural move in what follows—*Infans*—illuminates, Lyotard in no way means for us to understand that the writers and texts that the six readings consider were writers and texts that he read as a child. Rather, it is *through* them, he claims, that he hears the inarticulate voice of infancy.

What, though, according to Lyotard, *is* infancy?[2] Is it merely that brief period at the beginning of life outside the womb when we have mastered no articulate voice? Lyotard broaches this first question with crystalline density here, in *Infans*. More than just the earliest postpartum months of life during which one is "unable to speak," yet beholden to that condition with respect to the symbolic order, the first law encountered, "*infantia* [. . .] haunts discourse and eludes it" because, as he had written shortly before *Readings in Infancy*, it is "that condition of being affected, when we don't have the means [. . .] to name, identify, reproduce or recognize that which affects us."[3] He would define it with much the same terminology, but much more expansively, in *The Hyphen* (1993): "By infancy, I am referring not simply to an age that is, as the rationalists would have it, lacking in reason. I am speaking of this condition of being *affected* and not having the means—language, representation—to name, identify, reproduce, and recognize what is affecting us. By infancy I mean that we are born before being born to ourselves."[4] We have just taken the liberty of substituting "infancy" for "childhood" for, as is clear, Lyotard means *enfance* to name a *condition*

Foreword

driving a function—inarticulable and intractable—that may operate at any age whatsoever.

We might ask where and when this condition of infancy arose in Lyotard's thought as if to supplant previous guiding principles (such as the condition bearing the oft-misunderstood name of "postmodern"). *Infans*, Lyotard's opening here, was rendered into English by the regretted Mary Lydon—the initial translator, as it happens, of *Discourse, figure* (1971). It was precisely there, in the published version of Lyotard's belated doctoral dissertation, elaborated in the wake of May 68, that we may already detect stirrings of a fundamental function that would eventually take the name *enfance*. "Mai 68 would have been infancy exposed," Miguel Abensour once observed of the effect of those events on Lyotard.[5] For if, as the essays making up *The Inhuman* (1988) illustrate, infancy—which now, in the waning 1980s takes explicit center stage[6]—defies the predations of the human, then too, more than a decade before that, the mute affect that Lyotard named the figural resists and inflects discourse with the same tenacity from the position of "underdog." Both of these forces of resistance are intractable—a Lyotardian notion that particularly intrigued Miguel Abensour.

So also (still with Lyotard in the 1970s) pagan impulses push back against Christianity, just as here, in the pages that follow, when he reads infancy in *Ulysses*, "Jewishness (the Irish condition) produces a cleft or crack in the beautiful vase of the Homeric voyage."[7] This cleft finds an echo in the hyphen Lyotard saw both joining and separating Judaism and Christianity in the wake of Paul's caesarian of the latter from the former.[8] The work of anamnesis involved in the experience of *Nachträglichkeit*—said work and said experience both virtually inarticulable—also traverses Lyotard's oeuvre like an obsession. From "Anamnesis of the Visible" (that Lyotard worked and reworked all the way to his last breath) through "Emma,"[9] affect and wordless memory are preoccupations resulting from the conviction that infancy is an unrecognized redemption of the so-called humanity of our being. All of these lopsided dichotomies exemplify the strength of the weak at work. Declaring baldly that the postmodern is the modern in its infant state is to be in complete conformity with Lyotard's afterthoughts on the postmodern condition.[10] Even Lyotard's richly idiosyncratic reading of Kant's experience of the sublime could be said to work—in comparison to the conventionality associated with the beautiful—as if it were an eternally renewable infancy of judgment.

Pondering Ivan Karamazov's "protracted anthropological lesson on infantile mistreatment through the ages" followed by his "tirade on the

Foreword

innocence of children" in "The Grand Inquisitor" parable, Julia Kristeva affirms that infancy is "the only humanity worth saving."[11] Though Kristeva does not reference Lyotard, this declaration echoes Lyotard's thinking in the late period that concerns us. He asked anyone who would listen to consider not what an individual's infancy is (or was), not one's proto-childhood, not one's history before one is *one*, but rather what power is harbored by that state before a discrete being can subsist and resist in the person one becomes. Infancy is a function—the first function. Infancy is an intensity. Intrinsically affective—even if perhaps also mental—infancy is resolutely *before* consciousness. It is the earliest stage not just of childhood. The advent of language and, thereby, consciousness, while superseding it and harming it as it does, does not, cannot efface it. Infancy is a weak force that lingers in personhood. Speechless, however, it can only inform consciousness, if it does at all, in a state deformed by consciousness.

About the individual readings, I think it would be best—before you read them—if I did little more than suggest some "lines of flight," as Gilles Deleuze, his close colleague and kindred spirit in so many ways, might have said:

1. The phenomenon of return was central to Lyotard's thought from the beginning. As spatio-temporal operator fundamental to psychoanalysis, it was inevitable that someone who, like Jean Laplanche, would see potential for a more complete archaeology of the human in Freud's incomplete intuition of *Nachträglichkeit*, or after-effect. Here, committed as always to sounding literature for its philosophical wealth, Lyotard reads return as the thread binding Bloom, Joyce's Irish-Jewish-urban Odysseus, to Homer's. This abiding meditation on return and what it entails was, however, announced as early as 1972, in Lyotard's communication at a Cerisy symposium on Nietzsche entitled, "Notes sur le retour et le capital" (Notes on the Return and Kapital).[12] "Return" is also the title of §160 in *The Differend*—the section with which Lyotard closes one of the most ominous books of that magnum opus. That book—*Result*—is the one in which Lyotard excoriates Hegelian absolute totalizations and the resulting death-dealing deafness to differends.

2. As to the essay, here, ostensibly about the law in Kafka's *Penal Colony*, Jacques Derrida zeroed in on the importance of the operation named "prescription" in the words he pronounced at

a conference to pay homage to Lyotard and his thought, held in March 1999 at the Collège international de philosophie. Commenting on the phrase "There will be no mourning" that Lyotard inscribed toward the end of his contribution to a special issue of *Revue philosophique de la France et l'étranger* devoted to *his* thought, Derrida claimed that deciding whether the phrase was descriptive or prescriptive was impossible.[13] "Prescription" bears witness to Lyotard's excavation of this undecidability. That had not been the first exchange between the thinker of *différance* and the thinker of the *differend*. *The Faculty of Judgement* appeared in 1985. There, reflecting under the title "Préjugés" on Kafka's parable, *Before the Law*, Derrida challenged Lyotard through what he called "the postmodern signature."[14]

3. In "Survivor" we see evidence, I think, of what I once heard Élisabeth de Fontenay assert about Lyotard: that for a goy (I paraphrase), he was most sensitive and uncannily astute about Judaism and Jewishness, and that, as she stated in an earlier interview, there is a certain "becoming-Jew" to Lyotard.[15] In this regard (and I hope the reader will forgive the telegraphy), when we read in this reflection on Arendt that Hegel solves certain problems with "a 'we' consisting of him (me formerly) *and* me (now)," we are reminded of Lyotard's sustained critique in *The Differend* of presumption embedded in this pronoun by power—a critique that was not lost on Derrida, who in Lyotard and *"Us,"* eulogized Lyotard under the aegis of this very problematic.[16]

4. Lyotard's Sartre essay will perhaps *stick* out more than it stands out. It drips sarcasm and disdain. Steeped in the political implications of Sartre's vast oeuvre, meticulously referenced, it reads as an exercise in vengeance. And it is. More than Lyotard's deep disagreements with that dominant voice of the mid-twentieth century, his lapidary judgments are meant quite specifically to avenge the devastating ad hominem attacks Sartre launched in the early 1950s against Claude Lefort. As such, these "Words" ostensibly in praise of Hollier's book on Sartre are Lyotard's way of saying that *Socialisme ou barbarie* was ultimately right, while the obstinate fellow traveler of the communist party and "father of existentialism" was dead wrong.

5. "Disorder" in many ways anticipates Lyotard's work on André Malraux. Numerous steadfast readers of Lyotard expressed dismay at this apparently unforeseen interest in André Malraux, a novelist whose early antifascist positions and actions mutated into a Gaullism for which the Left never forgave him. The Malraux works that most intrigue Lyotard are his writings on art: a few compact, obscure essays written early and several massive studies published between the end of the Second World War and his death. What Lyotard shared with Malraux was an almost mystical belief, not in some redemptive power in art, but in its capacity to protect a space—against all extrinsic forces—in which innovative politics and ethics can still be thought and invented. It should be remembered that when Lyotard began discussing infancy with Jacob Rogozinski at the Centre Sèvres colloquium in 1987, it was in reference to *What to Paint?*—Lyotard's 1987 book on contemporary painters, Valerio Adami, Shusaku Arakawa, and Daniel Buren. In extremely different voices, employing disparate discursive genres, *Signed, Malraux* (1996) and *Soundproof Room* (1998) both significantly extend Lyotard's meditation on what remains intractable in the human, on what is inhuman in the face of inhumanity—infancy, in other words.

6. *Voix*—a word which, absent an article or adjective, is not obviously singular or plural—was one of the themes proposed for *Épreuves d'écriture* (*Writing Proofs*)—part of *Les Immatériaux*, Lyotard's 1985 exhibit and performance at the Centre Pompidou.[17] As such, the voice, voices or the voices in a voice quickly became a leitmotif in the exchanges between Derrida and Lyotard to which I have already alluded and which would transcend the latter's death in 1998. But the voice—especially the voice articulated in non-linguistic ways or even the voice barely articulated at all—fascinated Lyotard since his earliest writings. A 1973 essay on *Sequenza III*, Luciano Berio's 1965 composition meant for performance featuring the uncanny voice of Cathy Berberian, attests to this preoccupation with the infancy that remains with us vocally.

The potential force in absolute fragility and vulnerability of Lyotard's infancy is legible in more than one contribution to a recent two-volume publication by the Illusio collective on *L'Enfance au temps de l'humanité superflue*.

Foreword

A few, not all, because honestly, this title ought to translate as *Childhood* (not *Infancy*) *in the Era of Superfluous Humanity*. Most of the essays discuss that long formative period of our existence that arguably (legally, sociologically, politically) extends into early adolescence. As in Lyotard, however, a few of them dip into those weeks and months before language, before full initiation into the symbolic, that proto-childhood where a body experiences existence without the words to tell the story of that experience. Thus, Jean Baudrillard explores "The Dark Continent of Infancy," not that of childhood, which is a continent so much like the adult's, and in "From Youth to Infancy," Véronique Fabbri imagines the kind of salutary return by means of anamnesis that Lyotard advocated.[18] Thus also, in Illusio's second volume on the subject, Josep Rafanell i Orra sees infants as *anormaux*, according to Michal Foucault's definition, needing protection, Götz Eisenberg, studies the infant as a "bio-investment," while Augustín García Calvo attempts to answer the question "Que sait un enfant?"—"What does the infant know?"[19] Under Lyotard's conceptualization, the infant—that body whose being is conditioned by its infancy, by pure affect that cannot say its name—knows nothing. Knowledge is of the symbolic: it requires discourse, logos. The infant knows nothing because—so far as we *know*—it is pure affect.

Lectures d'enfance. I'm compelled to return again to comment a bit more on that title. This time, however, to focus on *lectures* rather than *enfance*. Like the latter, the former, too, is covered by two different words in English: it could be readings *or* lectures. It is quite true that all but one of the six essays that you are about to read were originally lectures, or at least exposés or "chats" [*causeries*], as Lyotard qualified the components of *The Inhuman*.[20] It is not, however, their original form or genre that strikes us as we read these reflections, but the speculative intensity, the interpretive verve—the power, in short, of Lyotard's reading in a metaphorical sense—that moves us as we move through these *lectures*.[21] And what about *d'* ? *In* infancy, we cannot even speak, let alone *read*. Infancy, thus, can only be spoken *about*, examined *from outside*, commented *on*, and speculated *about* by a subject of language in language. In this respect, we might just as well have decided that "readings *of* infancy" was as good a rendering or "readings *on* infancy" even fairer. And yet, didn't all of Jean-François Lyotard's philosophical enterprise consist in a protracted wager that the speaking and especially the writing subject both should and can espouse that which he is not or is no longer?; that he must try to engage in readings *in* infancy? Is that not the conviction driving the pathos-laden statement made in §19 of "Voices" that

Foreword

"All writing is this attempt to bear witness, by way of the articulated *lexis*, to the inflexible *phōnē*. Writing has a debt of affect which it despairs of ever being able to pay off."[22]

* * *

The readers of these readings may be sure that we have meticulously checked, harmonized, and revised—sometimes extensively—all translations. Before making the crucial decision as to whether to print "infancy" or, occasionally, opt for "childhood," we've gone case by case. As for the apparatus of notes, we have sleuthed and furnished dozens of page references absent from the original and even some lacking in earlier translations. We have strived to provide explanatory Editors' Notes as judiciously as possible where the English-language reader might miss an allusion or find obscure some name or other. I cannot help but state that since what I enjoy perhaps most and, in any case, without respite is Lyotard's lapidary and paratactic rhetoric, his allusive, ironic, parodic tone, and his irrepressible tongue-in-cheek humor, I just hope you readers will too.

One last word. Having always thought that the enigmatic *a.d.a.d.* at the bottom of *Infans* was code of some intimate nature and Lyotard having told me more than once of his resistance to prefaced interpretations of his work—a preference that I have now disrespected—I shall leave that enigma intact and break off this already lengthy foreword.

Robert Harvey

ACKNOWLEDGMENTS

Our most intensive work occurred after pandemic stay-at-home orders were issued, after which forays into our respective libraries were abruptly curtailed. So, without unfailing aaaaarg.fail, without Seagull Books, the Internet Archive, and the Interlibrary Loan services of Stony Brook University, we would have been up proverbial Shit Creek. Non-corporate persons we must thank are Geoff Bennington, Pascale-Anne Brault, Ed Casey, Thierry de Duve, Corinne Enaudeau, Ruth V. Gross, Philippe Huneman, Dolorès Lyotard, Alistair I. Macdonald, Lilian McCarthy, Roger McKeon, François Noudelmann, Nikos Panou, Florent Perrier, Tony Steinbock, Jean-Michel Rey, Sarah Richmond, Avital Ronell, Nao Sawada, Philippe Scarzella, Laura Silverstein, Lorenzo Simpson, and Adrian van den Hoven.

The editors and publisher gratefully acknowledge the permission granted to reproduce the copyright material in this book.

Infans.

Published as the preface to *Lectures d'enfance*, 9. This translation by Mary Lydon was incorporated into her article "Veduta on *Discours, figure*," *Yale French Studies* 99 (Spring 2001): 10–26.

Minimally revised by the editors for this publication.

Return: Joyce.

Paper delivered at the Eleventh International James Joyce Symposium, Venice, June 1988. Published in *L'Écrit du temps* 19 (Autumn 1988): 3–17 [as "Retour sur le retour," then as "Retour: Joyce" in *Lectures d'enfance*, 11–33. English translation "Return upon the Return" by Robert Harvey and Mark S. Roberts in *Toward the Postmodern*, 192–206. —Eds.]

Revised by the editors for this publication.

Acknowledgments

Prescription: Kafka.

Lecture given at the Franco-German conference organized by the Collège internationale de philosophie in March 1989, on the theme of "Morale et politique;" published in the journal *Rue Descartes*, 1/2, April 1991, 239-54 [as "La Prescription," then as "Prescription: Kafka" in *Lectures d'enfance*, 35-56. English translation "Prescription" by Christopher Fynsk, published in the journal *L'Esprit créateur* 31 no. 1 (Spring 1991): 15-32 and in *Toward the Postmodern*, 176-19. — Eds.]

Revised by the editors for this publication.

Survivor: Arendt.

Lecture given at the Goethe Institute in Paris at a "Hannah Arendt: Politics and Thought" conference organized in April 1988 by the Collège international de philosophie in collaboration with the Goethe Institute and published in *Ontologie et politique. Hannah Arendt* (Paris: Éditions Tierce, 1989): 257-76 [Lyotard's contribution was titled "Le survivant" in this collection which was subsequently republished as *Colloque Hannah Arendt: Politique et pensée* (Paris: Payot, 1996): 371-400. Published as "Survivant: Arendt" in *Lectures d'enfance*, 59-87, English translation "The Survivor" by Robert Harvey and Mark S. Roberts in *Toward the Postmodern*, 144-63. —Eds.]

Revised by the editors for this publication.

Words: Sartre.

First published as "Un Succès de Sartre," *Critique* 432 (February 1983): 177-89 on the publication of Denis Hollier, *Politique de la prose: Jean-Paul Sartre et l'an quarante* (Paris: Gallimard, 1982); [Published as "Mots: Sartre" in *Lectures d'enfance*, 89-106. English translation by Jeffrey Mehlman published as "Foreword: A Success of Sartre's" in Denis Hollier *The Politics of Prose: Essays on Sartre* (Minneapolis: University of Minnesota Press, 1986): xi-xxii, to which the essay was

Acknowledgments

appended as foreword. English translation © 1986 by the University of Minnesota —Eds.]

Revised by the editors for this publication.

Disorder: Valéry.

From a February 2, 1989 workshop organized by the Bibliothèque Populaire at the Centre Georges-Pompidou and the Collège international de philosophie. The "contestants" were Louis Marin, Jacques Poulain, and the author. [The workshop, titled "Ceci est de l'art" was proposed by Thierry de Duve. Lyotard's contribution was published in *Lectures d'enfance* as "Désordre: Valéry," 109–26. A version of this essay, translated by Robert Harvey, appeared in *Toward the Postmodern*, 164–75 under the title, "On What Is 'Art.'" —Eds.]

Revised by the editors for this publication.

Voices: Freud.

Paper delivered to the French Psychoanalytic Association, in Paris, in May 1990, part of the series titled "Case Histories" organized by the committee directed by Michel Gribinski; published under the title *Les voix d'une voix* in the journal *Nouvelle revue de Psychanalyse* 62 (Autumn 1990): 199–215. [Published as *Voix: Freud* in *Lectures d'enfance*, 129–53. English translation reprinted from "Voices of a Voice" by Jean-François Lyotard tr. Georges Van Den Abbeele, 126–45 in *Discourse: Journal for Theoretical Studies in Media and Culture*, 14, no. 1 (Winter 1991–2). © 1991 Wayne State University Press, with the permission of Wayne State University Press. —Eds.]

Revised by the editors for this publication.

Every effort has been made to trace copyright holders and obtain their permission for the use of copyright material. The publisher apologizes for any errors or omissions in the above list and would be grateful if notified of any corrections that should be incorporated in future reprints or editions of this book.

INFANS

Nobody knows how to write. Each one of us, the "greatest" most of all, writes to capture via and in the text something we don't know how to write. Which is not going to let itself be written, we know.

The narratives and essays that the present readings relate travelled along the trail of this poverty, this destitution. Like a frontier, at once inside and outside, the line of disappointment marks out an object for reflection, out there [*là-bas*], and works over the text up close, at the level of its very writing.

The thing that these various writings hold in abeyance, awaiting delivery, bears different names, names of elision. Kafka calls it the indubitable, Sartre the inarticulable. Joyce the inappropriable. For Freud, it is the infantile; for Valéry, disorder; for Arendt, birth.

Let us baptize it *infantia*, that which is not spoken [*qui ne se parle pas*]. An infancy that is not an age and that does not pass, with time. It haunts discourse and eludes it. Discourse never ceases trying to keep it at a distance, it is its separation. But it persists, by the same token, in constituting infancy, constituting it as lost. Unwittingly, discourse therefore harbors infancy: its remnant. If infancy stays at home, it is not in spite of but because of the fact that it lodges with the adult.

Blanchot used to write: *Noli me legere*, you shall not read me. Whatever does not permit itself to be written, in writing, calls perhaps for a reader who no longer knows or does not yet know how to read: old people, children in grade school, driveling, doting [*radotant*] over their open books : *a.d.a.d.*

RETURN
JOYCE

And then coming back was the worst thing you ever did [...]¹

Ulysses

1

How can one be sure that what returns is precisely what had disappeared? Or that what returns not only appears, but is reappearing? Our first gesture would be to challenge reality. What is past is not here, what is here is present. We require a sign—some proof that we are not dreaming—in order to be convinced.

As in a dream, Athena disguises Odysseus as a wandering and miserable old man to make him unrecognizable before he returns to his home in Ithaca.² Argos, the dog who has been waiting for him for twenty years, identifies his master (by his smell, I suppose), while the faithful old nurse, Eurycleia, identifies him by the scar on his thigh. As for Penelope, expert at deluding suitors, she only decides to trust him when he shows that he knows the secret of the conjugal bed's construction.

Indicators—smell, scar, sex—are proofs by the flesh. Only Telemachus takes his father at his word when he says that he is Odysseus. The nominative voice is a sufficient indicator. A son recognizes his father not by his body but by his name.

Several millennia later, here we are, the offspring of the *Odyssey*. We have to believe in the word. Joyce entitled a book *Ulysses*: we are in Ithaca; our father has returned home. From there, Joyce proceeds with his little travel narrative. Confidentially, he will reveal that each of the eighteen sequences of the narrative in fact bears the name of a sequence in the Homeric voyage. An entitled itinerary, the *Odyssey* returns to us in the form of *Ulysses*—or so the work's master assures us.

But how? Some god or goddess has metamorphosed the work to make it unrecognizable. The body of the text bears few indicators that would prove the event of return: no *Odyssey* is perceptible in the *Ulysses* narratives.

As to the name, we sons of Homer cannot trust it. The Greek father's name was *Odysseus*. *Ulysses* is a mere derivative: first from the dialectical Latin, *Olusseus*, and then to the English. The name of the book was deformed by crossing through two cultures, two worlds of names: the Romance world and then classical modern Northern Europe.

Moreover, Joyce's title designates no literary genre, as does the *Odyssey* or the *Aeneid*; these titles designate epic or romanesque cycles. His title indicates nothing of the book's mode of exposition. Some say that this type of title, using the name of the hero, is an old custom (from theater or the novel). But, technically speaking, *Ulysses* is not the name of the book's hero. Rather, it is Bloom, Leopold.

We could say that this is no great transformation: no one is fooled by it. But there is something shifty about it. The title shifts. It does not unravel. It is not a declension of the identity of the *Odyssey*. It evokes it, but in a blurred manner. It makes it equivocal.

Could we say that the journey that Homer traces has served as a model for Joyce and that, at the very least, the *Odyssey* accomplishes a return to *Ulysses* by lending it its compositional structure? We readers, true sons that we are, once in possession of a concordance between Joyce's work and the songs of the Homeric poem, will find it easier to spot the logic of return. But I fear that this ease might also be a trap.

Were we to follow the principle of correspondences, we would never finish counting all the displacements indicating *Ulysses'* divergence from the *Odyssey*. Some of these displacements affect the diegetic universe: namely, reference. Others modify the very story that Homer narrates. And still other displacements (and not the fewest) completely upset the narrative operators lending the *Odyssey* its epic status. I will leave for narratologists the task of counting up these displacements. Their number is such that we would have to wonder how *Ulysses* could ever be recognized as the offspring of the *Odyssey*, especially because the correspondences that we use to designate the episodes in *Ulysses* are only implicit in the text.

Further, the facility that correspondences offer us is an illusory one, for it only reveals to the viewer of classical painting the grid organizing that painting. In the painting, we rediscover the clarity of a *costruzione legittima*, the transparent logic of an ordered spatial and temporal placement. We know, of course, that Joyce employed this ordering not only to make it invisible but also to unravel it in detail, episode after episode. I am reminded here of something of which we are all aware: his proliferation of the most diverse modes of writing, the heterogeneity of genres and styles, something like a quasi-desperate effort to escape the logic of the artwork in order to render the book *inoperative*, to prevent it from closing itself into a beautiful totality. The work's construction only serves as a spur for deconstruction. It is not the logic of space-time that is at stake in *Ulysses*, but its paralogisms—paratopisms, parachronisms. While the beautiful classical form closes in upon itself, concludes, and thus makes its return, and while it *is* in itself the return, it is essential that Joycean writing place the cyclical motif under the rule of its disordering and its inconsistency.

Everything is familiar: times of day, places, people encountered, the most insignificant passerby, animals. The adventure is in the language, its proliferation, its dispersion, in the transgression of its horizons. *Ulysses* is not the story of a return: the hero has never left. He finds himself at once in the position of an immigrant or a ghost or even a wanderer [*métèque*]. Dubliner though he may be, he does not quite qualify for *being* from Dublin, nor does he manage *to be there*. He does not return: he errs; he is a *flâneur*. He suffers from a breakdown of presence. Each *now* evokes a *once upon a time* or another time; each *here* evokes a *there*. It is an intermediate state—half awake, half asleep—which can be likened to the reverie of a solitary walker. Everything that is perceived, well-known, too well-known, gives rise to an evocation, to an attentiveness, to a call from elsewhere. Thus, Dublin becomes a mere reserve, a depository of day's residues of which the *flâneur*'s daydreaming constitutes itself in order to free him from that city. T. S. Eliot said of Bloom that he "says nothing." In such a "*silent monologue*"[3] all the inner voices call out to each other oblivious to orchestration—a concert that will become the artwork or the subject.

If the *Odyssey* returns in *Ulysses*, it is in its absence. Ulysses wanders around Ithaca, a place inhabited by its people but deserted—peopled with phantoms. At home, he is not at home. Of King Hamlet, the father's ghost, Dedalus says (in the library episode), that his "speech (his lean unlovely English) is always turned elsewhere, backward."[4] His house is no longer his *oikos*. Thus, Hamlet shifts and thus *Ulysses* shifts its gaze toward the *Odyssey*. Hamlet only alluded to the beautiful protective abode and concludes his cycle only in order to direct his speech "elsewhere, backward," according to a space that is not there and a time that is not present.

2

The fact that Ulysses is called "Bloom" is a serious claim to paratopia and to parachronia, to the spatio-temporal breakdown that afflicts the ghost. It is a flagrant trace of the displacement that *Ulysses* imposes upon the *Odyssey* in order to recall it. Bloom the wanderer [*métèque*] par excellence, the converted Jew. A tradition of life and of thought evades the Greek *epos* by a type of being-toward-being that comes from "elsewhere" and from behind, and that is itself largely denied. This is a Ulysses who would shift, through today's Ithaca, toward the land of Canaan and toward a protohistory, without, for all that, returning. The interpolation of the Jewish theme into the Homeric motif, of which there are many occurrences in the Joycean text, should be examined under the title of the return. I will outline some of the characteristics of such an examination.

First, we should recall the parallel suggested by Erich Auerbach, in the first chapter of *Mimesis* (entitled "Odysseus' Scar") between the Homeric and the biblical scenes.[5]

At each instant and in every place, the Greek hero *is* entirely and expressly his role—the one that legend imposes on him. He saturates the situation with his own presence in such a way that he fulfills his destiny, fills it to completion. He is devoid of sentimentality, by which I mean he has none of the depth, the individual historicity, the unexpected, the "backward," the "elsewhere" that we moderns attach to affectivity, to the capacity to be affected.

The bard leaves no emotions, situations, or motifs in the shadows, none in reserve. Prosody, the recurrence of stereotypes, and ornamental description render states of the soul and states of fact equally visible. This clarity makes it possible to readily identify voices, references, intentions, and dramatic relations. On the stage thus overexposed, the protagonists are like pure *actants* by which Homeric poetics renders semiotics transparent.

"Homeric style knows only a foreground," writes Auerbach, where the recounting of events unravels a "uniformly illuminated, uniformly objective present," generating a world that "contains nothing but itself." Auerbach points out that "Homeric poems conceal nothing, they contain no teaching and no secret second meaning."[6] They leave no room for interpretation.

To himself as to us, Odysseus is none other than the ever-exposed identity of his role, of his "character." Specifically, he never ages. Athena must disguise him, twenty years after his departure, in order that he be unrecognizable. "Odysseus on his return," notes Auerbach, "is exactly the same as he was when he left Ithaca two decades earlier."[7] His return would provide an example of perfectly identical recurrence, except for the entirely circumstantial modification that the goddess imposes on him.

We moderns, sons of Ulysses, cannot believe that an expedition, an exile, experience in general would not imply some sort of alteration or alienation. Travel stories, *Bildungsromane*, Hegel's *Phenomenology of Spirit*—all odysseys of consciousness—accustom us to thinking that the spirit only conquers its substance and its final identity, its self-knowledge, by exposing itself to the risky adventure of all its possibilities. We think of the return not as recovered identity of the same with the same, but as the self-identification of the same with the "surveying" [*relève*] of its alterity. At the end of the voyage, the truth of Odysseus for us, is not the same as it was at the moment of departure: the voyage *is* that truth. The truth is in the method, as Hegel said, and the method—the passage through mediations and changes—is in no way extrinsic to self-knowledge (as Athena's metamorphosis of Odysseus is): it *is* this knowledge.

This amounts to saying that with modernity, what is true ceases to be a place, a dwelling—*domus* or *oikos*—from which some unessential circumstance (external war, the Trojan War) dislodges the master from the house: a place whose ownership could be restored by mere cleaning (massacring suitors, hanging unfaithful servants, and washing the floor)—a propriety that includes the nuptial bed, still resting on its olive stump, the token of an ineradicable reference.

In this regard, modernity owes the interiorization of war to Christianity. The return to peace in the house is prevented by an initial exile that drove us out and keeps us from returning. This exile is caused by an altogether internal transgression for which only expiation, the accepted suffering of exile—that is, sacrifice—can bring reparation and allow the return to innocence. The theme of self-sacrifice, of which Christ is the paradigm, subtends the speculative motif of an experience conceived as death and resurrection of the spirit.

Helen's beauty assuredly spreads disorder in Greek houses. Yet that beauty only gives rise to a distant war. Under the name of Eve, woman incarnates the primal figure of sin, the eternal source of the secret war that prohibits the spirit from returning to the house of the father. Yet, in the Christian *geste*,[8] the power of the "surveying" is such that Mary Magdalene, the evil Eve, attends the son in this agony. And thus the prostitute is redeemed. When that pagan-Christian and very Catholic Claudel reads the Homeric *nostos*, he makes sure that Penelope is the symbol of the end of this inner war. In his eyes, the olive tree of the conjugal bed, what he calls the "mediator between substance and heaven,"[9] is the figuration of the flesh's redemption and the true return.

Readings in Infancy

I am amazed that occasionally some commentator places Molly Bloom and her final "Yes yes" under this pagan-Christian motif of the Virtuous Mother and of shelter regained. Claudel, who was more clear-sighted, returned to Joyce his signed copy of *Ulysses*, labeling it "diabolical." It doesn't matter that Bloom was baptized three times (the same number of times that Peter renounced Jesus), the sacrificial and redemptive dialectic celebrated in the cemetery and the church that he visits remains foreign to him. And we well know that, for Joyce, Rome, every bit as much as London, was the name of Ireland's oppressor.

If there is return in *Ulysses*, that return is no more Christian than it is Greek. I return to Auerbach's parallel. He notes that the text of the Old Testament is a juxtaposition of little stories. Their conjunction requires no more than the "and" that lends order to paratactical time, without distinction between main stories and subordinate ones. These stories touch upon the most ordinary aspects of life. Far from being heroes, the protagonists are petty tribal chiefs or heads of families, shepherds threatened by scarcity, displaced here and there by migrations and by wars in the vast Orient. These brief narrations pass over anything having to do with the decor where the scene unfolds: no descriptions, not even ornamental ones, of persons or sites—just names. Hardly a word is exchanged. The injunctions, the entreaties, the decisions all appear briefly, leaving motives and arguments in obscurity. As in Beckett's theater, silence and a certain indetermination suggest that something is at stake that no one, actor or reader, identifies.

Homeric gods deliberate in council and then go out in person to support their protégés while they carry out the plan of strategy imparted to them. Unique and invisible, Yahweh (like Godot) forces, prohibits, promises, makes himself heard without explaining his goals—all this to a people that he holds hostage. "In the Old Testament stories the peace of daily life in the house, in the fields, and among the flocks, is undermined by jealousy over election and the promise of a blessing [. . .]."[10]

Auerbach concludes two things concerning this altogether different scenography. On the one hand, it opens onto a demand for realism, a concern for the concrete fact, an exactness stripped of all epic amplification in which he believes the rules of historiography have their source. On the other hand, the enigma surrounding the logic of episodes requires a ceaseless, perhaps interminable, effort at interpretation on the part of the reader or member of the audience—an effort that will engender hermeneutics.

I recall these few observations from Auerbach not because I subscribe to them, nor to discuss them, but because they explain the extent to which the interpolation of the Jewish motif into the return of the Homeric *epos* displaces it. The details of the demonstration need not be reviewed: impenetrability of motifs; attention to the most everyday detail, examined as if under the microscope; the solitude of characters; the difficulty of attributing to individuals the voices as they gossip, discuss, or "monologue"; ruptures in narrative rhythm; propagation of discursive genres and tones . . . while all of this does not derive from biblical writing alone, none of it belongs to the epic tradition.

Even though polymorphous or metamorphous prose, for example, must be attributed to the modern decomposition of literary languages, and therefore derives only indirectly from biblical writing, it must nonetheless be linked to it. For this labor of writing inscribes itself in an aesthetic or a counter-aesthetic (an an-aesthetic) of the sublime, which, since Longinus, through the Quarrel of the Ancients and the Moderns and Romanticism, has relentlessly assaulted signifying syntheses. This an-aesthetic not only assaults the rules that establish classical framing (notably spatio-temporal framing) and genres but also assaults the deeper cultural, ideological, and perhaps even ontological syntheses that fix the signifier (scriptural, pictural, and others) into syntactic and semantic groups ranging from the local trope or figure to the broadest finalities on manners of writing (or painting, etc.). These are the very syntheses that, again and again in ages past, lent their signifying value to the signifier as well as foundation and authority first to poetics and later to the aesthetics of the beautiful.

Now, this anti-synthetic work I have in mind, this work that strives to match the failure of representation to which the feeling of the sublime attests, has distant sources in the biblical text. Longinus, in his *Treatise*, points to this, but still confusedly. It comes to light, however, following Boileau (and notably in the French debate) on the subject of religious eloquence. Recourse to the *"je ne sais quoi"* creates at least the effect of intervention in order to confound "grand style," the "foreground" style, the Greek ideal of beauty, and the Roman ideal of eloquence. It opens a breach in the classical wholeness constituted of gods, men, and nature. Through this breach, one begins to perceive a non-world, a desert where a voice calls out in peremptory fashion, saying nothing more than, "Listen."

By the time Joyce wrote *Ulysses*, artists and writers knew (in divergent ways to be sure) that in a very broad sense the stakes of writing are (as they have always been, but now explicitly) not to create beauty, but rather to bear witness to a possibility to that voice that, within man, exceeds man, nature, and their classical concordance.

The aesthetics of a Baudelaire or a Flaubert already prove this. Everything, down to the motif of the city so predominant in *Ulysses*, belongs to the new stakes of writing. It is not enough to consider Bloom as a historian or a sociologist, as the literary counterpart of urbanization in progress. He is also and especially, I believe (with Benjamin), the return of solitude, of the desert, and of inoperativity [*désœuvrement*] at the heart of the community. The modern city is the operativity [*œuvre*] in the bosom of which the community and the individual are deprived of their artwork [*œuvre*] by the hegemony of market value. Far from being a free city, Joyce's Dublin is, to use Jean-Luc Nancy's words, an inoperative community [*une communauté désœuvrée*].[11] Bloom, the ad salesman, is witness to this painful futility. But rather than some officially sanctioned witnessing, it is the mere muffled mumbling of phrases free-associating "inside" when no one is speaking to you, when you're in the desert. Nor, further, must Joyce be allowed to constitute a work out of Bloom's witnessing. He can only bear witness to the fact that witnessing does not constitute a work—that witnessing is not Greek. *Ulysses* is one of the greatest works devoted to, consecrated to, inoperativity. The *Odyssey*'s framework returns in it only to be deconstructed and to leave room for the void of interpellation.

Witness the "Aeolus" episode: "We were always loyal to lost causes, professor [MacHugh] said [in the offices of the *Evening Telegraph*]. Success for us is the death of the intellect and of the imagination."[12] The name of this death is England: under its domination, Ireland is doomed not only to palpable misery but also to the same radical inoperativity as Israel in Egypt. At the college historical society, where assimilation has just been advocated, John F. Taylor explains that it is, on the contrary, by preserving and observing the tables of the Law "graven," he says, "in the language of the outlaw," by refusing the law of the empire, that the Irish people will, as the Jewish people had done before, succeed in escaping "their house of bondage."[13]

I do not claim that *Ulysses* is the book of the Law and the exodus. It is simply written in the writing of the outlaws that were Joseph's sons in Egypt and Parnell's sons in Ireland. In a bastardized [*météquisée*] Ireland on the flank of the empire; Bloom, the wanderer [*métèque*], is more Irish than the Irish. Being suspicious of his people, Moses looked askance at a people subservient to the idolatry of the false Roman god and to the interests of British power. But Parnell failed to deliver this people. And Bloom, a bad Jew and an ordinary Irishman, is incapable of holy anger. The only thing left in him of Moses' call to rise and leave is a disavowal of what is here, indignity at ordinary life, a cowardly concession of the soul to derisive reality.

"And yet [Moses] died without having entered the land of promise," says J. J. O'Molloy in the same episode. To which Lenehan adds, "And with a great future behind him."¹⁴ The exodus is perhaps a return. It is at least the promise of a return. But this promise remains, and must remain, held as a promise: never realized. Moses, Parnell: dying before fulfillment. The return's future remains hidden in the promise made long ago. The paradox of all ages is what structures the work of an anamnesis: what was announced in the past was that there would be a future to attest to it. Writing is this work of bearing witness to a presence that is not the "foreground" present. Once and for all, presence will have been promised; writing is devoted to not forgetting it.

Speaking to himself in the "Lestrygonians" episode, Bloom says: "Can't bring back time. Like holding water in your hand. Would you go back to then? Just beginning then. Would you? Are you not happy in your home you poor little naughty boy?"¹⁵ The enticing, vulgar interpellation comes from a woman's voice: the quote from a letter Bloom found at the *poste restante* from a correspondent, Martha, answering an obscene solicitation he had sent under the pseudonym, Henry Fleury.

Thus, two things find expression in the lowest of languages and feelings: the sorrow of captivity in Egypt and the misery of a false flight that would be no more than a repetition of the flight Bloom carried out in Molly's company and upon her person. Martha, Molly, the sirens, Bella, Zoe, Flora, Kitty, the girls on the beach—women never assist in the flight from Egypt: they *are* Egypt. Being unhappy at home means being unhappy at *their* home. One must not want or even hope to "repossess" this home of one's own, that is, to return to it. *Home* is not what was promised.¹⁶ Bloom will never again find Penelope. He will lay down, head to toe at her side (the Beckettian position).¹⁷ And he is not the one to whom she will say "yes yes."

There you go, pell-mell, and merely hinted at, these are some indicators for following the cleft or the crack that Jewishness (the Irish condition) produces in the beautiful vase of the Homeric voyage.

3

I should address the question of fatherhood [*paternité*] insofar as it affects the motif of the return in *Ulysses*. The question of fatherhood or lineage is also that of authority, or of the author, or, as we say, of creation. Under the title of lineage, Joyce lays out his poetics.

I will restrict myself to three observations, all of which concern the motif of return: To begin with, lineage conforms to the general principle of reversibility. The father is also son of his son, as the son is father of his father. They engender one another. We could say that they are the same individual, self-engendered.

This does not seem to be the case for the *Odyssey*. We do, however, find a trace of this principle in a fact well known to scholars. The "Telemachy" is an addition to Odysseus's voyage, placed prior to it in the narrative order. To complete this collage, Telemachus, who leaves for Ithaca in Song 4, only arrives there in Song 15, just shortly before his father. The son's adventures are like a pre-image of his father's.

Joyce respects this disposition in the composition of *Ulysses*. When Dedalus first meets Bloom at the brothel, only in the fifteenth episode, the question to be posed is whether, when this return of the son to the father and of the father to the son occurs, the father recognizes himself in the son, as if he were himself the son, and vice-versa. This is apparently the case in the Odyssey.

In *Ulysses*, the encounter, as we know, concludes with a separation. I would even venture to say that it begins with this separation. In the end, Bloom settles back into his home, while Dedalus leaves it. The lineage appears shattered, impossible. The son does not re-create his father. But it is precisely by this failure of identification that the true principle of generation is made clear. The authentic lineage requires the rupture, the interruption of the link between father and son.

Let me address the mise-en-scène of this rupture. In the Ithaca episode, Dedalus has just refused Bloom's hospitality, and they leave together, saying goodbye.[18] Bloom heads off first with his candle, followed by Dedalus, diaconal hat on his head and augur's rod of ash in hand (two props of the exodus introduced in the third episode, "Proteus").[19] Question: "With what intonation *secreto* of what commemorative psalm?" Answer: "The 113th, *modus peregrinus: In exitu Israel de Egypto: domus Jacob de populo Barbaro*."[20] Commemoration, secret, peregrination or pilgrimage, exodus—this text is that of the Vulgate Bible. In the protestant Bible and the Torah,[21] the rabbinical translation of Psalm 114 reads: "When Israel came out of Egypt, / the House of Jacob from a people of strange speech."[22]

Note, obviously, the resurgence of the "Jewish" theme at the precise moment of non-return. If the son rejects the father, the father also persists in returning toward the flesh of his house, toward his wife and carnal generation, that is, toward the Egypt of representations.

Return

I refer to only two indicators of this movement in the second part of Bloom's journey: to the fact that his meeting with Dedalus alters the figure of the father and that it renders it alien to the son.

At the moment that Dedalus finds Bloom, in the brothel, Bloom is in the process of reclaiming the potato (Irish misery, once more) from Zoe. He carries this potato in his pocket and had given it to her upon entering, like a fetish. He reclaims it in these terms: "It is nothing, but still, a relic of poor mamma [. . .]. There is a memory attached to it. I should like to have it." To which Stephen replies: "To have or not to have that is the question."[23]

To possess the memory of the wife and the house, to have it back. The son comes upon the father engaged in the imaginary dimension of this return—that of nostalgia. The scene of domestic jouissance and its appropriation, where this movement is completed, unfolds sumptuously in the Ithacan episode. The lady daydreams upstairs in the tepidness of intimate flesh and underwear. Downstairs, in the kitchen, her husband totes up all the petty modern (or postmodern) interests of a semi-skilled worker: puttering, minor patents, astronomy-made-easy, subway eroticism, playing the horses, moonlighting to supplement the budget, gardening, obtaining credit, seeking petty distinction. Already in the "Eumaeus" episode, we are reminded that Parnell has failed to free Ireland because of a woman. Flesh and incarnation, by their furor, cause writing and exodus to fail as soon as they offer themselves. Once one is satisfied, exaltation fails also, because it requires accounting. These are two meanings of the French word "jouissance." We also learn that Bloom has been thrice baptized: Protestant, English, and Egyptian.

A complementary indicator of the necessary separation between father and son can be found on the other side, in the son's story. From the beginning of the Telemachy, Dedalus is en route for, or rather, is rehashing, an irremissible inner exodus. I only mention one example of thousands of this distancing within apparent presence. Dedalus has sent Mulligan, whom he has just left, a telegram. Mulligan reads it aloud joyfully in front of the library debating club, which Dedalus himself has just met up with ("Scylla and Charybdis"): "*The sentimentalist is he who would enjoy without incurring the immense debtorship for a thing done.* Signed: Dedalus."[24] Literally: he who would take enjoyment [*jouir*] while shirking the endless debt incurred by the deed done.

This inscription from afar, this telegraphy (Does "Telemachus" mean "the end of battle" or "battle at a distance"?) recalls the indignity of all sentimentality: getting something for nothing. To assume that one is free from debt because one has paid the "returned" object through jouissance. But the debt is enormous, prohibiting the completion of this return that is jouissance. Through this, the flow of "sentimentality" that inundates Bloom, having returned from Ithaca, finds itself distanced.

A second observation. The thesis of fatherhood or true lineage is expounded, in this same library and primarily through Stephen's words, regarding the case of Shakespeare's identification with Hamlet. Elsinore is a failed Ithaca. The suitor has conquered Penelope, and Ulysses (the king) has been murdered. Penelope has been unfaithful like Helen. The father can only return to the son in absence, through his voice, which recalls the debt. You must revenge me, reestablish me, that is, engender me anew. Dedalus holds (without sustaining it) the thesis that Shakespeare was this absent, humiliated, cuckolded father, that he always played the dead king at the Globe, and that his wife, Anne, was, like the queen, a whore, a Molly.

In the end, there is no consubstantial fatherhood, except in the mystical sense that is also the highest degree of uncertainty concerning lineage. "Fatherhood, in the sense of conscious begetting, is unknown to man."[25] And further, "in the economy of heaven, foretold by Hamlet, there are no more marriages, glorified man, an androgynous angel, being a wife unto himself."[26] In the domestic economy, incest rages along all lines of kinship, except the father-son lineage. "They are sundered by a bodily shame [. . .]. What links them in nature? An instant of blind rut."[27] What links them separates them: the compulsion to copulate, woman, the "agenbite of inwit."

> Fatherhood [. . .] is a mystical estate, an apostolic succession, from only begetter to only begotten. On that mystery and not on the madonna which the cunning Italian intellect flung to the mob of Europe the church is founded and founded irremovably because founded, like the world, macro and microcosm, upon the void. Upon incertitude, upon unlikelihood. [. . .] Paternity may be a legal fiction.[28]

Lineage, or more precisely, true paternization,[29] is only the transmission of what I have called the calling. There is no carnal lineage between males: the feminine house is useless, even harmful to it. At Shakespeare's birth, "[a] star, a daystar, a firedrake, rose."[30] It is the star William follows upon leaving Stratford and the "arms" of his future. "A star by night, Stephen said. A pillar of the cloud by day."[31] Once again the theme of the wandering Jew. Shakespeare answers the call that comes to him from the desert. In fleeing from the incestuous and lascivious mother, Egypt, he also flees from the pretenders to carnal fatherhood. One leaves *here*, one goes over there, elsewhere, backward, toward the true past that is still to come.

A final remark on the question of paternity as return—unfulfilled return. What is said of the father and son must also be understood with regard to the writer and his reader. The reader engenders the author, and the author is the reader of his reader. But there again, a flesh interposes itself between them and impedes a pure genealogy: this flesh is language, the whore that language is. It can represent everything, say everything, and love everything. It is the Egypt of writing.

Language is like water, a kind of great profligate carnal sea that offers itself to everything, infiltrates everywhere, redoubles and represents everything. Writing (Joyce's), plunged in this water, tries to defer the effect of representation and ductility, to hold back the insidious tide. In the catechism recited at Ithaca, Bloom's elegy to water takes on the dimension of an inundation. Bloom surrenders himself to the immersion. But he is careful not to inform Stephen of his adoration and his drowning. The reason: "The incompatibility of aquacity with the erratic originality of genius."[32]

One must necessarily give in to language when one writes, but one cannot give in to it either. The defeat, which consists in the trust one puts into language, must necessarily be continuously defeated in its turn; the trust must remain suspended. "I believe, O Lord, help my unbelief. That is, help me to believe or help me to unbelieve? Who helps to believe? *"Egomen.* Who to unbelieve? Other chap."[33] What says *yes* to the permanent *yes* of woman-language is the Ego. As for the "other chap" (who tells him *no*, no, that's not it, you haven't got it, arise and leave), I hear in him the shattering voice that calls. ("To chap" is also "to split," "to cleave." And a "chap" is a "peddler," the traveling salesman.)

Literary genealogy responds to the same demand and runs into the same aporia as lineage. How, if one writes, is it possible not to say *yes* to the sea of language? Genius consists in inscribing within it what it cannot espouse. One thing that cannot be done with water is to part it. Joyce-Dedalus lacerates language. It closes up again immediately under his flamboyant style.

4.

I return to the catechism of the Ithaca episode. Question: "For what creature was the door of egress a door of ingress?" Answer: "For a cat."[34]

This is thus a final return, accompanied by this pussy-cat [*chatte*], a return upon and of sexual difference. An argumentative genre.

On the one hand, since the father is son of the son and the son father of the father, *male* is what engenders itself without sexual intercourse. Or, rather, engenders itself, in truth, according to the voice, only that which is male. From oneself, solely in obedience to the injunction issuing from nothing (fire and storm cloud) to listen—to write, that is. With regard to carnal paternity, the Holy One, blessed be He, can very well pull some Isaac from the withered belly of an old woman and make of him a gift to his old man. But there will nonetheless come a day when the voice will come to reclaim him, if not by sacrifice, at least by *aqedat*, by binding or alliance. This is a warning that males, the Ulysses and the Abrahams, would be mistaken to expect any revenue from what their wives claim to offer them. Bloom has lost his son Rudy. And Stephen has rebuffed the final wishes of his dying mother. Sexual generation is only the occasion for sin, for forgetting memory's debt. Remembering that nothing returns, that everything comes to be. This is what anamnesis means: a thinking back—back upstream—a return of which the work of writing consists. And this is endless. A peregrination without coming back.

But, on the other hand, there is the pussy-cat [*chatte*] (it is, as we know, a term of endearment the French give to the female sexual organ), which is the passage through which the father enters and out of which emerges his son. The pussy objects that it is, in the male-to-male lineage, the obligatory threshold, the inevitable path for the transmission of the seed. It argues that if the Lord has created us sexed, sectioned, and separated, and if he holds the power to reunite us according to the fire in our loins, it is not only to test us but also to expose the mystery of his ways. In particular, that the self-engenderment, of which sexuality is the sole heavenly guardian, resides (oh so palpably!) *ad portas mulieris*.

We see the argument. It is that of the Virgin Mother and the prostituted saint.

Now, what relation can this *disputatio* on sex have with the return and the return upon the return? That relation in which the things are not properly ordered: first, the adequation of the father-son, of voice and writing; second, the passage through the woman, the feminine passage, the concession and jouissance. No, it is the contrary, or, rather, not even the contrary: it is not even the same order returned on the same timeline, it is the initial definitive disorganization of that so-called timeline, which is only time consciousness.

Return

The question *Ulysses* poses in return is not even whether one can step twice in the same stream, which is a pardonable uneasiness of consciousness faced with chronological succession (that succession-forcing consciousness to forever defer its actualization, so that it must always catch up with itself, so that it must hold back at every step of its advance along the timeline). *Ulysses* poses another question altogether: Is not sexual difference the same as ontological difference? Is it not from sexual difference that the temporalizing separation of consciousness with itself is engendered? And from it that the unconscious as extra-memorial past is formed?—a past that does not last as past and that one cannot have back. Inappropriable. Is it not this immemorial that calls out? And is it not writing that attempts, desperately, to formulate an answer to this remainder to which the soul is held hostage?

Objection: Why would sexual difference occupy this eminent position in engendering when it has been established that, according to Joyce-Dedalus, true generation, fecundity, and propagation owe nothing to it and that it is carried out in the father-son identity?

Answer: It is readily demonstrable that the idea of male self-engendering—autochthony of warriors in the Greek version, the voice's injunction ("call") in the Hebrew version—only betrays (translates and disguises) the irreparable preeminence of sexual difference.

Argument: Homeric males go off to war to seek an unfaithful woman and Odysseus would simply have no need to return had he not taken part in this expedition. By this consecution, and also because the whore lies dormant in the matron, Helen takes precedence over Penelope. As for the Jews, their book recounts the fact that original sin—the offense of claiming to equal and substitute divine transcendence, for the voice—is the doing of a woman. By this consecution, and here because the she-devil lies awake in the wife, Eve takes precedence over Sarah. As proof, the laughter that overcomes the old woman when her belated pregnancy is announced: this is the same offense that Eve committed against the Lord. Another name for Israel is "he will laugh."

Concession: To be sure, this return that is the *Odyssey* attempts to form the scar of difference, and this exodus that the Pentateuch recounts attempts to free itself from it.

Conclusion: Both attempts bear within them the admission of an initial and recurrent servitude. This is why an originary position, before any mediation, as perennial source, must be granted to sexual difference. It is not because Joyce is overly obsessed, obeying some realist scruple or bent on shocking us, that there is so much sex in *Ulysses*. Rather, it is because the writing of Homeric return—even returned via the biblical exodus—cannot fail to come up against that difference, that more ancient, intimate obstacle that is opposed to return, to crash into it and ceaselessly return to it.

In returning upon and against the event of sexual difference—a difference that has no site, no representation, one that engenders uncontrollable anxiety—in reinscribing this event in language, whose ductile force ceaselessly immerses this anxiety and impotence, Joyce's writing announces the offense's irreparability and the return's impossibility. The writer can only bear witness to its remanence at the level of language. For it is not enough to take this anxiety linked to the irremissible hidden separation as the object of a discourse (as I myself am doing here). To truly bear witness to it, one must *anguish language*.

There is an eternal undoing of the spirit. We cannot avenge it. By avenging it, we repeat it, as Hamlet does. It is not situated in a temporality of successions. This anxiety, this obsession for pleasure and this horror, always begins again. This is what supports parataxis, the return of AND; this is what interferes with any return.

I shall end. Dedalus presents Shakespeare's initial undoing in these terms:

> Belief in himself has been untimely killed. He was overborne in a cornfield first (a ryefield, I should say) and he will never be a victor in his own eyes after nor play victoriously the game of laugh and lie down. Assumed dongiovannism will not save him. No later undoing will undo the first undoing. The tusk of the boar has wounded him there where love lies ableeding. If the shrew is worsted yet there remains to her woman's invisible weapon. There is, I feel in the words, some goad of the flesh driving him into a new passion, a darker shadow of the first, darkening even his own understanding of himself. A like fate awaits him and the two rages commingle in a whirlpool. [. . .] The soul has been before stricken mortally, a poison poured in the porch of a sleeping ear.[35]

Stephen slips this message to King Hamlet: "The poisoning and the beast with two backs that urged it King Hamlet's ghost could not know of were he not endowed with knowledge by his creator."[36]

Suppose now that the creator tells us nothing of the poisoning and that it takes us an entire lifetime to learn that we were not so much murdered as engendered by this poisoning of the flesh. Because the creator is not. Or at least does not speak, the voice having fallen silent.

It is then that Dedalus adds these words that will have served to return me upon the return, to return it and to attempt (with Joyce) to turn myself away from it: "That is why the speech [Hamlet's, Shakespeare's, Joyce's] is always turned elsewhere, backward."[37] Words that Dedalus comments upon as follows: "Ravisher and ravished, what he would but would not"; in other words, the very designation of the work of inoperativity.[38] With this one last joke: "He goes back, weary of the creation he has piled up to hide him from himself, an old dog licking an old sore. But, because loss is his gain, he passes on towards eternity in undiminished personality."[39] *Dog* is the returned truth of *God*, yet no writing can prevent *Dog* from returning, in its turn, into *God*. Return, nonetheless, of inoperativity. Amen.

PRESCRIPTION
KAFKA

In the Penal Colony will serve as a pretext for exhibiting some of the meanings of the Latin *praescribere*: to write (a name, a title, and so on) at the head of something, to prescribe or appoint, and, in a later form of Latin, to trace an outline in advance, to sketch out. There is also, of course, the meaning of the lower Latin, *praescriptio*, a "limitation," from which derives "prescription" in the French Civil Code, and which designates "the means of acquiring or of freeing oneself, through a certain passage of time, and under the conditions determined by the law."[1] The English "prescription" embraces nearly all of these nuances of meaning. As for German, that language does not confuse the "inquest" [*Vorschrift*], the "decree" [*Verordnung*], the "ordinance" [*Anordnung*], and the *Verjährung*, which is a statute of limitations on a right or duty.

As always, the violence and simple clarity of Kafka's text require no commentary. If anything, commentary will diminish them—a fact to which I resign myself. My excuse is that I think I can hear, and believe I can make heard, in those pages red-hot with hallucination, the echo of what has been called *the intractable*. I hear them saying that the intractable—that which resists all law—is also an absolute condition of the moral law.[2] And I think I hear something about the effects of this on politics.

The officer describes to the Western traveler—in French—the machine for execution and how its parts work: the tilting bed, the box of cogwheels called the scriber, and the harrow, with its glass needles irrigated by water. The machine writes the judgment [*sentence*][3] on the body of the condemned, recto and verso. Or rather, it cuts it *into* his body until he dies, bloodless. The coup de grâce is delivered by a long steel needle (the only one in the apparatus) that pierces his forehead. After which, the bed tips the tortured body into a pit.

The officer describes; the machine writes. The officer describes the machine; the machine writes the judgment. I'll return to the description. Let us consider the inscription.

The machine executes blindly: the program for the inscription corresponding to the judgment is placed in the box of cogwheels, and it carries it out. This box of cogwheels is what we now term ROM, or the "dead memory" in a computer, the text of the program being its "living memory," or RAM. Once the program is inserted, one presses the *Enter* key. The machine is blind not because it does not know how to read, but because it can read only the prescriptions written in the language of the former commandant. Let us say for expedience (too much expedience) that it only reads the prescriptions of the former law. The officer loves the machine because he loves that former law and because the machine is its automaton. This is an artificial intelligence whose memory operates only in the former language. The officer is the servant of this automaton. In his pocket are the papers on which are drawn all of the diagrams corresponding to all of the prescriptions, which in themselves constitute the entirety of the former law. He might be called a maintenance engineer.

Such tracings were termed, in lower Latin, *praescripta*, preinscribed lines; we would say "sketches" today, lines to guide an execution. This is a late (and apparently limited) meaning of *praescribere*—a spatial, and one might say, aesthetic sense of the term. The hand (as one speaks of the hand of the executioner)—here the harrow—will reproduce the tracings on the body of the condemned. It accomplishes its work according to the model or the template of the lines traced by the former commandant on the sheet the officer has in his pocket. It executes in the two senses of the word. Latin also gives for this term, *perimere*. *Perimere* means *to cause to perish* only because it means first of all *to acquire*, to take, or to buy . . . *completely*. The harrow executes thoroughly and without question, in a peremptory fashion, the reparation of the fault of which the condemned is guilty. The condemned pays with his blood, in full, to the point of its complete depletion. The authority of the forgotten, violated prescription costs him his life.

In this way, I rediscover the initial sense of *praescribere* and *prescriptio*: to write at the head, nearly "to entitle," and to enjoin. The commandment of the former commandant is a prescriptive sentence. Its form is: do this, do not do that, and so on. It would be appropriate at this point to examine the modalities of the prescription. I will designate all of these modalities with the letter *D*, which together constitute the spectrum of rights and duties: obligation, the forbidden, the permitted, the tolerated. Insofar as we are subject to these, we are the *destinataire* or addressee—we have duties. Inasmuch as we can subject others to one of these modalities, we are in the position of *destinateur* or addressor of the prescription—we exert the right to oblige, to interdict, to allow, and so on. As an order deriving from the former law, the prescription is translated aesthetically in the regulating layout [*tracé regulateur*] the *praescriptum*, which the machine will follow in order to execute the final *inscriptio*.

I say that the *praescripta* had an "aesthetic" sense for two reasons: one weak, the other strong. The weak reason is that the prescription of the former commandant must be transcribed on the basis of the words that compose it into lines by which the scriber must abide. We should reflect here on the relation between the letter and the design. Nothing ensures, if we follow Kafka's text, that the writing in use in the penal colony is alphabetical. Indeed there would not even be any need for a transcription if that writing were, so to speak, ideogrammatical, if it were related to the design, like Chinese calligraphy, or the Pharaonic hieroglyph. Thus, the writing is aesthetic in a noble sense of the term. "Noble" because we know, in particular from the Zen Buddhist tradition, that the forming of a sign with a brush dipped in ink requires of the painter-scribe a kind of ascesis, an inner emptying, an elimination of every idiosyncratic passion or intention. This is an aesthetic state of emptiness or absence of everything that is not, let us say, in the spirit of the sign to be inscribed. The body of the scribe must atone for the fault of living, feeling, and willing through a mortification. The required aesthetic is the elimination of what we call aesthetic, the preoccupying influx of the sensible. But the path opened by a writing-design is not the one followed by Kafka, so I will pass over it.

The strong, and this time the pertinent, reason for naming the work of the machine "aesthetic" is that its purpose is to make the verbal formulation of the law pass into a corporeal impression. Freud might say: a transcription of word-representations into thing-representations. But here it is a matter of something more than representation, even more than the representation of a thing. It is a matter, in fact, of something other than representation—something other than hallucination, dream, phobia, and so on. If we consult the Freudian catalog of symptoms, we will find "acting-out"[4] as a reasonable approximation of what is suffered by the condemned.

The body effects the law, immediately, *in actu*, upon itself—like the hysteric whose wrist is locked, whose nasolabial ridge contracts, or whose stigmata in the hollow of the palms begin to bleed. In his work, Freud observes a primacy of the body in the inscription of the unconscious—a privilege that is called hypochondria. The body (but what are we saying, exactly, with the words, *the body*?) exposes itself not only to display the infraction, the unbearable fulfillment of desire, that is, but also to pay for it by its suffering. Its most extreme disorder is death. Let me recall here the sequence of impassioned reasons for this argument: the hysterical symptom is found in all neuroses. As is the case with psychosomatization, hypochondria is always associated with melancholia, with a perpetually unresolved loss of a love object. The body accuses itself of this loss or at least assumes the accusation. It tries to redress the fault of the loss through its suffering and by recalling its perishable nature.

Why should this tissue of motifs, this *memento mori* be called "aesthetic"? To be, aesthetically (in the sense of Kant's first Critique), is to be-there, here and now, exposed in space-time, and to the space-time of something that touches *before* any concept or even any representation. This *before* is not known, obviously, because it is there before we are. It is like birth and infancy: there before we are. The *there* in question is called the body. It is not I who am born, who is given birth to. I will be born afterward, with language, precisely upon leaving infancy. My affairs will have been handled and decided before I can answer for them—and once and for all: this infancy, this body, this unconscious remaining there my entire life. When the law comes to me, with the ego and language, it is too late. Things will have already taken a turn. And the turn of the law will not manage to efface the first turn, this first *touch*. Aesthetics has to do with that first touch: the one that touched me when I was not there. This is not the place to develop this negative aesthetics that commands all great art, all writing, and that only reveals itself openly in modern literature and art. Its obligation, its constitutive prescription is to absolve itself of this insensible touch by means of the sensible.

The touch is necessarily a fault with regard to the law. It takes place and has its moment in a space and time foreign to the law—savage, peregrine. And to the extent that it maintains itself, persists in the mode of this immemorial space-time, this savagery or this sinful peregrination, it is always there as a potentiality of the body. If the law must both be announced and be obeyed, it must overcome the resistance of this fault or this sinful potentiality constituted at birth (by which I mean a potentiality deriving from the fact that one is born before being born into the law). For the law, the body is in excess. Aesthetics, even the negative aesthetics to which I have referred, cannot suffice to absolve the fault that the body *is* as the space-time of the touch. On the contrary, aesthetics might be said to exacerbate the fault. It repeats, at the very least, the savagery of birth-infancy. This loyalty is the fault of art. But the law must be concerned with this excess of the body.

If the law is to execute itself, it must, like a touch, inscribe itself on the body. The body of which I am speaking can hear nothing of the law; it hears nothing since it does not belong to the order of the address, to the transmission of *D* in accordance with rights and duties. Following its own cruel aesthetics, the body will have to be *touched*. It will have to be initiated [*entamé*]—that is, cut into and incised. The root of the very late Latin *intaminare* remains *tangere*: touch, a touch toward and within. Writing, the holy scripture, will have to be inscribed in the manner of a savage touch upon the body that does not belong to it. This body will be sanctified only by this prescribed inscription of the prescription. This inscription must suppress the body as an outlawed savagery. Only its death can redeem it, atone for it. Redemption requires peremption.

We speak of a "blood debt." But there is blood and blood. *Sanguis*—the blood of life in the arteries and veins; and *cruor*—the blood that is spilled. The first nourishes the flesh. It gives it its hue of blueness, its pinkness, its pallor, its sallowness, its early-morning freshness, the infinite juxtaposition of nuances that drive the painter and the philosopher crazy; an immaterial matter. As for the law, this innocence of the flesh is criminal. It must expiate this fleshly innocence. The blood that flows is called *cruor*. Expiation is cruelty, *crudelitas* versus *fidelitas*.

The machine of *In the Penal Colony* is the theater of cruelty—the aesthetics of spilled blood demanded by the ethical law when it is enacted. Between the first touch and the second, which is the last, the touch of the incisive harrow or the touch of the law, aesthetics changes meaning. Here, now, is that aesthetics, on and in the tortured body of the condemned, placed in the service of the former law.

The traveler asks the officer: "'Does he [the condemned man] know the judgment [*sein Urteil*]?' 'No,' said the officer." The traveler persists, "He doesn't know his own judgment [*sein eigenes Urteil*]?" And here Kafka inserts the stage direction: "'No,' said the officer again, then paused for a moment, as if demanding from the traveler a more cogent reason for his question."[5] The executor of the law knows that the infant body is ignorant of the law and can know nothing of it (in the sense of an explicit knowledge), unless the law is incised into it to the point where it draws blood. What it can know of the law, it can know only in the sense in which *sapere* means *to savor*, to be aesthetically passible, to be *touched*. Indeed, the officer adds, after this silence, "It would be pointless to tell him. After all, he is going to learn it on his own body [*Es wäre nutzlos, es ihm zu verkünden. Er erfährt es ja auf seinem Leib*]."[6]

The traveler persists: "'But at least he knows that he has been condemned [*daß er überhaupt verurteilt wurde, das weiß er doch?*]?' 'Not that either,' said the officer, and smiled at the traveler as if he now expected to have a few strange revelations from him." The traveler, the Westerner (let us remember that he is Western) goes on: "You mean [. . .] that even now the man still does not know how his defense [*Verteidigung*] was received?"[7] The response (and once again Kafka's indication regarding the staging or the one): "He did not have the opportunity [*Gelegenheit*] to defend himself,' said the officer and looked to one side, as if he were talking to himself and did not want to embarrass the traveler by telling him things that were so obvious to him [*dieser ihm selbstverständlichen Dinge*]."[8] The officer knows that his office, the office of the machine—that is, the necessity for the law to cut into the body to the point where it dies, to execute it in order to execute itself—has its reasons; reasons that are ungraspable to the Westerner. Because the Westerner has forgotten blood; because he believes that he has already redeemed the body once and for all through some incarnation (Jesus, or Louis XVI), that is, through a law that became flesh at the cost of spilled blood, a *cruor*—but once and for all. Such is the perfunctory attitude of the West regarding the law; such is its nonconfrontation with cruelty. It scarcely wants to know more about cruelty than about the cook's recipe. But you can't make an omelet without breaking some eggs.

The traveler becomes indignant. "But he must have had the opportunity [*Gelegenheit*] to defend himself."[9] And the officer, in the end, losing patience at the blind misrecognition that he nevertheless knows and recognizes—the misrecognition of the crime that *is* the innocent body, the misrecognition of the fact that, because of this body, the subject of the law and of duty, the subject D, is never obtained—the officer takes the traveler by the arm, shows him the condemned man who, in perfect compliance with his superior, salutes him and explains to the traveler:

> Here, in the penal colony, I have been appointed judge [*Ich bin hier (. . .) zum Richter bestellt*]. Despite my youth. For I assisted the former commandant in all penal cases [*in allen Strafsachen*], and also know the machine best. The principle according to which I decide is: "Guilt is always beyond all doubt [*Die Schuld ist immer zweifellos*]."[10]

I would willingly make this a "final word." It is, in fact, the word of beginning. The fault is certain—that we have been touched "before" the law touches us. The law can only re-touch us. This re-touching re-touches only if it is peremptory. That is, if it puts an end to the differend between the "before" that is the body and the "after," that is the law. I emphasize that this is the differend. There is no court that can take up the conflict between the aesthetic and the ethical and decide the matter. A *disputatio* would here be a lie. The body does not argue:

> If I had first summoned man and interrogated him, it would only have led to confusion. He would have lied; if I had succeeded in refuting these lies, he would have substituted new lies for them, and so forth. Now, however, I've got him and will not let him go [*halte ich ihn und lasse ihn nicht mehr*].[11]

The differend between the body and the law cannot be converted into a litigation. Only the sacrifice of the body maintains the sanctity of the law. Without deliberation or warranted judgment the sacrificial execution must be repeated automatically each time a criminal birth occurs. The cruelty will be machine-like. The condemned is not saved in another world—he is dumped, dead, into the common grave. It is the law that is affirmed in this manner, and in the world. If the law must execute itself, it will decide the matter upon the body, with the means of the body but against these means. With blood, but blood that will flow and drain out.

What the officer describes is the absolute condition of the moral law, and its cruelty toward innocence. Innocence is *in all certainty* the sin because it knows nothing of good and evil. It is not *jenseits*, beyond, but on the hither side, *diesseits*. The law prescribes, but not in the sense that it is inscribed in the rubric or the heading. The heading, what comes first, is not the commandment; it is birth or infancy, the aesthetic body. The latter is inscribed so much in advance, on this side, *diesseits*, that the law itself can only inscribe itself by reiterating on the body and in the body an inscription analogous to the one that instituted it. The law is always the body's afterword. It tries to preface the preface that is the *sanguis*. In doing so, it transforms it into a *cruor*, a blood that flows until death—the contrary of a transubstantiation.

I come back now to the *praescripta*, to the sketches that are traced on the former commandant's papers: the sketches the officer has in his pocket and to which he refers in setting the machinery of the scriber in such a way that they will move the harrow to engrave the words of the law onto the body.

In morals, it is not only a matter of making blood flow. The cruelty must be exhibited. This is its theater, its aesthetics. The body is seized here spatially as the surface into which the letters of the law are cruelly carved. But the time of the body must also be harnessed and touched by the retouching of the commandment. The law demands the death of a guilty innocence, but it also demands a time of death, and the agony of this innocence.

The officer shows the traveler the papers that bear the *praescripta*, the regulative designs that are traced out by the former commandant and that serve to program the movements of the harrow.

The traveler would gladly have said something in the way of acknowledgment, but he saw only labyrinthine lines intersecting at various points, covering the paper so thickly that it was an effort to detect the white spaces between them.[12]

The traveler confesses that he is unable to decipher anything. The officer laughs: "Yes [. . .], it's not a primer of beautiful lettering for schoolchildren [*es ist keine Schönschrift für Schulkinder*]. You've got to study it for a long time."[13]

This is not a writing to be read, nor a writing for learning how to read. The child cannot decipher it with his eyes. And yet it is this same indecipherability that will render it decipherable, eminently decipherable, exclusively and peremptorily by the infancy of which I am speaking, the criminal innocence of the body. This is a writing that has no need to be read and will never be. Rather, it is a tracing to be felt, a line [*un trait*] of suffering. What appears to the eyes as a scrambling or scribbling of the line serves to extend the ordeal of the body subjected to incision. The officer explains:

> Of course it can't be just a simple script; after all it's not supposed to kill right away [*Es darf natürlich keine einfache Schrift sein; sie soll ja nicht so fort töten*], but only over twelve hours, on average; the turning point is calculated for the sixth hour. So the genuine script has to be surrounded by many, many ornaments [*Zieraten*]; the real script encircles the body only in a narrow belt; the rest of the body is meant for the adornments [*Verzierungen*].[14]

The article of the former law to be engraved on the condemned man in the course of the execution attended by the traveler (and Kafka's reader) says, quite briefly in fact, "Honor thy superiors! [*Ehre deinen Vorgesetzten!*]."[15] If it were a matter of this sole text, the body would be quickly circumscribed with the incision. Would it even die? We could well imagine so. Our executions— those we carry out, we in the West—are in principle expeditious in this way.

The former law, on the contrary, requires a time lag of twelve hours. What is sought from this *post-scriptum*? Why this delay in inscribing itself? Why do the arabesques overlay the text of the law to the point of rendering it undecipherable?

The law requires and awaits another deciphering. The officer describes the agony of the condemned:

> But how quiet the man becomes around the sixth hour! Understanding dawns even on the dumbest [*Verstand geht dem Blödesten auf*]. It begins around the eyes. From there it spreads. A sight that could seduce one to lie down alongside him under the harrow. Nothing more actually happens [*Es geschieht ja weiter nichts*], the man merely begins to decipher the script, he purses his lips as if he were listening hard. You've seen that it is not easy to decipher the script with your own eyes [*mit den Augen*], but our man deciphers it with his wounds [*mit seinen Wunden*]! Certainly it's a lot of work [*Es ist allerdings viel Arbeit*]; it takes six hours before it's done.

After which "the harrow skewers him through and tosses him into the pit."[16]

According to the calculation of the Gospel of Mark, Jesus is crucified in the third hour, darkness spreads over the land after the sixth hour, and he dies in the ninth.

Six hours for the wounds to decipher the law, during which, says the officer, "nothing more [. . .] happens." The agony, properly speaking, the struggle of the body against the law, ceases at the sixth hour; and if nothing more happens, this is because the commandment's retouching, its remarking, has effaced the initial mark or touch. The immemorial *aisthesis* out of which the innocent body draws its savage resistance to any accusation, or judgment, is broken down, reduced, so to speak. The first six hours are given over, lost perhaps, to resistance, furious resistance, we say, from the Latin *forastica*, from the outside, foreign—resistance whose strength is drawn from outside the law because it comes from something on this side of it, *diesseits*; a torture imposed by what we politely call "moral education." As for sentimental education, there is none. Sentiment is either impolite or dead.

One might say that this time limit required by the law for its decipherment is needed not by the law but by the body because it remains hostage to a touch that is blind to all justice. French law defines *prescription extinctive* as a "freeing from obligations." It is determined by two kinds of conditions:

first, "the conditions determined by the law," which are inscribed here on the papers left to the officer by the former commandant. But in the terms of *D*, as I have said, the prescription is "a means of acquiring or of freeing oneself through a certain passage of time." This prescription is a phrase *D* that derives its authority from a temporal duration. Uninterrupted possession (thirty years, in French law) translates as ownership in matters of acquisition. And for the elimination of a debt, uninterrupted service (I suppose this is right: I say "service" for want of a better term), spontaneous subservience, and uninterrupted passibility translates absolution for some fault or offense. This meaning of prescription—*Verjährung* in German— the annulment of a crime by time, can even be applied to the punishment. We commonly speak of prescription when a deadline has passed and a crime comes under a statute of limitations that annuls it and renders the punishment inapplicable.

In the penal colony, at least as the officer wants things, this latter form of prescription can never be involved: the law remains imprescriptible in all cases, that is, always applicable. Every infraction is imprescriptible because it attests to the pre-inscription of an *aisthesis* that is indifferent to *D*, to rights and duties. And the application of the law always entails the same extinctive prescription: twelve hours of agony in payment for an indubitable offense, that of not having been born first to the law but, rather, to and through the *aisthesis*. In the program for inscription placed into the machine, the arabesques are the prescription of this prescription, the commandment of such a time limit.

Why does the former law prescribe that its execution, its incision on the guilty body, should be delayed in this way? Why not a quick death? Because death is jealous of birth. Or if you will: the law is jealous of the body. Or again: ethics is jealous of aesthetics. The law is jealous because it came second and because *sanguis* did not wait for it in order to circulate "freely." The body had its time prior to the law [*d'avant la loi*], a time when, not being addressed, it did not have to answer. This elementary time must also be paid for. In this way, the law's handicap will be eliminated. The law must be an excess of death for the body because the body has the advantage of an excess of birth over the law. The incision of the body by the law must be such that it delays the decision. The gap between decision and incision repeats and annuls the gap between the aesthetic birth and the ethical birth. It repeats it because it maintains the body in the aesthetic through the suffering caused by its wounds. It annuls it because this aesthetic of cruelty has its place and time only on the basis of the ethical.

In the last six hours, the law will have moved into first place, not only in the way it claims to but also as the body understands it. The body can decipher it only at the cost of spilled blood, and this is the only way in which the law is decipherable. In the eyes of incorporeal spirit—those of the traveler or the new commandant—it remains indecipherable, like the inexplicable tracings on the papers of the former commandant. As for the officer who knows how to read these papers and who serves the machine—he also knows that his reading has no significance, no value in regard to the law—it will be necessary—it would have to be necessary—for his body to be flayed by the teeth of the harrow for him to cease being the overzealous servant of the law and his machine and to become its victim, or better, its agent [*suppôt*].[17] To be just it does not suffice to be the officiant of the law: one must suffer from it. This is why the commandant will lay himself down under the harrow, as we know, after having set the scriber to the program corresponding to the article of the law upon which he infringes by serving it. And this article says simply: "Be just!"[18]

It must be recognized, then, that the law needs the body, its own dwelling upon the body, as well as the body's resistance to it, in order to inscribe itself, that is, to execute itself. And the law cannot be just without being cruel. If the law does not make blood flow, it is not decipherable and therefore *is not* at all, has no existence. This necessary cruelty is also the homage that the law pays to the body, its way of recognizing a more archaic pre-inscription than its own inscription, and its way of being just toward the *aisthesis* that was not born from it. The way of a jealous justice, which is just because it is jealous.

Latin ascribes the word *praemium* to that part of the spoils that belongs to the god or to the victorious general *before* the victors divide up the whole: a share set aside before the sharing. The aesthetic infancy of which I am speaking is a portion that has no part in the apportioning between good and evil. It is set aside from the address D. But cutting into this reserved part, the execution of the law stamps it under the name, or the title, of the *praescriptum*, the division. Thus, the body, set aside by its pre-inscription, is in principle placed back under the prescription of the law, obliterated and proscribed. As a *praemium*, it was not meant for D. The victor or the god to whom and by whom it was reserved is *aisthesis*. The god or the demon? Indivisible, it was intractable for the prescription of justice. From this difficulty, and with the wrong suffered by this body, arises the question of community and politics.

There is no way to avoid this aporia. The former commandant and his officiating officer set up what I called the absolute condition of the moral law such that the reinscription of the intractable under the title (that is, the *praescriptum*) of justice succeeds only by failing. The officer is aware of the aporia. And yet he persists. He recognizes that justice is "unjust" with regard to the pre-inscription of the body seized because it pays no attention to it. But if it gave up its necessarily torturing inscription by letting itself be intimidated by some *habeas corpus*, justice, he then thinks, would simply not take place. And it would be unjust in relation to the prescription that is the law. The law prescribes not only *what* must be done but also *that* it must be done. The judgments D that it writes, under the title of *juriscriptio*, demand that they be *enacted*, in the form of a *scriptio in actu*. The act differs from the code by reason of the support of inscription. The law is written on paper, the act of justice in the real. The machine effects the transcription of the one into the other. And the real is necessarily what resists it, innocently, being in no way addressed to it.

The delirious enthusiasm of Kafka's officer expresses this absolutely aporetic condition of the moral law. The execution of justice, in principle destined to efface an infraction, must automatically entail a wrong, a mortal wrong. The wrong is not occasional in character; it is constitutive of the essence of morals insofar as this essence is *enacted*. And the wrong is not a matter for the law. The law cannot treat it or redress it, because it is based upon it. Once again, this wrong is its condition, as when we speak of a condition of possibility through derealization, and also of the human condition. But in this case, it is an inhuman condition.

This aporia also finds its expression in the order of time, whose pertinence and importance I have tried to demonstrate. I stated that the time of agony was required as a compensation for the time of innocence, that is, for the enjoyment [jouissance] of the *praemium* "before" and outside the law of the division. But since it is a matter of enacting the law through the body, this enactment (which is a contradiction of justice as a wrong) must manifest itself in the order of time, which is, along with space, the order of the act. This manifestation occurs, however, in a manner that is temporally aporetic, that is, in an impossible torsion of time. I refer here to the third antinomy of the first Critique, recognizing, without further development, that the antinomy is not established on exactly the same contradictory basis as Kafka's. The moment when justice, as an actualization of the law, is inscribed on the body, which it wrongs and even tortures, cannot be *situated*. This moment consists, in fact, in an encounter between the time of an end and a beginning, on the one hand, and on the other, the time that has never begun or finished.

The justice exercised by the machine puts an end to an injustice, the identifiable infraction of which the condemned has become guilty, and, by making him pay for this fault, it absolves him of what was done, preparing him for action that is henceforth freed of this past. In sum, it frees him. Hannah Arendt often commented on this aspect of beginning, of novelty, even of birth, that is entailed by free action, and by the freedom of judgment in particular.

But in Kafka's problematic, this time of a renewal runs up against a time of an entirely different sort, that of the pre-inscription of *aisthesis* as body before the law. What I am calling "birth" or "infancy" has nothing to do, at first glance, with the birth entailed by the free act according to Kant or Arendt. With regard to reflective reason, the pre-moral, a-moral body is subjected, on the contrary, to the order of an irremediable heteronomy because it is constituted by having been *touched* even before being aware of it, before being able to produce a response to this touch, and having to be responsible for it.

And when I say, "having been touched," I am not even referring to the temporal status of this passibility, which could better be called "intemporal," assuming one collapsed temporality and chronology. But let us say rather that the heteronomy of the body, which is retouched by the harrow of justice, understands nothing of the succession of cause and effect, and nothing of the extemporaneous temporality wherein arises the causality without cause that is proper to freedom (a causality, that is, which is the effect of nothing). The heteronomy of the body understands nothing of physical time or of ethical time because the *aisthesis* that governs it is neither linked/linking (in the sense of intelligibility) nor unlinked/linking (in the sense of responsibility). The paradox of this body's time—insofar as it is constituted by its non-belonging to itself, its primary disseizure—is that it lacks the modality of any kind of linkage. This is, I think, what Freud meant when he said that "the processes of the system Ucs. are *timeless*."[19] I also think it is poorly stated. These processes are timeless in the sense that time is a chain, in the sense that time links. But time is also *stasis*.

We say that the pre-intelligible and pre-moral body *was* touched; I reiterate it when I use the prefix *pre-*, and Latin reiterates it with its *praemium*, a pre-purchase, an encumbrance prior to any division. In truth, this preordination to *aisthesis* is aesthetic subordination, and it is not liable to any alteration through the passage of time—it is imprescriptible. I would not even say that it is permanent. Nor primary either, since it is not inscribed in any succession where the secondary would come after it. Let us assume the paradox that, when it takes place, there is not yet any time that links.

In the sixth hour, justice passes upon, or into, the tortured body. This is an encounter between the time of redemption and the new beginning with the time of the insistence (or sistence) of the intractable. The officer describes (we arrive now at the description) how the great execution festivities were during the time of the former commandant. The whole population of the colony was assembled in a kind of amphitheater on the dunes surrounding the machine; silence reigned and the impassioned interest of the spectators was such that it obliged the officer and his guard to move aside those who wanted to see from up close justice pass over the body of the condemned. "[E]veryone knew [says the officer]: Now justice is being done [*alle wußten: Jetzt geschieht Gerechtigkeit*]."[20] Nevertheless, the children, according to the wise orders of the commandant, enjoyed the privilege of being able to come up close. The officer describes the scene to the traveler:

> I would often be squatting there, with two little children in my arms, right and left. How we all took in the look of transfiguration from his martyred face [*den Ausdruck der Verklärung von dem gemarteren Gesicht*], how we bathed our cheeks in the radiance of this justice finally achieved and already vanishing [*in den Schein dieser endlich erreichten und schon vergehenden Gerechtigkeit*]! What times these were, my comrade![21]

I shall leave aside for now the question of the little children. One can easily grasp the pertinence, the double pertinence of the privilege accorded to them: infancy of freedom, infancy of the body. And the officer is himself this *bifrons* infant.[22]

The rapture to which the former law has granted them privileged access is *ex-actly*, that is, it *en-acts*, the moment at which the two infancies merge. Out of this encounter there emanates a ray of light, and this ray is justice itself. The law is written in a writing the body can decipher: in bleeding wounds. This is justice "finally achieved," because at this moment the retouching of the body by the stylets of the law obliterates the instant or insistent touch that is its resistant pre-inscription. But it is also justice "already vanished" because this re-touching is mortal precisely in that it obliterates. How could an *aisthesis*, or its analogous engraving of the law, be decipherable by what it touches when it is this very touch that constitutes what it touches? The aesthetic body was not a support for inscription of the touch; it is a support for the re-touching, and this suffices to proscribe it. This is why justice fulfills itself only in passing. It *prescribes* itself in the three senses of the word: it is imperative, it has previously transcribed itself through its convolutions in a writing of the body, and it inscribes itself too late to be executable.

But at least the machine, when it was sanctioned in the old days, offered the community the opportunity for the parousia of justice. I stated that justice is not situatable. At the site of the desert hills packed with the community waiting for its law, justice cannot be incarnated, it cannot dwell. Justice is a fleeting gleam that passes over the face of the tortured criminal who is finally justified and almost already dead.

Politics enters at this point—that is, the new commandant. Politics abhors the machine and cruelty. The new commandant holds public council. Politics deliberates, the new justice provides matter for *disputatio*, for plaintiff and defense, for a trial, for respect of the rights of man even in the condemnation and application of the penalty. The new authority transforms the curious traveler who visits foreign countries into an international expert invited to examine the juridical and penal procedures of the colony's customs and to give his opinion—which can only be very unfavorable. The traveler speaks the language in which the rights of man were written. Women, who were so absolutely absent from the theater of cruelty, are admitted to the affairs of politics. Their delicate handkerchiefs are substituted for the wad of filthy cotton that the dying criminal desperately chews and rechews after a hundred others. As for these handkerchiefs, they wipe away any allusion, stifle any suspicion of allegiance to cruelty. At his death, the former commandant does not have a right to a consecrated burial. His tomb is hidden under a table in a bar pompously dubbed (by the women, I imagine), "teahouse," and frequented by the workers from the port, "poor, abused people," Kafka writes. The epitaph on the tombstone prophesies despairingly the resurrection of the departed: "Have faith and wait!" It indicates that those faithful to the former law "must now be nameless."[23]

These are all signs—each warranting analysis, but which I shall leave unexamined—signs that already the new commandant and the political order have triumphed, reducing the former to silence, to a clandestine existence, to pseudonymy and to waiting. And thus, signs that the community that gathered together around the machine for the cruel passage of justice has been suppressed. The community now comes together in another manner, through deliberation and tolerance. These are also signs that the harrow is already out of use, like the papers covered with arabesques, now indecipherable for the new man.

The officer knows all of this, he describes it. And yet he resists, with the resistance of which his body is capable. He asks the traveler to attend the deliberations of the new council and to give no opportunities to the new commandant, through his responses to the questions that will be asked of him, to officially condemn the former judicial process. He even asks him to cry out or to murmur (that would suffice) his "unshakable opinion" that the procedure is just.[24]

I cannot go into a detailed examination here of this double demand and the officer's hallucinated, anticipatory staging of the episodes of the scene. Nevertheless, it would be essential to follow all the traces of the contradictory, not to say schizophrenic, logic that governs the officer's strategy of persuasion with regard to the traveler. It is all too obvious that the officer doesn't want to know anything about the one to whom he is speaking, though he knows perfectly well who he is. In the excitement of this harangue, even more than in the melancholia of the descriptions, there is a strain of insanity, and above all a dreadful inanity—that of the body that understands that it is forever forgotten by the law.

Seized by the anguish of this prescription, in the sense this time of a peremption due to time (the new, modern time), the officer takes his place on the bed of justice after having dislodged the condemned man. First, he will have set the scriber in such a way that the harrow should inscribe on his body, with all the required indirection, the prescription of all prescriptions, the law itself: "Be just [*Sei gerecht*]!." In this manner alone can the law, being *enacted*, finally reveal itself through a perfect tautology.

For the law to effect the prescription "Be just!" it must engrave itself in the body, like every article of the law. But "Be just!" is a universally valid prescription. It is not normally invoked to punish a specific offense. However, it suits all offenses in that it applies to their essence as an offense, to the "certain offense," which is that of being "born before" the law, outside the law. The impeccable officer is guilty only of this certain offense. By submitting himself to the automatism of the sanction, he will verify one last time the justice of the prescription in relation to his own exemplary case (exemplary precisely because he is exemplary). Such is the tautology: by inscribing upon himself—a purely innocent person—the prescription of justice, he will establish the justice of the prescription. For the commandment and the sanction apply precisely to innocence.

The officer ceases, therefore, to officiate; he subjects himself to the cruel aesthetic of the ethical law. The machine, obviously, understands all of this; it does what is necessary *sponte sua*. Then, as you know, it breaks down, the box of cogwheels ejects its parts. The officer will be deprived of the agony that his offending body owes to the law. He will also be deprived of the fleeting instant when pure sanctity should radiate from his eyes. The steel needle pierces the skull and kills him, and the broken harrow holds suspended over the pit a skewered body.

So it would be true that the body is forgotten by the law, true that justice will not have been revealed, true that the new law has already triumphed, a law that has no need of the apparatus of cruelty to act. Adorno will say: true that death itself is dead.

But this is to rush too quickly toward a conclusion. I would end rather with the questions over which the body of the officer remains suspended. Is it true that politics—as it was once enacted and repeated by the Greeks and Romans, then by the Americans and the French two centuries ago—is instituted only at the cost of forgetting the absolute condition of the moral law, namely, cruelty? Is it true that if the law omits what is absolutely foreign to it—what I have named here the body of *aisthesis* and elsewhere the *intractable*—it fails to confront the status of its own transcendence and abolishes the support of its effectivity?

Or was that only a delusion, the antimodern, reactionary delusion, as we put it (or as it has been put to us; a delusion with fascist tendencies)? Is the truth of the law not, on the contrary, and as the modern commandant thinks, that it should be inscribed on paper under the title (*praescriptum*) of an axiom on how to divide—an axiom to which speaking entities (both subject to duties and holders of rights) will, after deliberation, have agreed? Does not justice consist in the meta-principle according to which the division applies to everything and must be as nonprejudicial as possible for each and for all? A meta-principle, according to which also, each and all are the sole judges of the division? And must not the good and the bad be understood as what is fitting and unfitting for the interests and expectations of each and all? Are not this good and bad all that is at stake in the question of justice?

Or, finally, must one distinguish between the justices of the new and former commandants, and maintain both of them, but separately? The one justice appropriate to morals and to its aesthetic of cruelty, the other justice to politics and to its aesthetic of representation? But then, what will be the relation between these two justices? Will it not be—is it not already—the relation between the penitential subject and the citizen? This relation itself, how can it be just?

SURVIVOR
ARENDT

I shall begin by recalling a few commonplaces—some well-known, others less so—relative to the very principle of what can be considered under a title such as "the survivor." This is necessary in order to clarify how I am approaching the thought of Hannah Arendt. The word "survivor" implies that an entity that is dead or ought to be is *still* alive. The concept of this "still," a reprieve, an *arrest* of death, brings with it a problematic of time—not just any problematic of time, but one that demonstrates its relation to the question of the being and non-being of what is. More precisely, of a time in which the being (the entity) [*l'étant (l'entité)*] is in relation with its beginning and its end, in relation with the enigma in which the entity *comes* to its being as entity and then *leaves* this being. It is therefore necessarily a double enigma, in that time is twice in relation with "its" non-being: it appears and disappears. But since when the entity is not, it also does not possess "its" non-being (since non-being is non-relation), the enigma to which I refer is that of a relation with what has no relation, that is, with an absolute.

A familiar observation, I dare say. Now to try to be less familiar, we must ask ourselves with respect to *which instance* the survivor survives. The survivor always survives a death, but the death of what life?

Hegel says that death is the life of the spirit. In phenomenology, spirit does not survive death; it is the sublation of immediate life, and thus spirit is both this life as (past) death *and* life revived and reliving. Spirit lives insofar as it is dead at the very moment that *it was* itself. Constitutively it is in mourning, in Freud's sense of the term. This implies that it is lost to itself insofar as, originally invested in a formation, it objectified that formation in order to know it, insofar as that formation then dies and represents death, and, finally, insofar as by these very facts, spirit returns into itself (narcissism of mourning) through a new formation. Spirit *is* only objectified or invested (this is what an entity is), and the new objectification comprises, contains, conserves the former one, but is now *conditioned* according to the mode of the *no longer*. This mode is that of necessity, or of the third person. The previous formation is no longer alive, the entity that I was can no longer say "I." *I* can only speak of it as *it*—in the third person. It *cannot* be other than what it has been (this is its necessity): it is in the state of having been ("being-been," writes Heidegger). Hegel solves this problem with a "we" consisting of him (me formerly) *and* me (now). Such a mysterious "and."

Survival is, according to this thinking in which *nothing* is *lost*, understood as being still according to modes of *power* (possibility, ability, eventuality: *event*, something indeterminate still happens), when in fact we should be beyond power, powerless, no longer able to take it.

The Hegelian sublation is that of one mode by another. In a sense, it expresses for thought the paradoxical constitution of the instant: it is not *t*, but always *t.dt*.[1] Heidegger's *being-been* implies in its determination both that it is no longer and thus could not be other and that it is the power (the derivative) of another instant (the "following" instant), at which point the being-been will give itself as no longer being.

The mathematical and phenomenological formulation of the instant *t.dt* thus furnishes an *intelligence* of survival. What is is alive. Yet, because it contains its own *not yet*, it is *already* dead. Time thus provides, at least for the spirit, the foundation of its idea of survival, in the philosophical problematic of spirit or consciousness. In a sense, Husserl's *Retention* holds the whole secret of survival. In the philosophy of ordinary language, time would be considered merely the play of modalities: for example, to *no longer* be capable *and* to be capable of this *no longer*; impossibility *and* the possibility of this impossibility.

This time is that of consciousness or spirit, and this survival is its absolute security, just as its death is insured—insured in that it is always a *belle mort*, because it is "retained" in the "we" composed of the me now and the former me.

One question, however, is whether something is not forgotten in this turning back on the *no longer*, something that therefore does not survive, a remainder that does not remain. What seems as though it must necessarily be lost is the presence *then* of what is *now* past. What is *now* necessary, unchangeable, was *then* contingent. What is now powerless (no longer *possible*), was *then* power or potential. There is a mortal sadness of the very thing that is retained and transmitted; the sadness of Minerva's owl, of what is *bound*. The tradition of what was then experienced in the present is its *betrayal*. The past is betrayed by the simple fact that the present it was is made absent. It lacks a certain mode, the tone of the quick, the lively, even as it is recalled.

In epistemological terms, this can be referred to as its contingency, what Arendt, referring to Kant, calls "desolate contingency." Desolate because it is absolutely resistant to the necessitating, universalizing linking through cause and effect. But desolate also in that the singular ontological savor—that *taste*—of being-there can only be lost to ordinary memory. (Does this savor ever *take place*? Is it not merely essential that it *took place*? Does this savor not merely result from the fact of remembering? Is it anything but a result of lack, the result of what memory misses in remembering? Is not every photograph, even a recent one, essentially faded?) The betrayal of the living consists in its being handed over by the survivor. This betrayal is necessary in order for some trace of the old, necessarily altered, "rehashed" present to persist. The witness is always a poor witness, a traitor. But still, he bears witness.

The question is thus posed within the framework of a philosophy of the subject or of spirit—in a phenomenology. It is the question of the synthesis of time in Augustine, Descartes, Kant, Hegel, Heidegger—which is also that of the subject.

We must now observe that if, within this problematic, the life of spirit is designated as a survival, then what is stressed is absence, or that which is lost in what is preserved. The world is gray for Minerva's owl. It is a disaster for Walter Benjamin's Angel, who is pushed backward into the future by the wind of the past. The Angel sees only disaster in the past, just as the owl is blind to the color of life. The Angel sees the past only as disastered present. The astral is the tone of the lively. And the issue returns as to whether the past really was a disaster, like the former present, or whether it is disastered by its re-view. Hegel would affirm the latter, Benjamin, the former. And this makes a difference—all the difference—between the speculative and the postspeculative. In Hegel, mourning gets accomplished; in Benjamin, it becomes impossible.

This impossibility of mourning the past presence (and reapplying its force, through new object, to the present self) is called melancholia. If it is not the impossibility of mourning, it is at least a stress placed on the irrevocable loss of presence, that is, on the death of what was there. And along these lines, even what is present now may be sensed as already doomed to no longer being there, becoming the object of a "preventive" melancholia. Is the apparently so lively not already dead?

Birth itself, the beginning, is reckoned, through melancholia, as an illusion. What comes to life—the instant as event, emerging from nothingness—is already doomed to return to nothingness. The only *being*-in-truth is not here. This inversion of appearances can give rise to metaphysics. The eternal present, the living present, is always absent. Being is not entity [*L'être n'est pas étant*]. This melancholia (which, since Platonism, has been called "Western"—for what reason I do not know) can be found in all thinking when it comes up against its failure, which is also possibility, temporality, modality.

Shunning all entities, while remaining melancholic and keeping watch over the perpetual retreat of true being, appears to be the way for thought *not to betray* presence. Series of entities, instants, and instances simply unfold innumerable false births—so many disappearances of the true. Present moments join the ranks of the "unemployed" of presence. A man says to a woman: "No, I don't want a child: he'll just be one more to add to the unemployed." This man expresses melancholia, a lack of faith in the being of being-there. He senses that the transmission, the handing-over of life is the betrayal of truth (which is other than life—"elsewhere"), and he does not want to betray. As for the authentic mode of presence (and who knows what that is?), every entity is a survivor.

I will now invert the stress on disappearance. Melancholia omits the other enigma in the relation of the soul with non-being or being—the enigma of appearance. Rather than nothing, being gives entities, instants, objects. Since being appears in "objects," it gets forgotten. Yet it *gives* objects, something *happens*. Expressions like "yet" are concessions to melancholia. But by conceding, of course, I am impugning; or, rather, I am emphasizing the impugnment that exists in melancholia. What melancholia impugns is the fact that there is "nonetheless" something rather than nothing, that this is why there is birth and death, even if the terms are inverted, even if one thinks of every birth as a death, and death as birth into truth.

The impugnment of melancholia or the refutation of nihilism consists solely in this humble question: If the truth is that there is truly nothing, how is it that there appears to be something? Or: Why does truth lie, why does death find itself deferred in birth and life? Even if we agree with the Freud of *Beyond the Pleasure Principle* that the difference between life and death is only one of rhythm (death hurries while life delays), why are there *two* rhythms? In the thermodynamic terms that Freud inherits from Fechner, *why* is there differentiation, complexification (neg-entropy), if the physical truth consists in moving to the most probable, simple, undifferentiated state, which is the death of the system (entropy)? This is, of course, only taking one step backward in order to take two forward. But why is it necessary to take two forward? The Freudian hypothesis of Eros is in keeping with the second law of thermodynamics. It still presupposes that complexity is *only* a simplification in suspense, that life is only a survival.

The fact remains that in examining the enigma of the *sur*-vival, of this *sus*-pense, Freud could never conceive of anything other than an *event*, whatever the name of that event—and there have been many, for example, the event of sexed reproduction in the history of living things. And in individual ontogenesis, the echo of sexual difference is the event whose savagery the whole life of the individual is unconsciously devoted to "regulating."

But what is this event if we strip it of its scientific or cognitive denomination? It is the enigma of there being a relation with what has no relation; that is, in knowing that it is born and dies, the soul (aptly named) bears witness to the fact that there is not only *what* is (*what* it is) but also the other of what is. Of course, this relation does not take place when it takes place, it *has* taken place and it *will* take place. Thus, it *will have* taken place all at once, appeared too late, disappeared too soon. And this is because my birth is always only recounted by others, and my death told to me in the stories of the death of others, my stories and others' stories. The relationship with others is, therefore, essential to this relation with the nothingness of its being that is reported to me (whence I come and where I am going), and also essential to the presence of the absence of which the relationship with *others* (this presence of absence) comes *back* to me. Essential, too, is the *fabula* to which the pulsation of beginning and end lends rhythm.

I must insist that, if being or nothingness is not the whole of truth, if the event is not entirely a lure, then I declare that the sense of "survival" can be inverted. Complexities, organizations, or orders can be formed, in which a power of arrangement or fashioning is affirmed, or, as Arendt says, the enigmatic faculty of *beginning* is exercised—a survival that can become truth as well, and alleged life can become the dead survival of that birth. Is this truth a truth of reason? What will be right and will have triumphed over any beginning, any *initium*, is the end and the end of ends, the annihilation of ends. The reason one can *have* or *give* can only reduce the most complex polynomials into the $a = a$ of equality without remainder. This reason will, in the end, deduce and reduce. But something must have raised the question. Perhaps it will be necessary to go to the depths of the last man's nihilism, the man who knows the "banality of evil," who suffers or administers it, or both, to find some *joy* (I am deliberately using Pascal's word, the word of the spirituals), the dark joy of a request made stronger for its being more improbable, and thus more threatened by annihilation and more openly confronted by the truth of nothingness.

In saying this, I do not intend to fall back into the restorative thought of a Hegel. I would simply say without further explanation, that this thinking about life as enigma of beginning is acceptable only if it is a matter not of a remission, nor of a challenge but of a *scruple*. The scruple of an *as if*, in which case the spirit thrust into the proof of nihilism, on the road to despair and skepticism (which is permanent), knowing that there is nothing to do or say, no valid entity, even which *is*, acts, *all the same*, as if there were one.

In no way is the effect of this clause cynicism. Cynicism remains derivative of nihilism and perseveres, through its activism, in the melancholia of *nothing's worth it*. The effect is neither a *ludic* form, where a corpse dons the colors of life in a grimacing and macabre irresponsibility. Nor is it an "artist's" metaphysics of will and values.

The effect is infancy. And infancy knows something about *as if*, something about the pain of powerlessness and the complaint of being too small, of being there late (compared to others) and of arriving too early, prematurely (in terms of its strength). It knows something about broken promises, bitter disappointments, failings, and abandonment—but also about dreaming, memory, questioning, invention, obstinacy, listening to the heart, love, and real openness to stories. Infancy is the state of the soul inhabited by something to which no answer is ever given. It is led in its undertakings by an arrogant fidelity to this unknown guest to which it feels itself a hostage. Antigone's infancy. I understand infancy here as obedience to a debt, which we can call a debt of life, of time, of event; a debt of being there in spite of everything, a debt from which only the persistent feeling of respect can save the adult from being no more than a survivor, a creature living on reprieve from annihilation.

It is true that one quickly learns that death will forbid paying off the debt, that it will always come too soon, and this alone can make one sink into melancholia or into that wickedness of trying to be the last one to die, as analyzed by Elias Canetti.[2] (I mean even that wickedness required by the will to bear witness, to survive so as to recount.) But infancy consists in the fact of being and of acting *as if* one could nonetheless pay off the enigma of being there, as if one could draw interest on the inheritance of birth, of the complex, of the event, not in order to enjoy it but to transmit it, so that it be passed on, returned. Interest drawn on the inheritance of birth is a function of birth's constitutive poverty and misery—like a *debt* of beginning, the passing on of debt, debt's tradition. Even the *belief* that the debt of birth will be paid off by the event of death, that the soul received will be returned—

this belief does not stand up to the harshness of an infancy without pity. Its "as if" blocks all righteousness.

How is Hannah Arendt's thought implicated in these few remarks? I am certainly not a *judge*, as she would have said, to decide this question. Not only because I have not sufficiently dwelt in her work, but also because the time I have spent there, although allowing me to recognize something very close to what little I have referred to under the term "survival," leaves me uncertain nonetheless as to whether I am faithful to her thought. I see three motifs as places to mark that uncertainty: the motifs of birth, tradition, and judgment. These really only constitute one motif, obviously, and I shall not manage to disentangle them properly.

The first motif, birth, concerns precisely the debt that I have just discussed—a debt to the non-being from which one has issued and of which infancy (having asked for nothing) is the altogether involuntary witness. It is well known that there is an ontological and historical melancholia at the heart of Arendt's thought. What I have outlined here (with the almost laughably scientific word "entropy") about the truth of non-being as ineluctable death is sometimes modalized by Arendt in related terms. For example, in this passage of *The Human Condition* on "Unpredictability and the Power of the Promise":

> And to a certain extent this is true. If left to themselves, human affairs can only follow the law of mortality, which is the most certain and the only reliable law of a life spent between birth and death. It is the faculty of action that interfaces with this law because it interrupts the inexorable course of daily life, which in its turn, as we saw, interrupted and interfered with the cycle of the biological life process. The life span of man running toward death would inevitably carry everything human to ruin and destruction if it were not for the faculty of interrupting it and beginning something new, a faculty which is inherent in action like an ever-present reminder that men, though they must die, are not born in order to die but in order to begin. Yet just as, from the standpoint of nature, the rectilinear movement of man's life-span between birth and death looks like a peculiar deviation from the common natural rule of cyclical movement, thus action, seen from the viewpoint of the automatic processes which seem to determine the course of the world, looks like a miracle. In the language of natural science, it is the "infinite improbability which occurs regularly" [. . .].

The miracle that saves the world, the realm of human affairs, from its normal, "natural" ruin is ultimately the fact of natality, in which the faculty of action is ontologically rooted. It is, in other words, the birth of new men and the new beginning, the action they are capable of by virtue of being born. Only the full experience of this capacity can bestow upon human affairs faith and hope, those two essential characteristics of human existence which Greek antiquity ignored altogether, discounting the keeping of faith as a very uncommon and not too important virtue and counting hope among the evils of illusion in Pandora's box. It is this faith in and hope for the world that found perhaps its most glorious and most succinct expression in the few words with which the Gospels announced their "glad tidings": "A child has been born unto us."[3]

For the moment, let me select the following formulations: "law of mortality," "inexorable course of daily life," the "rectilinear" movement of human life, like a "peculiar deviation from the common natural rule," which is cyclical, the "miracle" of action, "infinite improbability" compared with the "automatic processes" that rule the course of the world. All these terms refer, I think, without having to twist them to conform to a general principle of deadening, to the idea of a downward spiral that compels all entities toward the more probable, where they dissipate.

Arendt then opposes this melancholic principle what she calls "action," which, in the ineluctable and natural "ruin," would interrupt, begin something new, and be improbable, giving substance to faith and hope.

Let me note that the turn taken by Arendt's thinking here is explicitly humanistic: "men, though they must die, are not born in order to die but in order to begin." I would say that this is a resolutely anthropologized reading of the solution to the third conflict in Kant's Antinomy of Reason, the one that will rule over the deduction of a reality of freedom in the second Critique—much more anthropological than Kant's transcendental lesson. And of course, my reservation bears on this uncritical consent given the concept of a humanity of men defined as a vocation to begin something new. No doubt the Kant of the third Critique reaches an analogous conclusion, but one that hangs on the *as if* clause, which modalizes the regulatory Idea of a nature working for the benefit of freedom. Where Arendt is a realist, Kant is an analogist, that is, "infantile."

What seems more interesting to me is the role Arendt assigns in the economy of this negative entropy to the "fact of natality." In the text I have quoted, she states that the faculty of action is "ontologically rooted" in the fact of natality. How are we to understand this? As the "birth of new men," she writes, as the "new beginning," and finally in the news, the glad tidings, that "a child has been born unto us."

Here I would more than agree: a child is continuously born to us. Birth is not merely the biological fact of parturition, but, under cover and on discovery of this fact, the event of a possible radical alteration in the course compelling things to repeat the same. Infancy is the name of this faculty, in that it brings to the world of being the astonishment of what, for an instant, is nothing yet—of what *is already* without yet being *something*. I say this birth is incessant because it beats the measureless rhythm of a recurrent "survival." This "survival" does not prolong a life that is already dead; it initiates, in the death of what was there, the miracle of what is not yet there, of what is not yet identified.

And yet even in this ontological glimpse of a *birth* that *defies* the law of the return of the same, in which we can hear something consonant with what I have called *infancy*, I hesitate in my agreement. I said that we must emancipate the idea of a life as beginning, and not merely as survival, from the triumphalism of a challenge or the conviction of a remission. The passage quoted from *The Human Condition* grants to what Arendt calls the principle of natality and to the initiatory force of action the virtue of a redemption—a virtue I would call *protective*. Often it appears to me to govern the economy or the strategy of Arendt's thinking, through its detours, repentances, and hesitations, and to limit the stakes of that thinking. Here is the passage I omitted from what I quoted before:

> Action is, in fact, the one miracle-working faculty of man, as Jesus of Nazareth, whose insights into this faculty can be compared in their originality and unprecedentedness with Socrates' insights into the possibilities of thought, must have known very well when he likened the power to forgive to the more general power of performing miracles, putting both on the same level and within the reach of man.[4]

This passage refers to the previous section of the same book, "Irreversibility and the Power to Forgive." Forgiving, *aphienai*, unbinding and letting go, are understood by Arendt precisely as interruptions of the irreversible chain of *effects* of action itself in which action can only repeat itself mortally. Forgiving is a re-mittance, a new deal of the cards, what makes a cut in the consequence of necessities and begins—pardon versus abandon. The grandeur of Jesus—with respect to any tradition, be it Roman, oriental, or Jewish—is heightened by the fact of his teaching, by word and deed, and by the fact that it is within the power of the son of man to pardon offenses. What offends is always simply what is as having-been. The miracle of Jesus is that he is an event in the order of necessity. The good news, that a child is born to us, announces in truth that with Jesus it is birth that is born here and now, and that the offense of being there—in the world of entities—can be pardoned. Exercised here and now, the pardon whose birth is announced by the News is itself only the birth of the new, the crack of the not yet in the doleful world of the always-the-same. Thus pardoned, according to Arendt, "action" (power to begin) carries with it the promise of its emancipation from necessity, returning its effect to the nothingness of the same.

I do not claim that this humanistic, salvationist thinking is Arendt's last word. The text dates from 1958, ten years after the first German edition of *Die Verborgene Tradition* ["The Hidden Tradition"][5] and seven years after the first American edition of *The Origins of Totalitarianism*[6]—works that include the first meditations on the impossible "Jewish" condition. This condition, as we know, reserves for God alone the power to forgive, that is, to begin anew, and refuses the futile temptation of a restorative humanism. If I take as examples the four figures of this condition as Arendt analyzes them in 1948, the "Schlemihl" from Heinrich Heine's *Melodies*, Bernard Lazare's "pariah," Charlie Chaplin's "suspect," and "K" from Kafka's *Castle* (named by Arendt "the man of goodwill"), I can see nothing—or almost nothing—comparable to the faith and hope promised by the good news of birth in *The Human Condition*. Only the reading of *The Castle* (and I deplore this fact) seems inclined toward a certain optimism: by obstinately remaining in the village, K (in her reading) becomes the witness (though not accepted as such) to the fact that a debt remains unpaid in the order that the castle imposes on the common people. But to my knowledge, this debt, according to Arendt, is not the debt whose creditor is non-being, in the modality of its miracle, birth, or its threat, death. What the castle owes to the village is not the right to judge, to begin, but the right to live "as a human being" to have "home, work, family and citizenship."[7] Optimism is not Christ-like, but political. All these words would have to be overcharged with a somewhat arbitrary ontological connotation in order to make the elementary rights of "public man" express what Benjamin might have called the dependence of "action" on the event (*The Human Condition*). The village certainly survives the absence of these rights, but the enjoyment of these rights could itself be no more than a survival compared with "natality." I merely wish to state that even if it were democratic, this community would not escape the threat of banal entropy.

There is probably more "birth" in this sense in Heine's notion of the "Schlemihl," as raised by Arendt, but its tenor is so popular, not to say populist, and so poetic, in the sense of the comical paganism of Rabbi Faibusch (Phoebus Apollo), that I would not want to confuse this *gaiety* with the *joy* of which we were speaking. Yes, there is birth there, but birth to the presence "of such universal things as the sun, music, trees and children."[8] Hence the poetic life of Heine's people ("there is no poet without a people," Arendt repeats—what about Paul Celan?), the public life of Kafka's democratic citizen (oh, how often "revisited"); nothing in these figures is reminiscent of the inverted figure of survival to which I alluded: birth and the child as an interruption in the ineluctable process of deadening. A people's culture, democratic organization: are these not also possible modes of perpetuating identity? Possible figures for inert survival?

It is rather in an earlier text like "We Refugees," reprinted in *The Jew as Pariah* (1978), that something of the thinking of interruption returns.[9] It returns really without excuse, and at the very moment when the community of pardon in the person of its pope, Pius XII, will have "forgotten" to pardon. Here Arendt makes no mistake when she sees, in the fate dealt upon Rolf Hochhuth's *The Deputy* in 1964,[10] the response to one who has just been influenced by her *Eichmann in Jerusalem*.[11] For there is no refuge offered to these *refugees*, not even that of assimilation, whether poetic or civil, to the people of their land of asylum, which is to say no inscription into a premodern (pagan) or modern (republican) tradition—or, least of all, into a Christian one. It is impossible to survive like this in Europe (she writes in 1943, at the moment that the *Judenfrage* is about to find its Final Solution), because "the outlawing of the Jewish people in Europe has been followed closely by the outlawing of most European nations."[12] So that the refugees "we" are represent "the avant-garde of these peoples," and Jewish history thus ceases to be separate from that of nations.

We can see at what an appalling cost the interminable hesitation between tradition and assimilation finds its "solution," if I dare use this now accursed term. This text, "We Refugees," has something terrible about it, and its content and tone contain a dreadful bitterness. Arendt mocks the Jews who are *Doktor* in Berlin and *Schnorrer* (freeloaders) in Paris, whose spokesman says: "We have been good Germans in Germany and therefore we shall be good Frenchmen in France,"[13] who no longer *succeed* in being *successful*, in assimilating to the bourgeoisie. They have to flee too fast, things move too fast. And anyway, as she said in *Rahel Varnhagen*,[14] Jews cannot assimilate without assimilating anti-Semitism at the same time. As for their own tradition, it cannot be maintained. The shtetl and the ghettoes are burned, and the communities expelled, deported, or massacred. But more than this, the very principle of an installation probably does not conform to the strange tradition in which the kings and the political men will always have been denounced by the Prophets in the name of a Word which de-installs. The Jews do not constitute a people in the sense of a *nation*. They are without *nature*, without land. They are linked only by the law of the book and the debt of an alliance and a promise.

Arendt does not make this explicit in "*Die Verborgene Tradition*," but her eulogy of Bernard Lazare's *pariah* in another text authorizes me to express it for her here. For if in 1943 she can see in Jews the "avant-garde" (terrifying word) of a Europe persecuted by Nazism, and if she can hope in desperation for their inscription into modern history, it is precisely because they are not a natural or national people and because they prefigure a state of being-together to which all European peoples are and will be committed by the totalitarian disaster—a being-together without roots—that behaves according to judgment alone, without any established criterion, the last resource of the survivor. There is no necessity, no being-in-need, that could in principle deprive the mind of the ability to distinguish between good and evil. The diaspora, persecution, the Shoah, all these accelerated modes of dispatching into nothingness, leave the soul without the support of an established tradition; they leave to its desolation only the responsibility of saying yes or no to abjection, only the infancy of the mind, which is the ability to judge, the true lineage. The reminder of a promise of alliance, and thus a reminder of birth, may be heard, stammering feebly, in the night of a young Elie Wiesel, in his supplication, "Why have you forsaken me? Does it mean that you do not exist?"

In the end, Arendt will obviously seek this mind in an embryonic state in Kant's "Analytic of Aesthetic Judgment." Even if she does not see it this way, the fact is that each time, singularly, what is at stake in this reflective judgment is the birth of a subject and thus of a community, but only of a *promised* birth. With the beautiful, it is pure happiness, the miracle of promise. (But with the sublime, it is its impossibility, the imminent threat of non-being. The beautiful is an event of birth; the sublime, one of death. In the seminars of 1970,[15] Arendt was not preoccupied with the "Analytic of the Sublime" through which, however, there reverberate the horrors of abandonment. The reason, I think, is that the desire to protect and to be protected against the unbearable is stronger in this case than the persistent intrepidness of her inquiry.)

Problem of survival: every mind is the child of its parents and survives them. Arendt's mother never abandoned her, and she never abandoned her mother. What mind can declare itself free from defense mechanisms, from forgetful resistance to a total melancholia? One writes because one's attempt at suicide has failed. Arendt says a great deal about Jewish suicide in "We Refugees."

(Let us recall that the last Jewish survivors in the caverns of Jotapata besieged by Nero's troops in AD 67 discussed whether they had the right to commit suicide. Josephus, the leader, the traitor, and the survivor favored the "solution" (exactly) that each should kill the other in turn, and be killed by the next. Josephus managed to come out last in the drawing of lots and negotiated his fate with the Romans. He then wrote *The Jewish War*. Arendt writes in her *Eichmann in Jerusalem*: "There will always be a survivor to tell the tale."[16] How does she know? How do we know? Because of the Shoah, which is an almost perfect *Vernichtung* in that it would not have taken much more for there to have been no one left to tell of it. And the witnesses who speak are horrified at having been chosen by the evil of survival to tell it. To be "selected" in the final round.)

(We should also recall that *we* write and think in a state of relative peace, without having to listen for the doorbell at 6:00 a.m., without the immediate, constant threat of the most abject of annihilations. Protection against abandonment loses some of its urgency with the thought that persecution is held at bay. Thinking can advance a little more in the direction of catastrophe, of the sublime for example, and of non-being, because no one today, with the exception of a few terrorists, "refuses [to the thinker] the right to share the earth" with him, as was the case with Eichmann.[17] Rather than "share the earth," I would prefer to speak of the right to *share the story*, the birth and death of the improbable: of sharing judgment. Regarding the refusal of this sharing, this abandonment, who can pardon it? Who can set it right [*remettre*]? And does not Arendt's gesture of protection derive from her proximity—greater than ours today—to the horror engendered by this refusal?)

To return to tradition, it is always threatened with being merely a survival. Through tradition, a state of complexity, a state of textual corpora is maintained from one generation to another (at least). As a result, children lodge their complaints and take their responsibilities on the basis of a sophisticated and well-founded arrangement of knowledge, know-how, opinions, or of being-together in the most general sense. Here I would refer to the fine pages in *Between Past and Future* on Roman *auctoritas* as foundation, tradition, and religion.[18] As tradition is enriched, as it gains authority, so infants are born less naked—less and less from nothing. They may even lose the feeling of non-being, ensured as they are of being inscribed within a continuity overarching deaths and births, that is, any relation to nothingness, to what is without relation. Yet, even in the most "augmented," authorized, and "linking" tradition, the enigma of a something to which there is no response must continue to inhabit the mind secretly (the question of "why me?"), the enigma of the singularity of birth, which cannot be shared, like that of death. The persistence of this enigma can make the mind accessible to something that is prior to the world of culture and tradition, keep it in a state of infancy, that is, unprepared.

Only in preserving the possibility that this enigma may come to mind can tradition be other than the placidly implacable survival of what is already there, and death be inflicted upon the improbability of being born. But by the same token, if its possibility is preserved, uncertainty, whether melancholic or wondrous, persists through the generations to shake the hold of tradition and of the consensus that feeds off it.

I would like, in short, to situate certain aspects of totalitarianism, as analyzed by Arendt, in relation to this problematic of a tradition of the beginning. In *Between Past and Future* (1961, 1968), the organization of the totalitarian system, already explored in *The Origins of Totalitarianism* (1951),[19] is compared to the structure of an onion. Authoritarianism organizes power in a pyramid, whereas tyranny suspends it with equal indifference over everyone. Arendt notes that the totalitarian onion has the following property: examined from the center, where the leader resides, each stratum appears more "realistic," less "radical," in proportion to its distance from the center. Seen from outside (from "reality"), on the other hand, each stratum looks more committed, more militant, "harder" than the strata whose surfaces precede it. (Esoterism/exoterism: Is the Pythagorean distinction between the *mathematikoi* and the *politikoi* with respect to their initiation into doctrinal radicality authoritarian? Or is it already totalitarian?)

My questioning here concerns the "realism" of the analysis and, in general, of Arendt's thought.

She writes: "The onion structure enables the system, by its organization, to be resistant to the shock with which it is threatened by the factuality of the real world"—"resistant to," in other words, sheltered from.[20] This is a system that deadens events and confrontation. Totalitarianism is thus a vast organism serving as a protective "shield," in Freud's sense of the term.[21] But I think that we must then understand "factuality" not so much in the sense of the fact established by the historian (as described by Arendt in the chapter "Truth and Politics" that she added to the later editions of *Between Past and Future* after the uproar provoked by her *Eichmann in Jerusalem*), but rather by accenting what she herself stresses at the end of this chapter: factuality is "what we cannot change."[22]

Hypothetically, politics could change reality; totalitarian politics could change it totally: whence the onion, a system of complete (two-way) filtering of the real, with the aim of transforming reality into ideology or culture. Bearing Freud and what I consider essential in mind, the reality that needs filtering is not a so-called brute fact (in Clemenceau's sense: no one can or will ever be able to say that Belgium invaded Germany in August 1914), but its degree of anxiety, its quality of attraction and repulsion, its force of excitation. This quality of the fact does not stem from its established factuality, but from its eluding repression and crossing the strata of the protective onion. The "real" should be understood as *the fact* of desire and not as *a fact* established in the referential field of a cognitive discourse. For the so-called real fact only possesses this power of anxiety because it has an ally at the center of the onion. This ally is the something to which the mind remains hostage and to which there is no respondent (in Freud's terms, no representative), with which it has no (narrational) relationship. It is the "presence" of nothingness, of birth and death, and of indivisible singularity. So much so, that defense against what is called external reality is only necessary insofar as it can awaken this "truth" deemed internal, this something that, more than anything else, cannot be changed or exchanged. The categories of external and internal are practically useless here. When I say that external reality can *awaken* inner truth, the metaphor of awakening (so dear to Proust) places me in a space-time that cannot be divided up or clearly decided, that is "outside" or "before" the scene, in the double sense of the theatrical scene and the time of a short story,[23] whether fantasized or not. *Before* and *outside* are misnomers. Simply stated, the decoupage of places and moments does not take place or have its moment when it is a question of the Thing. Hitler, burrowed down in the center of his onion, is no less exposed to the Thing than a humble Swabian student on the outside. The self is always naked with regard to birth and death and so also to difference, sexual or ontological. But the leader wants to forget and make others forget the terrible nakedness constituting infancy. Thus, for such a powerful instrument of foreclosure, of forgetting, as totalitarianism to be fabricated, the Thing must appear extremely threatening, the relation of desire to the real must be one of extreme defenselessness. That is where the origin of totalitarianism is to be found.

Yet, in reading *The Origins of Totalitarianism*, one comes across—to my knowledge—few indications of this "origin" of totalitarianism. The description is essentially an external one, from a historico-political point of view. Even terror is analyzed mainly in terms of its use, as the means of breaking with the preceding legality. But the following observation is an exception: "terror is *needed* lest with the birth of each new human being a new beginning arise and raise its voice in the world."[24] Yet "fear" seems to me to express little, and the remark conserves a certain natalist tone.

This objectivation and realism, predominant in the 1951 text, certainly in no way detract from the importance of the analysis. But they do limit its significance for us. For if it is true that the totalitarian tendency has to be grafted onto a heightening of anxiety unequaled in the cultural, political, and philosophical history of the West, then the defeat of the totalitarian *regimes* alone will doubtless have been insufficient to exhaust the source of totalitarianism's spirit.

I would point to three paths opened to the resurgence, to the survival of this spirit after the political totalitarianism analyzed by Arendt. She shows that, in order to realize the system of total domination, there is no need to have recourse to "the mob" and that Himmler's power was due to his knowing that "the masses of coordinated philistines provided much better material and were capable of even greater crimes than so-called professional criminals, provided only that these crimes were well organized and assumed the appearance of routine jobs." What Himmler understands, she adds, is that "most people are neither bohemians, fanatics, adventurers, sex maniacs, crackpots, nor social failures, but first and foremost job holders and good family men."[25] In other words, they are ordinary folk who don't want to understand anything about the relation to nothingness and the debt of infancy, and who "distract" themselves from these things by keeping busy. Now this state of mind, which refuses the debt, seems to me just as true, in fact more so, for developed societies at the end of this century as for the Europe in crisis of the 1930s. The massification and activation of the forces of thinking, their exclusive devotion to what is nowadays called active living, are they more completely accomplished than then? And is it the same for what Arendt calls "loneliness"? The question must be asked. For if the "factuality" is that of the Thing, it is not enough to destroy the totalitarian "onion" for the anxiety to disappear and for the reactions that it induces to cease, even by other means.

I will now proceed to a second persistent germ of totalitarianism today, what Ernst Junger called total mobilization:

> In the interpretation of totalitarianism, all laws have become laws of movement. When the Nazis talked about the law of nature or when the Bolsheviks talk about the law of history, neither nature nor history is any longer the stabilizing source of authority for the actions of mortal men; they are movements in themselves [. . .].
>
> Terror is the realization of the law of movement; its chief aim is to make it possible for the force of nature or of history to race freely through mankind, unhindered by any spontaneous human action. As such, terror seeks to "stabilize" men in order to liberate the forces of nature or history. It is this movement which singles out the foes of mankind, against whom terror is let loose, and no free action of either opposition or sympathy can be permitted to interfere with the elimination of the "objective enemy" of History or Nature, of the class or the race [. . .].
>
> Terror as the execution of a law of movement whose ultimate goal is not the welfare of men or the interest of one man but the fabrication of mankind eliminates individuals for the sake of the species, sacrifices the "parts" for the sake of the "whole." The suprahuman force of Nature or History has its own beginning and its own end, so that it can be hindered only by the new beginning and the individual end which the life of each man actually is.[26]

Several decades after Hitler and Stalin, the contemporary system surely no longer invokes History or Nature in order to leave behind legality and the capacity to judge. It does not have to tear up treaties and contracts or exterminate lives. The principle rendering humans superfluous as juridical, moral, and particular persons (Catherine Chalier) inhabits the very "acts" of administrated life (Theodor Adorno), creating a void in the minds it administers. This principle is called Development. It is an entity no less abstract or anonymous than Nature or History, and it maximizes the effect described by Arendt: setting things in motion totally and mobilizing energies. Neither political organization layered like an onion nor the use of terror to break up legality and the debt of birth are indispensable to it.

On the contrary, as Junger knew by 1930, in democratic forms and in the constant adaptation of laws to attain greater well-being, the "law" of development finds both a means and a mask even more powerful (because more acceptable to "philistines") than the totalitarian organizations of the 1930s. Crude propaganda is discreet in democratic forms: it gives way to the inoffensive rhetoric of the media. And worldwide expansion occurs not through war, but through technological, scientific, and economic competition. The historical names for this good-natured "totalitarianism" are no longer Stalingrad or Normandy, and least of all Auschwitz, but Wall Street's Dow Jones Average and Tokyo's Nikkei Index.

We all share the ideology (but is it an ideology?) that we must, at any cost, develop and complexify in order to survive. The enemy is not human, it is entropy. Entropy is at the terminus of what remains of human history, in the form of the explosion of the sun into a black nova in four-and-a-half-billion years.[27] Development is the reply to this immense challenge. And it alone is just, since it is necessary for survival. The faculties of judgment, imagination, and paying homage to birth again are more solicited than suffocated in this process, but solicited in the suffocating busyness of performativity, a busy survival. We should at least, on the basis of this diagnosis, look again at the question of ideology. Development is ideological not because it is out of control in relation to the reality of things, but because it forecloses the anxiety of birth and death as an ontological enigma.

A last observation on the same lines: one inevitable effect of totalitarianism is that children are not allowed enough time for infancy, in the ontological sense in which I have been using the word. In "The Crisis in Education," Arendt writes:

> The more completely modern society discards the distinction between what is private and what is public . . . the more . . . it introduces between the private and the public a social sphere in which the private is made public and vice versa, the harder it makes things for its children, who by nature require the security of concealment in order to mature undisturbed.[28]

I interpret this formulation as follows: the contemporary system maintains the totalitarian principle of the multiplication of interfaces, but nowadays as a network, not as an onion. The "institutions" (school and family) where infancy securely sheltered its insecurity, its questions without answers, while learning adult answers and their inadequacy, where the fate of tradition vis-à-vis anxiety was in play, are destroyed by the contemporary system (it is enough for it to deflect their ends). And they are destroyed because the system places infancy in immediate contact with its demands, which are its responses to anxiety. Infancy has to immediately take its place in the communicational networks that have replaced the onion's strata, to function there as efficiently as possible, that is, to become the carrier of the messages that are circulated there and optimize their information. No time to challenge the old-timers or tradition; on the contrary, save time, to avoid the return of what has to be forgotten—the squatter within the soul.[29] "Let the dead bury the dead" is today understood as the abandonment of the body to administration by undertakers or to medical schools. One either gets rid of dead bodies or makes them serve development.

As for infants, so for the dead ... always. They are the two aspects, in the tradition itself, capable of appealing to the intransmissible.

In the preface to *Between Past and Future*, Arendt recalls the two enemies that the character in Kafka's parable fight simultaneously: "He has two antagonists: the first presses him from behind, from the origin. The second blocks the road ahead. He gives battle to both."[30] It is not just a question of the past and the future, but also of death and birth. What Arendt fails to state, however, is that if the dead here press upon, oppress the soul, and if infants block its escape, it is because they all weigh upon it with the force of what *already* is what it is. The past is saturated with its consequences and the future with its programs. The castle imposes the reign of its administered time on the soul's time.

There remains the interstice, without extension, which is the instant of judgment, reading, learning, and writing, of "growing up undisturbed," for the infant (who only blocks off the future if it is integrated too fast into what the constituted social offers it). It is also—for the tradition that pushes its way up from the depths of time with all the weightiness of the already judged—the time of being questioned. Between infants already dead, in a hurry to be (that is, to become "mature" adults), and yet-still-living-corpses—the two groups that *survive*—thought, in a hurry to get there, "to be there," struggles to bar access to its truth, to its condition of being hostage to something that has not been and will not be, but to which it must bear witness. It renders this witnessing in that it "judges." For it judges from nowhere, and in the name of nothing and no one, past or future, testifying by this that at the heart of necessitating and necessitous immanence, an obedience to what is *unbound* can be justified.

The temporal state of urgency, decision, effectuation, demanding unfailing adhesion of one instant to the next, corresponds to the multiplication of mediating layers or media networks in the spatial totalitarian organization. Freud said that, in the end, time, too—sequential time—must be conceived of as a "shield." This would be a time of the complete, of the dense—saturated, and sufficient to the point of satiety—stripped of any modality of possibility (past or future); in short, total in its seriality. Thus, non-being is excluded from it, as are inquietude and angst, and, to be sure, the faculty of judgment.

It is the effects of this saturation, I imagine, that indicate to Arendt that man without qualities, Eichmann in Jerusalem, is what she calls the "banality of evil." The totalization of time by the homogenization *of* times, by their banalization, banishes the *Urteilen*, the distinction between what is good and what is evil. It is evil because it eliminates the ability to discern between good and evil. At the end of *The Origins of Totalitarianism*, Arendt calls this state "loneliness," the opposite of solitude.[31] It is simply the complementary inverse of the massing of singularities: the massing of time. It is a *new* evil. The old evil requires that, in what is still experienced as the relation to non-being, privilege reverts to disappearance and death, and thus to the melancholic or criminal idea of survival. Nazism not only said "Thou shalt kill," but also "Let them disappear so that we may appear." Similarly, the old good, according to the same disquiet, is the avowal of and respect for a debt of apparition or infancy. And this is judged without any criteria. But the malignancy of contemporary Development is that it eases the very disquiet of apparition and disappearance.

Massification and survival, mobilization and saturation, and foreclosure are obtained more efficiently by an organization through communicational networks than by totalitarian politics. I know how brutal this diagnosis is. I know very well that development is indeed a development with regard to a traditional society. I am aware of the advantages of democracy: that it provides more opportunities for judgment than Nazism and allows us not to tremble at the sound of the doorbell at dawn. Proof of this is that we are here, in the Goethe Institute.

But, even so, I still wonder whether "birth" (the ability to judge, the vocation to begin) makes "administered life" feel just a survival in comparison with the true life of the soul. I wonder if, from this still possible miracle, we can expect any alternative to the system.

One example among others. In the proliferation of initiatives and civil institutions, particularly in the United States, Arendt saw a sort of protection or resistance against the threat of the totalitarianism of the nation-state, that is, against the forgetting of non-being. In the conflict and crisis surrounding the busing of black and white schoolchildren, she supports resistance on the part of families, and local activities against the application at all costs of federal laws designed to assure the integration of school populations. From civil society's capacity to spontaneously come up with organizational modes protecting individual or local concrete freedoms (especially important here because they concern childhood) against a law decreed from afar (as indeed is often the case in the United States, most notably in the 1960s and 1970s), Arendt hears the echo of a power for judging concretely, radically, without theory or criterion, a power that is mutually shared. This is the "common sense" or good sense whose basis she finds in Kant's third Critique.

I repeat that this conclusion is only at the cost of an abusively sociologizing reading of Kant's *sensus communis*. Kant's text undoubtedly lends itself to this, since it is not stripped of anthropology in the way that a transcendental analysis would have required. But I do not want to get into a philosophical discussion of Kant's last seminars; I just wonder what this reading of "good sense" still owes to the ideology of workers' councils to which the 1956 Hungarian revolution and, before that, through Heinrich Blücher, the experience of the Spartacus movement lent a sort of authorization.

I say this as someone who, like others, including some much better than I, let myself be taken in by the movement at the time. The interpretation of the Hungarian Councils in these terms can certainly not be recused. What can be recused is the possibility of concluding from this that what has been called the self-management of being-together (wrongly named, I think, because it is a sort of *Sebstbehauptung*) could of itself constitute a political or social alternative to totalitarianism, of whatever type. With the destruction of totalitarian systems and their replacement by "permissive" neototalitarianism (or, rather, possibilist neototalitarianism, since the slogan "anything is possible," which Arendt picks up from David Rousset and which is essential to these organizations, underscores this side of the question now more than ever), the very idea of an alternative is extinguished, and with it, that of a revolution. And that is just as well since that idea is itself totalitarian.

Birth or infancy, beginning, and finally the ability to judge, surely remain, but in *loneliness*. Without ideology we could not transfer to the possibility of spontaneous, local initiatives—which are in any case useful for the institution of the contemporary system, that is, the democratic one—the hope that was once placed in workers' councilism as the means of organizing the struggles of the oppressed. The transfer of the forms of revolutionary resistance to the free exercise of citizenship within the frame of democratic laws is still too protective a transfer, and in this sense ideological. It is a surviving [*survivance*].

In a reality that is principally turned toward the survival of complexities in the physical world, the other survival, the openness to non-being (under whatever name) is a debt that persists, in which Pascalian joy and Kafkaesque melancholia take refuge. But they do so in solitary fashion, in the desert filled with loneliness. And based on this inventory of the soul, the question of community, of being-together, can and must now be posed.

WORDS
SARTRE

I confess that he was neither my favorite novelist nor my favorite philosopher, playwright, or political thinker. To put it bluntly, I did not like the air of capability his writings exuded. Hollier alludes to the crisis Sartre went through in the early 1950s and to which *The Words* bears witness.[1] A doubt began to undermine the redemptive role he had accorded to the writer ever since the revelation that befell him during his captivity. Yet he did not elaborate on that doubt, but rather rid himself of it by shifting from the writer's activity to that of the "intellectual," an identical responsibility for curing the world of alienation. That bit of acting out resulted in a number of unworthy texts (in both tenor and tone), such as "The Communists and Peace" and "Reply to Claude Lefort."[2] In reading them, the militant I then was (alongside Lefort and several others[3]) experienced the same vague, menacing feeling I had felt ten years earlier as a student of philosophy on reading *Being and Nothingness*.[4]

In each case, negativity was unceremoniously annexed by human freedom, and dialectic by the project. The latter availed itself of the former in order to justify its cropping up everywhere. In the face of which, passivity was banal, shameful, and as tempting as a sin. Of their own accord, Being and the world (merged) collapsed into an abject viscosity. The summary diagnostic bearing on the in-itself (said to be nonsense) found its rhyme in the clear verdict in favor of the unitary Party (capital P) against the spontaneous inconsistency of "class." Left to itself, the latter fell to (nauseating) pieces, "molecular swirls, a multiplicity of infinitesimal reactions which reinforce or cancel each other out, producing as a result a force more physical than human. It is the mass. The mass, that is to say precisely the class denied."[5] *The Transcendence of the Ego*,[6] which I read later on, completed the picture: "I" am nothing, therefore I can do everything.

And the plays? In the age of Artaud, Brecht, and Beckett, of the meditation on signs, representation, and events, his plays were as edifying as those of Diderot, with the single difference that in Sartre's case, sentimental domestic tragedy had yielded the stage to sarcastic political comedy: *Dirty Hands*, *The Condemned of Altona*.[7] The theater of the bourgeoisie continues to exist, he thought, but in a moribund state. But how does one know that a class is dying? That he was passionately bent on it is all that is certain, and that desire was itself the mainspring of his politics. But it was not clear that that excellent sentiment would yield decent results on the stage.

As for the novels, the generation that was mine discovered Dos Passos and Faulkner, to be sure, but also Thomas Mann, Joyce, Beckett, and Proust. But what was *The Roads to Freedom* compared with them, I wondered.[8] Where did it lead that one had not already been taken by *Man's Fate, Wind, Sand and Stars*, and *Les Misérables*?[9] In what way did his novelistic prose reveal itself to be commensurate with the "Mallarméan" crisis? Sartre later declared that he had wanted it Einsteinian, as opposed to the Newtonian universe of the classical novel. But what was at stake in the novel from the time of Joyce and Gertrude Stein was no longer best conceived under the sign of the relativity equations but of the uncertainty principle. The *nouveau roman* set its clock according to Heisenberg and the pagan Danes rather than the pious Einstein.

Later there was a love for *The Words*, which gaily confessed the extravagant pretension of its subject to save the world, in the guise of Pardaillan. Sartre seemed to be realizing that something was toying with him. But he quickly couched the matter in the past: "I have changed. I shall speak later on about [. . .]. The retrospective illusion has been smashed to bits [. . .]. I see clearly, I've lost my illusions [. . .]. I've been a man who's been waking up, cured of a long, bitter-sweet madness."[10] He was dreaming, to be sure, while writing that, and believed nothing (or almost nothing) of it. All the same, he believed just enough of it for *The Words* to be possible, had just enough self-deprecating irony and just enough indulgence toward that irony to make of the book a splendid introduction to his Confessions. Writing is a sweet delirium, I agree, but I write as much. It is not Philoctetes, as he believes, but Epimenides, in the version of the liar's paradox quoted by Aristotle—I declare myself on oath to be a perjurer, which in the case of Sartre becomes: I am a traitor, but a self-confessed one. On the last page of *The Words*: "I sometimes wonder whether I am not playing a game of loser wins."[11] Indeed, with the sole reservation that it was not *I* who was playing, but writing, and that to believe it was *I* was already to leave the sweet delirium beyond cure at the very moment it was diagnosed.

Without the slightest conversion, the heroism of fiction was transferred to that of action, from *Troubled Sleep* in 1949 to "The Communists and Peace" in 1952.[12] Sartre's writing once again spared itself an analytic phase and enlisted an excellent reason—modesty—in justification: "my madness

[. . .] has protected me [. . .] against the charms of the 'elite.'"[13] As in the case of many others, "politics" enters into play in order to blind the time and place of analysis. That blindness is called lucidity. Under the names of almost random adversaries, praxis is always opposed to the same enemy: Being-in-Itself. In *The Words*, Sartre polemicizes against another Sartre, the childhood one, and it is in order to shut him definitively up, as may be heard in the very disposition of many a sentence: a brief description of a fact, a short pause, and the (absurd) meaning Poulou attributed to it.[14] There is a repression of anxiety in that demonstrative syntax and in such lapidary "cautionary" tales. Childhood, the figure of disquiet, is vigorously put in its place. It is a matter of affixing, stapling meanings to things in order to be done as quickly as possible with that ultimately unessential phase, which is to be bypassed since it is past, and is of necessity laughable.

Now the arrogance of the polemic is of the same vein as the stylistic regimen administered to Poulou. Allow me to insist on this, somewhat more than Hollier: the discord was painful. Lefort was treated as though he were suffering from the same fantasy that haunted Karl Schweitzer's grandson: escaping from his situation, "to be missed, like water, like bread, like air, by all other men in all other places."[15] Lefort wants to know nothing of his situation—to know neither who he is nor where and whence he is. It frightens him. And that is because "Being situated would teach you that you are neither Hegel, nor Marx, nor a worker, nor Absolute Knowledge, but rather that you are a remarkably intelligent, young French intellectual who has ideas about Marx like those men had about women circa 1890."[16] In parentheses, Lefort's situation declares what it is and isn't, thanks to Sartre's pen. Sartre can write what is missing. And it is not Lefort (but bread and water?). Lefort is but a minor elitist or thinking situation, as antiquated as that of the feminists of the end of the century, having nothing to do with the movement of history, with its crude male hands ("woman," a subject for intelligent ideas, like Marx: the parallel justified Hollier's making short order of it).

If the young man was to be shut up for good, it was because the immanentist notion of history and its struggles that Lefort was in the process of elaborating deprived the Sartrean stage of its principal protagonist, the Absent One, crucial to the sublation of the viscosity of the particular to universality and of the dispersion and contingency of experience to the status of a single drama. In the new Sartrean cast, the Absent One (who, before the crisis of the 1950s, was the writer) is called the Party. If I don't intervene to plead the role of the Party, Lefort will pounce on history, refusing it that lack which the mediator is called on to fulfill. A hole is needed in every lock because a key is needed in order for it to work. "What you refuse on principle I accept without difficulty. I admit that there are in the working class memory partially or temporarily unintelligible experiences whose key can be found in the hands of the Kominform or in those of another proletariat."[17] One is not very demanding when it comes to opening the lock. The passkey can be called Stalin, Togliatti, or Mao, as one prefers. What is important is the hole. The situation may be deciphered "by means of a mediation." A mere possibility? No, the liberality continues, this time with reference to modality in addition to name. "It is permissible, if not necessary, to ask for help." The Kominform or,[18] if you prefer, Togliatti. Mediation as possible or, if you prefer, necessary. In addition, there is no question of "a party can only try its keys; it cannot force them."[19] That was in 1953. The Stalinist apparatus had been trying out its keys for almost thirty years in the locks of the workers' movement, that was all. No forced entry anywhere. Rest assured.

The attempts, in the last analysis, were even fruitful in proportion to their failure, since they left the "call for help" emanating from the working class still gaping and consequently, the need for a supreme locksmith unsatisfied. With "Lefortism" in politics (as with Merleau-Pontyism in philosophy), with the opposition between nothingness and being neglected in favor of more local distinctions and the gaping hole receding, who then would forge man? If the Party were no longer missed by the masses or felt to lack amid contingencies, Lefort's proletariat would remain inert like a woman unaware that it was hers to await fulfillment, a "frigid woman." Which is why, "if I were a 'young owner,' I would be a Lefortist."[20]

I am not recalling these oddities of diction in order to relaunch the polemic. Not that Sartre ever made honorable amends. In 1975, he would still not yield an inch. Contat told him: *Socialisme ou barbarie*, in the 1950s, was right in its opposition to you, and the libertarian socialism that you discovered in 1968 had been promoted by that group for twenty years.[21] Had he not "taken advantage of the passage of time"? Didn't Cohn-Bendit "offer proof of it"? And Sartre responded: first of all, it was "really a two-bit nothing." (To which Contat: And aren't your Maoists today in the minority? Pretending thereby to overlook the fact that the central issue was the role of the Party, in which—since the Maoists were Stalinists—Sartre could be a Maoist.) Second, the group is right today but was wrong then. It was imperative to defend the USSR. "Truths have 'become,' and what counts is the path leading to them, the work one does on oneself and with others in order to get there."²² The path of my freedom at the time passed through Moscow; today in 1975 it passes through Peking, and if you tell me that Peking is no better than Moscow, you will be wrong, even if you are right, because you are moving against the flow of my praxis. How did the exorbitant privilege attached to Sartre's praxis—which made him deaf to everything—achieve legitimation? It was the praxis, he thought, of the most unfavored individuals, the little men of the everyday sort. The responsibility to everyman is set up against the imperative of truth. A humanist ethic or an intellectual cynicism? In any event, the response sheds light on another problem, that of notoriety: if Sartre was popular, it was because he was a populist.

There can thus be no question of reviving the polemic; Sartre is dead, "he succeeded in depriving us of himself," as Hollier puts it, and this is no time for disputation.²³ I am less sure than Hollier that he deprived us of himself. At one and the same time, it was always the case from the beginning, and it will never be so. Which is what he wanted. He must be having a hearty laugh at the sight of me trying to come to terms today with his immortality. A circumstance he will have owed to Hollier's book. I'm coming to it, but one more preliminary in order not to conceal anything of my prejudices. What was at stake in the polemics (of which the one with Lefort was exemplary) was neither the proletariat, nor Communism, nor the direction of history, but the metaphysics of the subject of will. Sartre was the name of that subject. Even as the autobiography of *The Words* was a polemic, the polemics were always an autobiography of that subject. Beneath the adversary's mask was concealed a face from Sartre's hell. Other people are hell because they are those faces of identity, of the past, of the inert, passions that the temporality of will deposits—being, degenerated into itself, that the nothingness of the future never stops transcending.

The polemics were negativization in action, the sleight of hand allowing pure lack to hold off the viscosity of all that does no more than be. Sartre himself observed that he had no "ideological debate"²⁴ with Lévi-Strauss, Aron, or even Merleau-Ponty, who all the same argued with the intent of refuting him. It was not a matter of being true, convincing, or even persuasive, but exemplary in one's transcendence of the situation. It is not through debate that freedom is defended and expressed, but in running an adversary through. Bourgeois is the name of that which is to be pierced, the secular name of the in-itself. And how does one know that one is exemplary in transcending situations when one does not have at one's disposal, as do the Germans, a dialectical logic and a labor of the concept? Through the "work done on oneself and with others," through the suffering felt when one thinks "against oneself" (against viscosity), through the popularity that welcomes you and that is the sign that the common run of humanity recognizes its freedom in your gesture.[25]

Hollier plainly did not have to overcome such prejudices to approach Sartre. He does not debate "in depth" the affairs concerning which the prosecutor has argued. He does not seem to believe in depth. He attempts, rather, to outpace the prosecutor. He follows the thread of denials, occasionally right to a series of minute unperceived nodes, but without either love or hatred. He is gay, alert, without disdain, without demagogy, at times amused to the point of disrespect, always guided by a meticulous consideration of the surfaces of the text and the life, with a touch of the rake in his delicacy. I write these notes solely in order to understand how or why, aside from his talent, Hollier succeeded in having his curiosity shared by the worst reader of Sartre that Sartre could conceivably dream of. Might it be that he related to the work in the same way as he related to Bataille's, so diametrically opposed to it? *The Politics of Prose* is not a biography or a psychoanalysis of the man or his work; it is neither a study of literature nor a history of ideas nor an erudite essay in textualist criticism. It is an attempt at a portrait of commitment [*engagement*], or rather of its impossibility.

Hollier does not analyze commitment as a philosopher; he rather composes its portrait in small strokes. And the face that emerges from his sketches is then exposed to a devastating light; its grain reveals unexpected asperities, a different face begins to surface within the one we knew. In the triptych entitled *Mirrorical Return*, which Ruth Francken designed from Sartre's face as an old man and which furnished the special issues of *Obliques* with their unforgettable cover, the active and rather good-old-boyish gesture of negativization finds itself similarly infiltrated by an "I don't know," worse yet, by an "I can't" that both anguishes and delivers, like a caress. The writing of commitment is accompanied by its own impossibility. Such is the "collapse" that Hollier pursues throughout Sartre's text, exposing it to a light that comes from Blanchot in its essential aspect, but he is not conscientious in the manner of so many epigones. More feminine. In the manner of Paulhan, perhaps.

Commitment does not take place. It presupposes a present, a situation construable as a presence, a future end, beneficiaries, a concerted action. But there is no presence at the outset, if the formula be permitted. Roquentin writes: "I am in the Café Mably; I am eating a sandwich, everything is more or less normal." And Hollier: "More or less, he says. The sandwich in one hand, the pen in the other? But which one in which? With which hand does he eat and with which does he think? Try it [. . . .]"[26] (It is as though one were reading Guyotat.[27]) At the beginning of *The Imagination*: "I look at this white sheet of paper lying on my desk." How might one write that without looking at the sheet on which one is writing? Sartre thus begins with perception, by what he believes (as a good phenomenologist) to be reality. Second sentence: "But now I turn my head away. I no longer see the sheet of paper."[28] This worries Hollier: the "I" that doesn't see the sheet of paper cannot be the "I" writing that he doesn't see it since, in order to write as much, he is obliged to see it; or perhaps there are two sheets, the one on which I write and the one I no longer see but imagine. (This slippage, which governs every phenomenology, replaces the referential—deictic—value of the term *I* with its autonymical value, *the I*.) Hollier dubs the episode "allegorical."[29] Sartre perpetually believes that he is starting with reality in the phenomenological sense, and later in the Marxist sense. He begins with a brief story, a "fable" forged to demonstrate that reality must not be confused with imagination. But the story designated to present reality is itself imaginary. The subsequent political texts, submitted to the same analysis, reveal the same sort of fictioning [*fictionnement*] of the real through writing, the same type of uncontrolled sophism.

And, second, there is no present, "Committed fiction [. . .] should present the present," writes Hollier, then quoting Sartre, "it should become 'the reflective self-awareness of a classless society [. . .] the world aware of itself.'[30] But the present is not up to presenting itself."[31] The "enormous presence" of existence is unpresentable: Roquentin observes that nothing escaped presence, except for itself. "A viscous temporality [. . .]. The time of time's absence," as Hollier concludes.[32] The present is gnawed at by the future and the past, by the nothingness of freedom and the massive inertia of the already accomplished. And yet the idea persists that it is here and now that praxis has its place and time. The presentation of *Les Temps modernes*: the future that interests us is only "the future of *our* time," "a limited future barely distinguishable from it" (from the future of that era, that is).[33] The extasis of temporal instances within time has been a matter of course at least since Saint Augustine. Sartre's "sweet delirium" does not lie therein but in the denial of the temporality of writing. Hollier clocks the time of the narration of the lunch with the Self-Taught Man, which is in the present. Thirty pages to describe the two hours of the meal. But since they are theoretically written in the present tense of absolute simultaneity (the persistence of the imaginary deictic), Roquentin would have had to spend no more than two hours to write the thirty pages (while eating). "Atopical and without extension, the narrative is also instantaneous: it takes neither time nor place. Costs nothing. Its writing, utterly gratuitous, claims not to enter into account."[34] The narrator forgets himself and has himself forgotten. When he writes in the past, he is free to take all the time he wants, and even sustain losses in relation to actual time, like Tristram Shandy or Marcel. But writing in an absolute present entails that writing does not take any time, that the story is directly inscribed in the narrative. As in the principle of the tape recorder, or oral history, "the free direct style,"[35] as Hollier dubs it rather nicely. That style obeys a vow: I, the writer, do not write because I am not; I merely exist. As an aspect of negativity or negativization, writing is the instant of the for-itself, and if it is to be, it has neither body nor duration nor place.

And, third, there is no end. Hollier underscores that all of Sartre's books end with a "to be continued," presenting themselves as unfinished. They are merely, he writes, the serialized installments of a future work. He sees a correlation between that incompletion, the genre of the novel, and the Sartrean problematic of the series. The serialized world—of separation, of idiocy or schizophrenia, of nonsense—which is also the American space deployed by the novelistic technique borrowed from Dos Passos, Faulkner, and Hemingway for *The Roads to Freedom* is opposed to the fusionary world, the being-together of the group reconciled with itself and with meaning, of a free and socialist humanity. Sartre responded to a militant imploring him to write a truly popular work (instead of the Flaubert): "A popular revolutionary novel can't be read by everybody off in their own little corner: they would have to be able to read it *together*."[36] But reading cannot be done together, Hollier observes; what can be done together is attending a play or a movie. In the dark, one escapes from the other's gaze, from serialization. Once socialized, the addressee becomes obscure. There is no end for writing because it fails in the presentation of presence; onto the text are grafted other texts, as many texts as there are readers, and diverging in every direction; that proliferation consecrates in Sartre's eyes the regime of seriality. Socialism would be the end of that writing, whose terrain, temporality, and audience are bourgeois. Sartre writes for the bourgeoisie, which instituted seriality, and against the bourgeoisie, in order to effect its undoing. The crisis of 1940 reveals to Roquentin the existence of the group in fusion, the prison-audience for *Bariona*. The crisis of 1952 is gripped by the question: How might one emerge from the idiocy of separation by means of writing, which entails that very idiocy? To which the abbreviated fiction of "the people," and those most unfortunate, offers a response: write in the dark, think like the majority, be affected like the most wretched. From there comes political writing not in the service of the Communist Party, but rather having as its horizon that community for which, in Sartre's eyes, it bears responsibility. What Sartre wanted was epic and an audience that was also his hero, the masses. Which he always confused with the proletariat, which he in turn confused with its leaders.

Fourth: was there at least action? But how might what is pure negativity transform inertia, the past, the passive? Where might be the point of application of what is not on what is? Hollier devotes two chapters, "A Study of Hands" and "Insinuations" to that question. The only body that the for-itself can stand is that of the striated muscles. Those organs which are not under cerebral control are a defiance to freedom, its very failure, and are rejected in a spasm of nausea. Things are instruments for the pure project; they must not touch it; it can touch them, but at a distance. They are outside, as objects, at the end of intentionality's focus. In Berlin, Sartre read Husserl and was jubilant to learn from him that consciousness is not inhabited by impressions or sensations, as the English claimed, but that it manipulates at a distance and even constitutes eidetic objects. When a thing touches, penetrates, or inhabits you, the result is nausea: the striated muscle, like an intestine, escapes control. In a caress, a hand is touched at the same time that it touches. It is animated by involuntary movements, mired in the viscous. Similarly, an act is opposed to a gesture: the latter is an "act *become object*";[37] it "has already been done,"[38] is not freedom, but archaic tradition, seductive nature, dangerous for freedom, magic, as is said of emotion in *Sketch for a Theory of the Emotions*.[39]

The caressing-caressed hand undergoes the fate of a sexual organ; it acts only insofar as it is affected and, consequently, passive. Hollier composes a bouquet of philosophical, political, novelistic, and critical texts in which that schema is repeated; they come from every phase of his work. The anxiety linked to the feminine (as we shall thus term an "impure" negativity) is constant, the horror of "pursu[ing] in the dampness of the bed the sad dream of absolute imminence."[40] After 1968, Sartre's texts, for the most part, stem not from his hand, but from his mouth. From tape recorder to megaphone: the immediate phonation of intentionality without flesh. There are equivalences here—which should be pondered—between, on the one hand, time, passivity, immanence, the feminine, and writing and, on the other, the act, transcendence, the virile, and voice. I admire the delicacy and elegance with which Hollier plucks these flowers and assembles them—I was about to say, without touching them.

What is at stake in all these impasses is not sex but writing. And at this point, at the cost of an additional step, that Michel Enaudeau helped me take a while back,[41] one realizes that the politics of prose, perhaps even in its failure, reveals poetry's success. Sartre's theory of language, wrote Meschonnic in a 1979 issue of *Obliques*, is "the most conventional variant of the theory of the sign."[42] According to Sartre in *Saint Genet*, meaning is "a certain conventional relationship which makes a present object the substitute of an absent object."[43] The present "object," be it word or sentence, is a sign; its true value is the object it signifies. Thus "if you direct your attention to the signification, the word is effaced; you go beyond it and fuse the meaning with the thing signified."[44] Such is the norm assigned to writing by Sartre after the "crisis of language" of 1948. As may be recalled:

> The function of a writer is to call a spade a spade. If words are sick, it is up to us to cure them. Instead of that, many writers live off this sickness. In many cases modern literature is a cancer of words. [. . .] There is nothing more deplorable than the literary practice which, I believe, is called poetic prose and which consists of using words for the obscure harmonics which resound about them and which are made up of vague meanings which are in contradiction with the clear signification.[45]

That latter dimension "is conferred upon the object from without by a signifying intention."[46] I intend to say such and such a thing, and in order to do so, I employ such and such a word or sentence, "for I consider myself to be the signifier."[47] From there, an entire philosophy of language can be derived—a politics of prose. "The art of prose is interdependent with the sole regime in which prose retains a meaning: democracy. When one is threatened, the other is, as well." Individual subjects communicate meanings through language, that is, intended objects. Names of objects give way to the transcendence that names objects. In prose, freedoms communicate. But in prose insofar as it is an art.

Hollier reminds us that at the time Bataille was publishing *The Hatred of Poetry* and Caillois *Les Impostures de la poésie*, Sartre, at the beginning of *What is Literature?*, was analyzing poetry as a language become natural, turned back on its own words and turned away from meaningful objects—perverted speech, "language inside out."[48] Like many others, Hollier understands this analysis as an appeal to committed literature to rid itself of its poetic narcissism. Poetry would be an aristocratism of language: the words are there for their own ends, not for the emancipatory ends of its speakers. Meschonnic sees in that self-reference the origin of the litanies of "enclosure," of the "rhetoric of limits, of the play of madness," of the "literature of noncommunication" denounced by Sartre.[49]

But matters are not that simple. In capitalism (and this is one of the issues at stake in the Flaubert study[50]) prose has ceased being, for Sartre, the medium within which transcendences communicate. It has become the accumulation of established meanings. We no longer speak within it, but are rather spoken. The rule is no longer free usage, but the constraint of commonplaces and received ideas. The crisis of democracy and the decline of the bourgeoisie consist in this collapse: meaning, becomes immanent, slips away from signifying subjects. And it was in vain that the poetic withdrawal into language games tried to pass itself off, with Mallarmé, as a literary revolution; from Sartre's point of view, it was but the flip side of the opaqueness to which prose had fallen victim, an all too simple manner of overthrowing the literature of consumption and amusement, an acceptance of language's neurosis. Meschonnic concludes from that analysis that Sartre, all things considered, with his refusal of the cult of writing, is perhaps more lucid than the philosophers of writing's self-enclosure and the politics of the revolution of poetic language. At least, he writes, Sartre is not like them: "deficient in historicity."[51] I wonder if in order to save the thesis attributed to Sartre it is worth paying the price of abandoning the entire critique of subjectivity! Which is not, as Meschonnic seems inclined to believe, a vagary of philosophers and writers. The politics of prose runs smack against the impasses enumerated by Hollier—presence, the present, the reader, and so forth. But its failure reveals at the core of language an essence that is more than—or different from—a function of signification, and which Sartre did not fail to perceive.

In *Saint Genet* he opposes meaning [*sens*] to signification [*signification*] in these terms: "By meaning, I understand participation in a present reality, in its being, in the being of other realities, be they present or absent, visible or invisible, and thus, little by little, in the universe itself [. . .] meaning is a natural quality of things." Signification "is a transcendent relationship between one object and another," meaning is "a transcendence that has fallen into immanence."[52] The question is the following: Is this fall no more than that accompanying the growing inertia of linguistic praxis, the fact that once the word has lost its arbitrary character in relation to the thing itself, we traffic in words as though they were the things they designate? That would amount to the alienation of language in the already spoken, its ideologization. That meaning of meaning would be the opaqueness within which the spark of freedom is extinguished. But meaning is also its total opposite: the compost of signification.

Verstraeten asked Sartre in 1966: Do you devalue poetry?[53] Sartre, astonished, clarified his thought: In prose, words are exchanged between interlocutors, between author and reader, such is the democracy of prose. In poetry, the author reconquers "what is for all of us a moment of solitude [. . .], the moment, precisely, in which words refer us back to the solitary monster that we are."[54] It is a different communication than that effected through prose: in a movement of a narcissistic identification, the reader enters into resonance with the sentence. A frequent phenomenon, declares Sartre, and a regrettable one, if the resonance is not "contained within certain limits."[55] (We should not lose sight of the subject's rights over the associations to which the devil prompts him.) Already in 1948, Sartre had given Leiris as an example of a "search for lost time" by way of words charged with affective implications. The moment of solitude may indeed be constantly transcended, but one is constantly "obliged to come back to it again." And why is that? Because even in prose "there is a perpetual exceeding of simple signification. It might even be said that everything exceeds signification, and it is that everything which founds communication, or better put, deep communication."[56] Already in 1948, an excess within poetry itself: "The word, the phrase-thing, inexhaustible as things, everywhere overflows the feeling which has produced them."[57] Perfect communication, the republic of freedoms would require that interlocutors exchange the entirety of their respective situations, one whole world for another. In theory that takes place only in the writing of prose, in its art-form at least, if not in commonplace prose. And in literary prose, it is precisely the "indispensable," the "absolutely indispensable" poetic moment that lends prosaic communication its depth. Prose is the transmission of significations outside the self; in prose, poetry is "the moment of respiration in which one returns to oneself," in which resonances are attended to and liberated (within certain limits); it is a stasis in which Desire (capital D) or History (capital H) is acknowledged.[58] History or desire slips into the articulations of the language of signification in order to give voice to the "inarticulable."[59]

Those specifications come much later than the 1940s,[60] which interest Hollier; they are from the 1960s, and the echo of Lacan's thought can be heard in them. The instrumentalist thesis by then had lost something of its contours, and the transcendentalist critique lodged in 1944 against Ponge's materialism at the end of "Man and Things," for example, could not be maintained.[61] When one calls a spade, one is not calling a spade, but a world, a "microcosm."[62] The arrogance of the for-itself is given rather harsh treatment. An aesthetic that is more ontological than humanist begins to surface. By which I mean that poetry may be a failure (Ponge, Baudelaire, and all of modern poetry as a conflict with the religion of success), but it is such from the inarticulable.[63] From the perspective of being, it remains a success. That aesthetic had already brought with it into the 1948 text expressions such as "a face of flesh"[64] of the word, its "physiognomy,"[65] its "particular affinities with the earth, the sky, the water, and all created things,"[66] with the result that if poetry indeed "misuses language"[67] it is not to be understood as an abuse or aberration, but as a different situation, a different project than those called into play in the polities of prose. And even as a different style of commitment, if one likes, the modem poet is "man committing himself to lose"; he doesn't contest modernity any less than the writer of prose, but through different means "the contesting of prose is carried on in the name of a greater success; and that of poetry, in the name of a hidden defeat which every victory conceals."[68] It is consequently imperative to observe "an absolute difference" between prose and poetry, as Hollier says; Sartre maintained that it was a matter of "complex structures,"[69] but it is no less the case that each is, he added, "impure, but well-defined."

If I insist on what is a constant in Sartre's commentary on poetry (the failures of Baudelaire, Mallarmé, Ponge), it is because the diagnosis ends up spreading, via the *prosateur* par excellence named Flaubert, to Sartre himself. Immediately after the 1940s, he became aware that there was no way to win, that words could not be dissipated in the transparency of a signifying intention, that capitalist modernity, but perhaps also the being of language itself, was part and parcel of pure communication and freedom. But if the performance principle requires speech to attain expression in a wooden language, triumphalism is doomed to aggravate that alienation, for one can triumph in such language alone. The proper strategy, instead of choosing to ignore the thickness of words, would be to explore it since history and desire are embedded therein.[70] And that one become the witness not of constitutive freedom but of the intermediary realm, of combinations of being and nothingness, of viscosities, of the entire transitional region which is the business of poets. A politics of poetry? That would be saying too much and saying it poorly. But does not the work of Sartre as a writer—

in its incompletion, in the very impasses revealed by Hollier, and even in the secret dissonances that he "insinuates"[71]—bear witness to a success carried off by language against him who wanted to turn it to his own use? At the foot of the popular, populist, political Sartre, huge circulation, huge contestation, the shadow of a different Sartre—withdrawn into himself, secret, captivated by failure, unknown, and never managing to recognize himself in the words that came to him or, rather, failed to. The shadow wins out over the hero toward the end, when the committed writer lays down his pen, renounces in favor of his comrades, advances in the wilderness of the Paris suburbs with a megaphone in his useless hands, only to realize at the end that his prose has no audience at all and that the poetry in his work would have won out over his life's work. It would be a marvelous story, to which I am prompted by Enaudeau, behind Hollier, in which the subject is defeated by words.

DISORDER
VALÉRY

Thierry de Duve proposes a commentary on the sentence: 'This is art.'[1] My thesis is that this sentence is consistent by its very inconsistency. I shall begin by analyzing the sentence's properties. It is simple to show that it is *not consistent* (in the ordinary logical and epistemological sense) when taken *literally*, without concern for the connotations that the history of modern art attaches to art's "creation" and its "reception" (what Paul Valéry terms, respectively, "production" and "consumption").

I shall then attempt to show that the motives one may invoke for detecting the inconsistency of the sentence "This is art" are quite possibly traits characteristic of the reflexive status of the artistic operation (writing) and of its reception (reading). In this second step I will tacitly seek help from Kant, but above all from Valéry—even though his approach may seem altogether different.

Finally, it would be appropriate to draw from these brief analyses a few observations relative to disorder and order, to nothingness and the witnessing of nothingness, to singularity and consensus. These observations will only be lightly sketched.

1. Inconsistency

Here, I use the term "consistency" for the properties expected of a sentence claiming to state what is true or false.

I use the term "cognitive" simply for this family of phrases claiming to state that something (obviously) is true or false.

I do so knowing, like everyone else, that this claim is not the same as to verify or falsify a mathematical statement or, let us say, a "physical" one (that is, one possessing a referent reputed to be real, which is not the case for mathematics).

I will limit myself here to taking a cognitive physical utterance for a term of comparison by supposing that the sentence "This is art" applies to a real object (referent).

"This is art" appears, at the very least, to be a partial determination if not a definition (defined as a complete description). The sentence attributes a predicate ("art") to a propositional subject ("this"). (This could be expressed otherwise, for example, as a Chomskian *noun-phrase* "this" and *verb-phrase* "is art."[2] Linguistically, this would be more interesting, but, for that very reason, less enlightening logically or epistemologically. It could also be expressed in Frege-Russell notation.) What is usually called knowledge resides in this attribution of a predicate to a subject. Knowledge is the recognition that an object (referent), named by the propositional subject, belongs to the class named by the predicate. The object named "this" belongs to the class "what is art."

From the vocabulary of *The Differend*,[3] I shall recall the three operations that appear to me indispensable to cognition and recognition. I shall not, however, expand upon the problematic that led me to these conclusions: suffice it to say that, considered within a language-like perspective, it is the very problematic of the possibility of knowing a *reality*.

In order for a sentence to be cognitive, that is, apt to indicate the truth or falsity of what it signifies concerning its referent:

It must first be endowed with a meaning. In other words, it entails the connection of one term with another, and this connection must take place by means of connective operators (Kant called them synthetic) that are reputed to be rational, or at least reasonable. These are the operators that Aristotle, and Kant after him, called categories. In modern logic (which is extensional), the symbol of inclusion ($\supset$) designates the connection of one term with another; the nature of this connection being specified by the play of symbols of quantity, quality, and relationship (parentheses, equals signs, and so on).

The existential "this" belongs to the universal class of "what is art."

The second (properly physical this time and not merely logical) condition for a cognition is that the logically conceived sentence must be confronted with "reality." Practically speaking, this means that *cases* must be presented that appear to verify the meaning of the sentence in question (or at least to falsify the sentence that contradicts it).

I stress the term "case," and here is how we find it glossed in contemporary logic: "*there is* a certain x" and "this x belongs to y" (to what is art, for example).

This *there is* obviously eludes the signifying capacity. It belongs to the capacity for *showing* or *indicating*. It presupposes that "something" particular is given, here and now, to the speaker (and to the addressee, who must be able to ascertain that *there is*, really, *this*, an x).

The cognitive procedure thus demands that deictics ("here," "now," "this," "that," "I," "you," etc.) be used.

In the sentence under question, "this" is precisely such a deictic.

For the third condition, you may notice that the deictic "this" only refers to a "there is something" to the extent that it is *currently* indicated by the *current* sentence.

I must forego the issue of this *current* moment. Suffice it to say that it is the *in actu* or the *actu*, the *in situ* or the *situ*, of artists or *performance* arts. This raises difficult problems concerning space-time, or, more precisely, concerning not the time *in which* the sentence is located, but the time *marked by* the sentence—often marked by its very presence, sometimes by its presentation. When we find the term "now" (or any of the deictics adjacent to this term: "here," "you," etc.) in a sentence, it indicates the instant contemporaneous with the time in which the current sentence takes place; contemporaneous, but "measured" (if I may express it this way) *on the basis of the time* of this sentence. To say "today" (a case analogous to "now") is not the same as saying "2 February 1989."[4] In the latter case, the measurement of time is carried out by means of a calendar (years, months, days).

A calendar is an evenly divided grid of proper nouns enabling us to indicate all of the "nows" in a solar year by making them independent of their current designation. When I say, "2 February 1989," I am not saying that it is "now" or yesterday or tomorrow. And if it happens that it is in fact "now," the indication of this "now" by its date detaches it from the current moment of the deictic sentence and fixes it on a grid of proper nouns whose interrelationships are ordered in a fixed manner independent of deictics.

Like all proper nouns, dates are only designations (they have no meaning). But, unlike deictics, dates are designators that fall under the category of what Saul Kripke terms "rigid designators," which I understand to mean that the designated is only designated (and not signified), but is identical to itself regardless of the current sentence that designates it.[5]

Thus, proper nouns keep their designative value from one sentence to another and from one speaker to another.

Each of the nouns and symbols used by science are such rigid designators and thus proper nouns. For example, the nouns designating units of length, intensity, weight, mass, velocity, etc.

Without this "rigidity" in designation, it could not be proved that *this* (a simple deictic) confirms the assertion that x is y or that "this is art." For we must be able to place "this" in a world of nouns (a grid, for the calendar, but this goes for all tables of designative regularities) independent of "performances" (sentences insofar as they are current), in order to be certain that both the current sentence p_0 and the *later* sentence p_1 still have the *same* referent. This, I shall not develop further.

It is now obvious what makes the sentence "This is art" inconsistent. To be precise:

1. It is not inconsistent because it presupposes the class of "objects that are art." For recognition to take place: an inclusive relationship must be established between the object under examination and a class to which it is judged to belong. This class is thus defined beforehand. We may accept that *in this respect* the sentence is consistent, provided that the class of "what is art" be known.

   When the receiver (the public) protests that "this is not art," it has an explicit or implicit definition of the class of "what is art."

   The receiver cannot be accused of being wrong unless we accept that the definition of this class may change, or, in a case of major importance, if we accept that the "this" in question can contribute to a modification in the definition of this class. In themselves, neither of these presuppositions (neither a modification of the definition of art nor a modifying role played by "this") leads to an inconsistency. A model analogous (but only analogous) to this modification and this modifier may be readily located in the history and epistemology of science. Here too, the definition of classes (what is electric, what is dense, what is interactive, etc.) may be expanded; in science too, it is "this," a designated (and *also*, of course, named, that is, communicable) reality that may be the modifier of it. This is called discovery and/or invention.

2. Where inconsistency intervenes with respect to our sentence's truth or falsity, is that it lacks *the name* "this." It is inconsistent, in this sense, because it is incomplete. It should be linked to another sentence like "The Venus de Milo [proper name] or the Large Glass [proper name] is this [deictic], and this is art." Without the so-called proper nomination (the exclusive one, that is, locating "this" on a grid of regularities: the nominal catalog of works belonging to the class of what is art, for example), we do not know *what* we are talking about when we say, simply, "this." There is no guarantee that the speaker of (our) sentence p_0 designates by "this"

the same referent as his addressee. And if they converse together, each in turn becoming speaker then addressee, from sentence to sentence, they will never know if they are speaking about the same referent.

3. Yet this defect is only a fault within the framework of the requirements of a cognitive phrase (one whose purpose is to tell the truth concerning a referent). Now, my thinking (following many others) is that the question as to whether this is or is not art (assuming that "this" is *named*) can only be settled cognitively to the extent that "this" (under its name) is posited as an *object* to know or to recognize, as a *referent* that belongs or doesn't belong to the class of "what is art."

Under this supposition, "this" (under its name) is posited as a thing (a positional operator called "modality")—that is, as a material object, a "physical" object in the sense discussed earlier, a "sensible" object if one prefers—to be classified in a set.

That artworks may thus be taken as things to be recognized and placed in known and defined sets, there is no doubt. A major portion of literary and art criticism is engaged in this project. This is also the main concern of museum curators and librarians.

Let's listen to what Valéry has to say about this procedure in his course in poetics:

> There remains the work itself as a perceptible thing. Here we have a third consideration very different from the other two.
>
> In this case we regard a work as an *object*, as pure object, that is to say, we put into it no more of ourselves than may be applied indiscriminately to any object—an attitude that is adequately characterized by the absence of any production of value.
>
> What power have we over this object which, regarded in this way, has no power over us? But we do have power over it. We can measure it in space and time; we can count the words of a text or the syllables in a line of poetry; we can note that a certain book appeared at a certain time; that a certain element in a painting is copied from some other painting; that there is a hemistich in Lamartine that can be found in Thomas, and that a certain page in Victor Hugo was written as early as 1645 by some obscure Père François. We can point out that a certain piece of reasoning is a paralogism; that this sonnet is incorrect in

form; that the drawing of that arm defies anatomy, and that a certain use of words is not customary. All these conclusions result from a kind of mechanical operation which amounts to superimposing the work, or parts of it, on a particular model.

This way of dealing with works of the mind makes no distinction between them and all the other possible kinds of works. By giving them a *definable* existence, it ranks them with things. This is the point to remember:

Everything that can be defined is ipso facto *dissociated from the producing mind and set off against it.* By defining it the mind turns it into raw material on which it can operate, or an instrument with which it can work.

Thus the mind puts what it has defined out of its own reach, thereby showing that it knows itself and trusts only what is other than itself.[6]

Valéry suggests that the definitional (which is also referential) procedure stands in *opposition* to what he calls the "producing mind," that is, the mind insofar as it "creates" (to use that old term), and that opposition, according to Valéry, is as present in the "consumer" (the receiver) as in the producer (the writer, the artist).

Insofar as the mind is concerned with art or, rather, with making art, it proceeds so little by means of definition, reference, or conceptual determination, Valéry further suggests in this passage, that if it posits or apprehends works as things, if it places them "out of its own reach," it is because it "knows itself," because it "trusts only what is other than itself."

To put it another way, "this" is proposed to the cognition of things because "this" *is not* a known thing, neither is it a knowable nor even a recognizable thing to the mind that "produced" this. Moreover, the question whether "this is art" is only posed precisely at the instant where "production" (or what Valéry also calls *poetics*—I would say *writing*) *ceases* and makes way for classification.

2. Consistency

My punctual and awkward recourse to Valéry already brings us into the zone of consistencies attributable to our inconsistent sentence.

That sentence—"This is art"—is not, I repeat, consistent from a cognitive point of view. It therefore is not even classifiable within the sort of critique that Valéry exemplifies in the text as we heard it. The unnamed "this" is the point at which it fails vis-à-vis cognitive consistency. And it is with this point that I shall begin to ascend again toward its "poetic" or written consistency.

1. To carry out this anabasis, I will seek help once again from Valéry, for the insistence of "this" in our sentence seems to me entirely congruent with the stress Valéry places on what he calls *act* or *in action*. I have remarked that any deictic—and "this" is a deictic—only refers to a situational element (a person, a time, a space, an object) by placing it in relation to the actuality of the sentence in which that deictic appears: to the *current* sentence or the sentence *in action*. On this point, Valéry writes:

   > Everything that I have said thus far may be summed up in these few words: *a work of the mind exists only in action*. Outside of its action nothing is left but an object that presents no particular relation to the mind. Transport a statue you admire to a country sufficiently different from ours, and it turns into a meaningless stone; a Parthenon into nothing more than a small marble quarry. And when a piece of poetry is used as a collection of grammatical difficulties or illustrations of rules, it ceases immediately to be a *work of the mind*, since the use that is made of it is utterly alien to the conditions under which it came into being, while at the same time it is denied the consumption value that gives it meaning.[7]

   It is pointless to belabor what is clearly understood here: this (passably enigmatic) *act* or *in action*, this act *of the mind* (a no less obscure entity that is properly "the work of the mind") is (negatively) first circumscribed as what is not the work as *object* or thing. The work as act is not the work as object.

   As object, the work is named and signified, or signifiable. Conditions are placed on it; it is subject to rules of cognitive belonging in one or more sets.

   The mind that recognizes or strives to recognize it ("Is it art?") is not the mind—the poetic mind—that makes it. The poetic mind is only in action, that is, here and now: the mind has neither permanent sights nor a permanent grip on it, because the mind does not hold a defined and constant identity for it.

Valéry expresses it even better in the following passage which may be considered a definition of undefinable actuality or presence:

> But regardless of the clarity, evidence, force, beauty of the mental event which puts an end to our expectancy, which completes our thought or dispels our doubt, nothing is irrevocable so far. The following moment still has absolute power over the product of the one before it. For the mind reduced to its own substance cannot do anything finite and is absolutely unable to tie itself down.[8]

According to Valéry, the state of the poetic mind affects the consumer as well as the producer. That poetic state is not, properly speaking, a state, but a mode of temporality remarkable for its discontinuity and discreteness. It is a sort of spasm in which what has been done does not govern what is yet to be done. "[T]he mind [. . .] is absolutely unable to tie itself down." Neither the linkages nor the connections between one word and another nor the connections between one part of a visual or sonorous figure to another are fixed, and, at each instant, there is a "decision" to be made as to how to create linkages. Forming a form (for there will be, in the end, a form) is not bound to a project.

2. The use of the terms "expectancy" and "doubt" should be noted in the earlier passage from Valéry. I have said that a "decision" had to be made. In the uncertainty where the disconnection of moments thrusts the mind—a disconnection that is, thus, a proliferation of possible linkages between one moment and the next—the mind awaits this decision. A decision one waits for is not a decision one makes.

The *act* or the *in action* thus takes on a meaning that is not immediately a temporal one, but one of *exis*, of being-there, or perhaps even of *ethos*, of disposition. Let's say a manner of being, of being with respect to time, of course, but, for this reason, a manner of being with respect to linkage. (And I stress that this is not a manner of being with respect to being.) And it is assuredly not a manner of being with respect to the *object* (even a future, anticipated, or projected object): there is no object in this *exis* or *ethos*.

What the writer, composer, painter, or filmmaker (or even the reader, listener, or spectator) waits for is for "it to come." It is the event of the "decision" that enacts and ends the infinity of possibilities. It should be recalled that "the mind reduced to its own substance cannot do anything finite." It desires or waits for it but does not have it at its disposal. It is not the mind that will complete the form.

For the mind is the indefiniteness and infiniteness of linkages, indetermination, and what Valéry, in short, calls disorder:

> To raise the question of the mind is to call everything into question; all is disorder and every reaction against disorder is itself disorder. But this disorder is the condition and promise of the mind's fecundity, which depends on the unexpected rather than the expected, on what we do not know (and because we do not know it) rather than on what we know.[9]

This disorder is also the mind's "freedom." Others have referred to free association or *aura*.

The act that decides is not an *action* in the strict sense of the term—it is an event. Valéry refers to "the clarity, evidence, force, beauty of the mental *event* which puts an end to our expectancy."[10]

It may well be that "our only means of direct action on our mental system is to curtail its freedom." (Strange system.) "But," Valéry adds, "as for the rest, the modifications and substitutions that still operate despite restrictions, all we can do is wait for our desideratum to turn up. *We have no way of finding within ourselves exactly what we want.*"[11]

I believe I recognize in this "freedom" or this "disorder" what I, for my part, call passibility; a disseizure.

"Instability, incoherence, inconsistency," writes Valéry, "constitute [the producing mind's] habitual way of life" when it is reduced to "its own substance."[12]

3. Yet this is a disseizure and a passibility in anticipation of their end. Something is *wished for* in this expectation. Not something from the regime of voluntary action, where it is *I* who wishes. Something is wished for that is not I, something that is not the finished object, which immediately becomes the simple referent of cognitions or possible interpretations.

These, in turn, pay indirect homage to indetermination through an indefinite proliferation of their determinations and explanations: in one sense, this is or is not art; in some other sense also, this is or is not art. Commentary would be interminable and, especially, futile (incapable of building an inheritance, a capital of clear judgments). This is an eminent difference between the history of commentary on poetic works and that on natural effects.

What, then, is "wished for" at the heart of uncertainty, in the proliferation of imaginary possibilities? What is desired? Simply the event of an end. In a sense, a death. Yet is it the death of what is simply possible, in order to give *birth* to the artwork?

Here we must introduce the necessarily concomitant *topos* of the expectation of the act at the heart of disorder, the *topos* of fatigue.

Valéry discerns *two* kinds of fatigue: one through art and another through poetics:

> Whether I chain myself to the page I wish to write or to the page I wish to understand, in either case I am entering upon a phase of reduced freedom. But in both cases the limitation of my freedom may take two opposite forms. Sometimes the task itself incites me to pursue it, and far from feeling it to be a burden, a deviation from the more natural ways of my mind, I abandon myself to it and advance so eagerly along the path laid out by my intention that my sense of fatigue is diminished—up to the moment when it suddenly beclouds my thoughts, muddles my ideas, brings back the disorder of normal short-term exchanges, and restores a state of dispersive, restful indifference.
>
> But sometimes the constraint is the main thing; I force myself to maintain a direction that becomes increasingly painful; I am more aware of the effort than of its effect, the means fight the end, and I am compelled to preserve the tension of my mind by more and more precarious expedients, having less and less to do with the ideal object whose power and action must be maintained at the expense of a fatigue that soon becomes unbearable. Here we have a striking contrast between two ways in which the mind may operate.[13]

Unable to give this text the commentary it deserves, I will merely stress that good disorder does not fatigue; exhaustion befalls you.

It's a happy ending. But the specter of the act that we try to bring on through endless rule- and constraint-making is a desiccating, desertifying fatigue, a fatigue caused by the will and an obstinacy that moves us toward sterility. This is a fatigue effected by rules and perhaps by the breathlessness caused by having to produce a work just the same. It is a fatigue caused by requirement.
4. Let us take up again this term of sterility. In any "this," is it not, at bottom, a question of a banal analogy with the pain of childbirth and with the impatience to give birth.

When Valéry writes "To put this briefly: in the production of a given work, *action comes in contact* with the indefinable,"[14] is he stating anything other than that the phallus comes to touch the lack thereof?

And by this touch, assuredly *killing* the hysterical agitation of forgotten renewed beginnings, of misrecognized disorders, of panic before virtual linkages, but also *engendering* an infant: the work. As soon as it is born, the infant can be subsumed under the rule of knowledge. At the cost of misapprehension, however, it will remain, like an infant born of inconsistency, as long as it has not engendered in the "consumer" this very agitation and expectation of the end of agitation from which the work was born.

Besides his *Cahiers* (*Notebooks*),[15] many texts, starting with *La Soirée de M. Teste*,[16] demonstrate how this sexual difference (let us call it sexual for the sake of convenience) occupies and undoubtedly preoccupies Valéry's thought in its *entirety*. We know his bewilderment before femininity and aversion to the possibility of disorder (a male, cognitive term) in his house, the mind.

As much could be said, although in another register, of the Kantian preoccupation, the Kantian *division* between imagination and reason. With the *beautiful*, it lies in a division or an emulation that is moderated by agreement; with the *sublime*, it lies in a conflict brought to a breaking point where the proliferating network of imaginary possibilities becomes frayed and the act of understanding appears as it truly is in its princely principle: not the rule of knowledge but the transcendental and unknowable law, the event itself and the act that is incomparable to any regularity.

I am not particularly beholden to this division of labor between imaginary and symbolic under the regime of the real, as Lacan would have said, and that Valéry, a bit naively but unfailingly, calls desire.

I simply state this: "this is art," a cognitively inconsistent sentence, is consistent with regard to the *double inconsistency* of art (or writing). There is an "initial" inconsistency (sorry for the poor term) in the indetermination of possible linkages—that is nevertheless not just hysteria, itself infelicitously determined in its repetition (here, one would have to refer to *unbinding*)—and the "final" inconsistency of an event of determination that produces the work, "from time to time," not as an object but as an occasion, a case, a "this," here and now—an occasion to reiterate the same conflict, sweet or furious, in the said "consumer."

3. Reflection

I promised to approach the question of reflection. The time of reflection escapes or has escaped me, as always.

As always, because reflection (which I mean here in the Kantian sense) is of the order of a time in relation to which what we call "physical" time, clock time, also called (by antiphrasis, I suppose) "real time," never ceases to escape us. The time of reflection, in the broad sense that Kant lends the word (under the rubric of reflective judgment), is exactly what I have discussed, in reference to Valéry, as the time of the work.

As I said a while ago, determining an object—"it is art"—supposes that we *already* possess the rule of its signification: the class to which it belongs and the categories of that belonging.

Reflection supposes that we do not possess that rule. Consequently, we do not even possess the object since we are not yet in a position to signify or name it. We can just barely indicate it as "this," as a case or an occasion. This is what Kant says of the object from an aesthetic point of view: it is only occasion.

So, we do not have the rule, not yet, we await it. Actually, in Kantian orthodoxy, it is not the rule of understanding that we await but, where art is concerned, the form imagination might take. But the case (if I may call it such) is no less convincing in that reflection is uncertainty, expectation and uncontrolled ramblings among analogies. No less convincing because it is poorer for the fact that what will act is not even the concept, but the form.

In Kant's first Critique there are strange, nearly impenetrable, but decisive, pages on the amphibology of the concepts of reflection. I would have liked to have given them some commentary, they are very illuminating, but I will forgo that wish.

I will just say this: reflection is a disposition of the mind by which it judges without concept. To judge, that is to settle [*trancher*], to decide, to cleave: the power to cleave, *Urteilskraft*, is also that of bringing together, *to synthesize*. What Valéry calls *act*.

And if this takes place without concept it is because previously, before the advent of a decision, nothing occurs but the rambling flow of every linkage possible—Valéry's "disorder," to which the comparison in Kant or the analogy—the common demon—would correspond.

We see that this reflection is not a flexion of thought back upon itself, but rather a flexion within thought of something that seems to not be itself since thought cannot determine it. Yet it is the *flection* of a something that is possibly more "inside" thought than itself.

Now, this further inside is nothing other than feeling, *Empfindung*, or, as we say today, affect. Valéry writes:

> A poem on paper is nothing but a piece of writing, subject to all the uses to which such writing can be put. But among all its possibilities there is one, and only one, that creates the conditions under which it will take on the force and form of action. A poem is a discourse that demands and induces a continuous connection between the *voice that is* and the *voice that is coming* and *must come*. And this voice must be such as to command a hearing, and call forth an emotional state of which the text is the sole verbal expression. Take away the voice—the right voice—and the whole thing becomes arbitrary. The poem becomes a sequence of signs, connected only in the sense that they are traced one after the other.[17]

Excitation of the affective state. I will not insist: we are indeed speaking of the same thing, of a "this" that is in no way a thing, but rather an occasion for a "pure" feeling in the Kantian sense—pure in that it is unmotivated. The voice, the double voice, the one that declares that this is beautiful and the one that calls for this feeling-judgment to be shared, that voice may also be found in the Kantian Analytic of the Sublime.

Again, and to conclude, Valéry: "Works of the mind, poems and all the rest, relate only to *that which creates what created them*, and to absolutely nothing else."[18]

A sentence understood clearly as follows: this is art if "this" gives birth to the pure feeling (disorder, expectation of its end, and hope of its transfer to a receiver) from which "this" was itself born.

Such is the *resistance* of art—a resistance in which all of its consistency consists: determination should never *exhaust* birth.

VOICES
FREUD[1]

> I shall not in the present paper attempt any discussion of the psychological significance of obsessional thinking. Such a discussion would be of extraordinary value in its results, and would do more to clarify our ideas upon the nature of the conscious and the unconscious than any study of hysteria or the phenomena of hypnosis. It would be a most desirable thing if the philosophers and psychologists who develop brilliant theoretical views on the unconscious upon a basis of hearsay knowledge or from their own conventional definitions would first submit to the convincing impressions which may be gained from a first-hand study of the phenomena of obsessional thinking. We might almost go to the length of requiring it of them, if the task were not so far more laborious than the methods of work to which they are accustomed.[2]

1. There are always three states in the inscription of a voice, three scenes: the public report, often published, that recounts and sets forth the case and the cure; the sequence of analytical sessions in the course of which the patient's suffering life is supposedly recounted; that life itself. —You might say: three life "histories," the latter one supposedly exempt from all mediating relations. Well, that's a narratologist's banality. It's likewise a banality to remark upon how the voice and the characteristic of the voice change from one scene to the next. And banal to remark how each of these changes corresponds to a work, a manner, shall we say, an art. —I take the case of the Rat Man. Here's an example of the kind of question raised by this art: is it really Ernst's voice (the name he goes by in the *Journal* of sessions kept by Freud), the voice of Ernst himself, that Freud hears on the couch? Is this the voice Freud makes heard at the Salzburg Congress and in the *Jahrbuch* article?[3] —In order to

answer this kind of question, a supplementary witness would be needed, an extra voice, one above all suspicion and having a perfect knowledge of which voice is the voice of Ernst in himself, which is the voice of Ernst addressed to Freud, and which is the voice reported by Freud. A classic problem: when the truth of subjective certitude must absolutely be guaranteed, a bearer of absolute knowledge is called upon. But this bearer of absolute knowledge is in turn only the object of a subjective certitude. —What is banally limpid in this distinguishing of the three scenes and in their interrelations stems from the following ideology: there is a voice, it belongs to someone; which is to say that this someone knows what he or she says by means of this voice; and this voice is addressed to someone. —And, by way of a complement that is no less ideological: that someone who has a voice also has a life which is recounted by that voice. —But the clinical *prattein* (see §22) is by itself the critique of this ideology.

2. It isn't easy getting rid of this ideological complex. But the notion of *case* bears upon it. Latin says *casus* and Greek *ptōsis*, from *piptō*, to fall. These terms are used in the most ancient treatises on medicine and grammar. They signify an inflexion, a flexing (all the way to a fall) in relation to some norm, to some non-cased state, which serves the function of absolute witness. In medicine, this is health. In grammar, Aristotle finds an example of a non-cased phrase, of "simple and proper" discourse (*haplos logos*), in a proposition like *Sōcratēs peripatei* (the noun in the nominative singular; the verb in the third person singular of the present indicative). —Would there likewise be a zero degree or "simple and proper" state of the voice? And what would it be? An atonal voice, without intonation, which would hide behind what it says, would not let any of the speaker's feelings appear, would do no more than transmit the message to an addressee in such a way that it is received without misunderstanding? More or less the ideal of information theory. Hello, Timid Fawn, do you read me, I repeat, over and out, received five by five. —But that voice is itself a case, the non-tone is still a tone. As opposed to medicine and grammar, *Tonkunst*, the art of tones, music that is, does not admit a non-cased state, of a zero tone. And consequently, not of inflexions either.

3. So much so that when we accept that Ernst's voice (eventually Freud's too) is modified when it crosses from one scene to another, we ought to say what kind of change is going on: is this one of those *case* changes in the health of language, I mean a flexing vis-à-vis a simple grammatical state? One or more *inflexions*? Or is it the tone that *jumps*, without one being able to say that that jump is an inflexion? —I would say that according

to the first hypothesis, the voice is supposedly *articulated*, in *arthron* as the Greeks and above all Aristotle used to say. The voice is formed by *articuli*, by little members deprived of signification in themselves, conventionally put together in order to form words, *onomata*, which can refer to the objects they designate because they are their arbitrary representatives. Their referential value is agreed upon by the speakers who exchange these words. Aristotle consequently names them *symbols* (*symbola*), since their "passive" value (at the receiving end) can always be applied without remainder to their active value (at the enunciating end).[4] —Without going any further, it suffices to say that the articulated voice, which I shall call *lexis* (something akin to "enunciation"), goes from an addressor to an addressee and transmits to the latter a meaning on the subject of what it is referring to. It is thus articulated along two axes: its destination or *addressedness*,[5] and the referentiality of meaning. The pragmatic axis and the semantic axis, one would say today. It is on the basis of this structure, which would be like the non-case of sentences, that an inflexion is conceivable and that a modification in this voice can be conceived as an inflexion.

4. Freud likes to clarify his conclusions about a case through inflexions of the articulated voice. So he does with the phantasy of a child being beaten;[6] even more so, perhaps, with Schreber. He doesn't start from some zero case, at least implicitly, but on the contrary from the case of the *lexis* that he thinks is the clinical *case* itself. For Schreber, the case is articulated according to the *lexis*: "I (a man) love him (a man)," which would be the key inflexion. Starting from this case, Freud reconstitutes the sentences, always articulated, which come to hide (inflect) this first voice and which correspond to the symptoms: "I do not *love* him—I *hate* him, because HE PERSECUTES ME"; "I do not love *him*—I love *her*, because SHE LOVES ME"; "It is not *I* who love the man—*she* loves him"; "It is not *I* who love the women—*he* loves them"; "I *do not love at all, I do not love any one*."[7] — In the vocabulary of metapsychology, there is a distinct name to designate each of these inflexions. But in any case, these inflexions are all allowed by the flexing abilities of the articulated sentence: in gender, in number, in person, in voice (active or passive). —One of these abilities is nonetheless not used here, the one that allows for inflecting the tense of the verb (for conjugating). All the sentences are in the present indicative. This is no accident.

5. Meanwhile, it does not seem difficult to place each of these states of inflexion onto each of our three scenes. In "Schreber," Freud presents them

in a genealogical order, that of the *ratio essendi*: the *lexis* first cited is the oldest. But according to the *ratio cognoscendi*, it is the last to be formulated, as the meaning of the case finally identified; it is on this score that it is brought out onto the public stage, in the published case. The other sentences are elaborated during the sessions, as symptomatic utterances that give the case away to the extent that they reveal it in the course of hiding it. Finally, these utterances are elaborated on the basis and on the occasion of those sentences said to be taken "from life," the little narratives recounted by the patient. —You narratologists can keep your cool.

6. But now, what about the other voice, the voice of the tone, that does not inflect, or that does not let itself be inflected? Sure, I know that every kind of music has tried to articulate it, to furnish it with discrete units, such as notes, with chromatic scales, with harmonic and melodic rules, and to constrain it by forcing its vibrations through sets of strings whose settings are calculated on an ad hoc basis. But I also know that contemporary music, more attentive to the event (is that a case?) of the timbre itself, seeks to evade its bondage to legible *lexis*. —The voice as timbre is what Aristotle called the *phōnē*. It is not articulated. It is therefore not arbitrary. It does not refer to an object whose meaning it would transmit to an addressee on the part of an addressor. —But if it has neither *addressedness* nor referentiality, how does it differ from a noise? (There too, contemporary music has much to teach us about so-called noise.) —It is a voice because it makes sense. It is a *sēmeion*, a signal. It is not the arbitrary sign put in the place of a thing, an *onoma*. It is sense itself inasmuch as it signals itself. What sense? A *pathēma*, says Aristotle, of pleasure, of pain, according to their singular nuance. Their timbre, precisely.[8]

7. By its very hypothesis, it is not easy to articulate and argue about the *phōnē*, which is supposedly inarticulate. I cloak myself in the authority of Aristotle. —It is continuous sound, it cannot be broken down into what we call phonemes. This sound can be in every possible timbre. The voice is deaf, mute even (silence is a voice). It can sound with all the tones that connote in Indo-European, the root *mu* (*mut*), which indicates the sound obtained by closed lips: *to moan, to mutter, murmeln, murmurer, mugir* (in French, even the word for word, *mot*, comes from this root, *muttum*). The voice is choked up, it explodes, it is blank, it whines, sighs, yawns, cries, it is thin or thick. I connect it to *mu-*(*mut-*) and to mutism because, whatever its timbre, it always muffles the *lexis*. But in each of these occurrences, it is also wholly its own timbre. In this, it is identical to an affect, which is wholly what it is, with one fell swoop the state of the

psukhē and the signal of this state. The *phōnē* is the affect insofar as it is the signal of itself. The affect is its immediate manifestation. Aristotle writes: "Even inarticulate noises [*agrammatoi psophoi*] (of beasts, for instance) do indeed reveal something [*dēlousi ti*]."[9] All animals have *phōnē*, since all are capable of affects, or affectual. Human animals also have it. But on top of this, they also have the other voice, the articulated voice, that of the *logos*, the *lexis*. With the *phōnē*, they show; with the *lexis*, they communicate, reply, debate, conclude, decide. They can tell tales. —The *phōnē* has no history.

8. Temporality is inscribed into the structure of the articulated sentence. It is intrinsic to it. A minimal example: the personal pronouns, in our languages. What is *I*? That in whose name the sentence is currently articulated, its speaker right now. What is *you*? That to whom the current sentence is addressed, but also that which, *later*, in a moment, or in a very long time, it matters little, will come to occupy the place *I* during a later sentence. And if this latter sentence is a reply to the first one, then at the same time that the preceding *you* is changed to the current *I*, the first *I* now becomes *you*. *I* and *you* are thus potentially exchangeable along the poles of address. Or, more precisely, the personal pronouns designate these poles, and the proper names are exchanged in their places. —Now this ability immediately entails a consecutiveness of the two sentences, a temporalization. In addressing itself to *you*, *I* expects a sentence to come, where the two names will be in reversed positions along the poles of address. —This disposition is the kernel of temporality in the phenomenological sense. (I note along the way that the failure of Cartesian or Husserlian thought in the elaboration of the problems of time and otherness results from the aberrant philosopheme that the Cogito is: an *I* without a *you*.) And this phenomenological "inter-subjective" temporality, as it is called, is transformed into ordinary or objective chronic time (that of the sciences, and particularly the history-*Historie*) by the switch from *I* to *you*, and from their temporality of expectation and memory, to the third person. *You* as my future now, *I* as your past now, become *them then*, for *I* who currently tells the tale. This is the setting into reference, into diegesis, of a past historicity, by the present narrator. —But this narrator is currently addressing a *you*, to whom he recounts the story, and who will link onto it.

9. If they are not articulated, the *pathēma* and its manifestation, the *phōnē*, escape from this dialectic of temporalization and historicization. Freud writes that "the processes of the system *Ucs* are timeless," that "reference to time is bound up [. . .] with the work of the system *Cs*."[10]

Elsewhere, he says that the only known time of desire is now. The affect does not accept inflexion. Aristotle writes: "Of pleasure the *eidos* [proper essence] is complete [in the sense of perfected, of having realized its finality, *teleia*] at any and every time [. . .]. Pleasure must be one of the things that are whole and complete [*holon ti*]." Pleasure would not be pleasure if it were missing something. It awaits nothing therefore for its completion. It requires no supplement of duration; "it owes it nothing." It is now, and "that which takes place in the now is, so to speak, a whole."[11] It is outside of movement, thus unaware of inflexion and of diachrony. For the same reason, it has amnesia. It is singular, inflexible, incomparable, in the very strict sense that the English-language speaks of a *singleton*. —I could say just as much about pain. It would take longer to develop, because part of its *eidos*, part of its essence, would seem to be in demanding its cessation, in awaiting its ceasing, and thus in articulating, be it ever so brief, a duration proper to suppress it. But I believe that, by qualifying it in this way, it is already articulated as suffering, that is, as a pain that is addressed, and perhaps even referred, to an object. Taken as a "pure" affect, pain is undoubtedly no less inflexible than pleasure. It is right now and whole. —The temporal paradox, the parachronicity, of affect and *phōnē*, is remarked upon by Freud under the rubric of *Nachträglichkeit*, by Lacan under the rubric of the *Thing*. —I insist: the affectual now is not framed by a *before* and an *after*. It is not the now of the temporalization and historicization deployed by the articulated sentence, or by the discursive voice, that is in-between a protention and a retention. —All of which in no way prevents this voice from *speaking about* the affective voice, from recounting its story. Discourse can and ought to try to say everything. —But then, it speaks about the affect in the third person. An affect is like death and like birth: if it is thought, articulated, recounted, it is that of the other, of others.

10. In Freud, it is not the opposition between conscious and unconscious that covers more or less the same ground, it seems to me, as the distinction between *lexis* and *phōnē*, but rather the opposition between *Vorstellungsrepräsentanz* (which represents through representation) and the affect.[12] —There again, it would take too long to develop. But one can say that an affect is in effect a witness, since it is manifested by way of a *phōnē*. It is even, within its own order, a witness that is above suspicion: being wholly what it is, and as a signal, it doesn't know how to lie. But its order is not that of *Vorstellung*, which requires a referential and even an addressing articulation. An affect, be it pleasure or pain, signals pleasure and/or pain, but it does not signal *who* signals, *to whom* nor *about what*

it signals. It is tautegorical.[13] In terms of discourse, (*logos, lexis*) it is deaf, or dumb. Consequently, it is eminently equivocal. And, therefore, it can lie.

11. *Whose* voice is the *phōnē*, you might ask? The question is inconsistent if it is true that an affect bears no indication of address. Ernst tells Freud that "though he considered himself a moral person [*eine sittliche Person*], he could quite definitely remember having done things in his childhood which came from the other person."[14] Freud had just been telling him about the splitting of the personality: the evil Ernst complains of comes from his other self, from the unconscious. Freud congratulates the student for having identified this other person: it is *das Infantile*, third person neuter. —*In-fans*, it has a voice but doesn't articulate. Non-referential and unaddressed, the infantile sentence is an affectual signal, pleasure, pain. Freud circumscribes its double paralogism with respect to the *lexis*: absence of the referent and of the addressee, such as the pre-objectality pinpointed in 1905 in the essay on infantile sexuality; absence of the addressor, that is the primary pre-egoic narcissism elaborated in *On Narcissism: An Introduction* in 1914. — The idea (a pure Idea, in the Kantian sense) can thus be forged out of an affectuality (*affectedness*)[15] stripped of the "normal" (non-cased) valences of reference and of address. *In-fans* does not have the means to *reply* to an articulated sentence that addresses it or refers to it by inflexions bearing on the I and the you (address) or on the he or the she (reference). So has it come into the world of the *lexis* immediately referred to (even before being born) and addressed to by adults. Such is its *Hilflosigkeit* [helplessness]: it can't "help itself" for its being taken into reference and address. By these is it taken hostage, as Levinas would say. *In-fans* understands nothing of the adult sentences, and it doesn't hear its own affectual *phōnē* since it cannot put itself into the I/you position. The encounter of *phōnē* with *lexis* is thus inevitably traumatizing and seductive. Is this the "scandal" that "must needs be" done to children, as Jesus says in Matthew 18? *Skandalon* is an offence done by means of a trap. —One would not say that *in-fans* speaks another language, since any language is by definition translatable into an already known language. Nor is *in-fans* for that matter another person. According to this idea, what can affect its affectuality in the articulated sentences that come to it, is the *phōnē* that they bear. For the adults who speak to or about it are themselves always, *right now*, hostages of former adult sentences and of the affects they bear. *Phōnē* thus traverses generations, chance and necessity, an unheard tradition. —Moreover, it is only the adult who contracts this transmission of traumas, seductions, and scandals, for *in-fans*

itself does not belong to the inflected time of genealogies, for want of being able to articulate.

12. I'm stiffening the opposition to clarify things (following the compulsion proper to philosophers, their compulsion for what is proper). Moreover, *phōnē* is scarcely heard of outside of *lexis*, where one who speaks articulates. *Phōnē* can be heard, even as silence, *within* the *lexis*. The inarticulated voice gives timbre to the articulated one. When, for example, I say: the compulsion to oppose and to appropriate, I confess that there is some of this timbre even in the clarity of the well-articulated. Affects silently *squat* the explicit referential meanings and addresses. —Two temptations need to be avoided here: that of hypostatizing the *phōnē* into the metaphysical entity of an "absolutely other," and the temptation to bring the *phōnē* back to articulation by means of a rhetoric of the passions, by a treatise on tropes (be it reduced to the skeletal state of metaphor and metonymy . . .) where affect is thought out of principle as if it belonged to articulated signification. —Suffice it to agree that *phōnē* "makes up stories" for discourse, in *lexis*. *Phōnē* pierces its eardrums, or plugs them up. "Too terrible for the ear," says Macbeth.[16] No need for *phōnē* to break it down or mistreat it massively. It can infiltrate a given place in the articulated structure, a given linkage, *without being heard*, precisely without inflecting the good order, and thus without having to reflect it. This is the specialty of obsessive neurotics. "They dissimulate," writes Freud in the published case history. Their "dialect" is "more nearly related to the forms adopted by our conscious thought than is the language of hysteria."[17] We understand (*begreifen*) nothing of the leap, the *Sprung*, the hysteric makes into the somatic, but that leap is manifest. One can say, on the other hand, that the obsessive is gifted with the exceptional "endopsychic" ability,[18] as if he knew his traumatisms perfectly, and as if, Freud writes, "[his] unconscious mental processes occasionally break through into [his] consciousness in their pure and undistorted form."[19] And despite it all, he concludes that the obsessive neurotic is much more impenetrable and inaudible than the hysteric.

13. Ernst, the Rat Man, tells Freud: "I used to have a morbid idea that my parents knew [*wissen*] my thoughts; I explained this to myself by supposing that I had spoken them out loud, without having heard myself do it [*ohne es aber selbst zu hören*]."[20] —At this moment, Freud is with Ernst on the scene where the supposed story of his life is told, the scene I call the dramatic one and whose archive is the "Original Record of the Case." (But the episode is reported the same way in the published case.) —His thoughts, Ernst *knows* them, he recognizes them very well: they are all about seeing *Mädchen*

(young women, maids too) completely naked. He unpacks these thoughts for Freud from the very first session, he imputes them to an initial scene or scenes where the maids seduce the child he was back then. He tells his little "life" story, and in a completely articulated way, in such a way that he knows his interlocutor, Professor Freud, whom he has already read a little (of whom he has thus already been an addressee), will not fail to hear it, will not fail to lend an ear to his narrative *lexis*. The respective axes of reference (women) and of sense (to see them naked) on the one hand, and of address on the other hand (I, Ernst, am telling this to you, Freud), are clearly distinguished and saturated. Then he mentions his "morbid idea": his parents *knew* (*wissen*) his guilty thoughts that he sought to silence and believed he had silenced. Problem: how is it possible for a sentence that has not been proffered to be nonetheless heard? Solution: it has been proffered, but the speaker did not hear himself proffer it. Question: if he doesn't hear himself speak, how does he know that his parents hear what he says? Answer: he doesn't *know* it, it is an "explanation" he gives himself (*was ich mir erklärte*); it is "morbid," he recognizes. Such is the dialectic of the reasoner.

14. What is it that is "morbid" in this explanation? The *lexis* in question, the one Ernst presently addresses to Freud, was and is normal or non-cased in terms of its reference (women) and its sense (to see them naked); but it was bent out of shape or inflected in terms of its address: it was addressed to addressees to whom it wasn't addressed, and shouldn't have been, namely the parents. In fact, this sentence shouldn't have been addressed at all, Ernst shouldn't have said it, and the parents shouldn't have known anything about it. —By its very principle, this "pragmatic" mutism betrays the affectual (sexual) content of this sentence, thus deprived of half its articulation. If he wants to look at naked women, it's no one's lookout but his own—such acts address no one other than oneself. After all, I can address a sentence to myself, or if you prefer, the you can bear the same name as the I. This is not a pure tautegory of affect but the autologism of the interior monologue, which, in the order of what is articulated, is closely akin to the mutism of the *phōnē*, at least in terms of address. Its model is to be found in Molly Bloom's monologue, in the final episode of *Ulysses*. This autologism sets up house with autoerotism, for Ernst as well as for Molly. One has there an acceptable characterization of a phantasm: an intense *phōnē* which concedes its reference and sense to *lexis*, but refuses to it the possibility of addressing another. Thus, two paths are in one. —Only, Ernst's articulated voice betrays his affectual one, by addressing it to his parents, since they

know Ernst's thoughts, his phantasm. Comes along the "explanation": the phantasm was articulated out loud, and therefore addressed to another. But by that itself and by the same stroke, it ceased to be addressed to the self. Ernst did not hear himself address it "out loud." The I no longer hears itself, it is no longer its first you. The you is this he, the father, that the autologism tried to keep apart. —Did the avowal or the confession of the phantasm take place then? Without a doubt, it was proffered by the teller (the patient, the sinner), but not heard by him. The mark of disorder due to an affectual *phōnē* has been displaced at the same time that a *lexis*, the articulated voice, appears to reassert all its rights over it, I mean to say the duty of address. This disorder now affects the very place of the addressee. If my father hears my thoughts, I for one do not hear myself tell him. —Such is the inflexibility of the affect. Its timbre deafens the ear of the other. And if it is assured that the other nonetheless hears, this timbre makes my ear deaf. The *phōnē*, intact, has leaped from one pole of the articulated *lexis* to another, from addressee to addressor.

15. Being a good connoisseur of his symptoms, Ernst knows that the inflexible remains intact in the attempt at inflexion, since he tells Freud that the explanation is "morbid." I hear him ascertain this rather phlegmatically. That indicates that Ernst does not understand what the explanation means. But this time, this deafness is spoken on the dramatic scene of the analysis, and no longer on the so-called scene of "life." Now, the analytical scene presupposes, by its very construction, that every sentence that comes to it, *lexis* and *phōnē* all mixed together, is addressed to the present interlocutor. New inflexion: the phantasm is *addressed*, here and now, to Freud. But it is the *signification* of the fact that the phantasm was not able to be addressed to the other (in the mute address) or that it was without knowing (in the deaf address)—it is thus the signification of the failure in the address which presently is addressed as failing, as raising a question. A question addressed to Freud. Which thus places Freud in the position of a *you* that knows the answer and that, in its response, when he says *I*, will indeed answer. The exchange satisfies the rules of discursive address, and even those of dialogue. It is a matter of discovering between the two of them the meaning of a referent (the scrambling of the phantasm's address). A dialogical inquiry ought to commence on the model of *Oedipus Rex* or of Plato's Socrates. *Phōnē* and affect appear to have no place in this, they are only (under the auspices of the scrambling effect of the address) taken as referents for which their sense needs to be found. And they in effect will work with representatives-representations. The latter are furnished by

the excursions into the associative tissue that Ernst furnishes to Freud by answering the latter's questions and that is woven out of the little stories (dreams, phantasms, narratives) Ernst reports about his "life."

16. We know, notably from the minutes of the meetings of the Vienna Psycho-Analytical Society, that the psychoanalysis of the Rat Man inaugurates, within Freud's clinical adventure, the systematic use of the technique of free association. This fact is underscored by Otto Rank, who edited the account of the oral presentation of the second session on October 3, 1907.[21] Now, the use of this technique has, among others, a bearing upon what I call here the axis of address of the sentences proffered during the session. By refusing to "command," as he did when using hypnosis or again when applying the pressure of the hands to the forehead, the analyst slips away or tries to slip away from the "you who know" place assigned to him by the patient. The you seeks to remain unnamed, its place is not occupied in advance, it is a simple pronoun offered to a multiplicity of addresses. Freud thus weakens the function of the interlocutor, and that of an interlocutor gifted with a knowledge imposed upon him by the dialogic relation. This neutralization has the effect of giving to the affectual voice, scarcely or not at all addressed, a wider field in the strongly articulated voice of the discourse. —Thus, by the same stroke, this favors transference, defined then as *phōnē* in the process of articulating itself. Besides, the elaboration of the clinical function of transference thereby marks the psychoanalysis of the Rat Man as the midpoint between the failure of the Dora case in 1905 and the article on "The Dynamics of Transference" in 1912. The published case history gives notice of this.

17. Despite a disposition propitious to manifestations of the affect, Freud lets himself be seduced by Ernst's articulatory, narrative, and argumentative resources. The associational tissue keeps spreading and accruing density. With the word *Rat*, Freud, stirred up by the game of disentangling, thinks he has found the name of the shuttle that runs from one thread to the next. He writes, underscoring it, at the end of the session notes for November 30, 1907: "The rat-story becomes more and more a *nodal point* [*ein Knotenpunkt*]."[22] The Notes [*Bemerkungen*] (the published case, the public stage) deploys the polyvalence of this "nodal" signifier: it signifies the officer, money, syphilis, the penis, the anus, the child. The lexical thread is of a surprising richness. But Freud is no less awed by the procedural ingenuity of Ernst's unconscious syntax. There is, he writes, an obsessive *Gefüge*, the stringing together and the accumulation of arguments and plotlines, the rationalizations are so inextricable that finally all these voices

so well-articulated render inaudible, to the patient himself, the affectual voice they cover over. I am going to tell you, I would like to understand, it's necessary to know why I am deaf to my voice, —and it is this impulse to know (the *Wisstrieb*), to protect, to cover (in both senses of the word: to inform and to hide) which in and of itself bears the deafening *phōnē*, in silence. Freud calls this nuance an *ellipsis*: the voice chased out remains inside, *elleipein*, by omission, by desertion.[23]

18. Perhaps it is precisely in this elliptical non-place that one needs to introduce what Blanchot, in one of the texts from his *De Kafka à Kafka* (a title in the form of an address that itself merits some commentary) calls "narrative voice."[24] Narrative voice is neuter, he explains. It says nothing by itself, adds nothing to what there is to say. Rather it upholds the nothingness, the silence, into which every speech proceeds. It understands nothing. Every attempt to endow it with a narrative identity betrays it. It remains in suspense in the narrative without either appearing or disappearing there, for it has nothing to do with the visible and the invisible. Suspense means that it is only in the narrative to the extent that it is outside of it. It is ignorant of mediation, attribution, and community. It is that indifferent difference which alters the voice of persons, and the infinite distanciation wherein narrative distance is at play. Let's say it is a specter or a phantom. —This neutral voice is not to be confused with the impossible zero tone I imagined earlier.

19. Freud tries to lose nothing of the lexical and syntactical complexity of the obsessive text, of the representational network. He writes, at the end of the third session's notes: "Not well reproduced [*reproduziert*]; I missed [*vervaümt*], or wiped away [*verwischt*] many of the case's singular beauties [*Schönheiten*]."[25] Singular, *eigentümliche*, these beauties make for the singularity of the case, its incomparable character, not inflectable into a typology or nosography, they are foreign, ringing with an unexpected voice. While closing the dramatic scene, Freud as a writer then makes a critique of his writing. All writing is this attempt to bear witness, by way of the articulated *lexis*, to the inflexible *phōnē*. Writing has a debt of affect which it despairs of ever being able to pay off. While preparing the *Bemerkungen*, the published case history, Freud writes to Jung on June 30, 1909: "My energy is pretty well exhausted, except for one undertaking [. . .]. This one undertaking is my paper about the Rat Man. I am finding it very difficult; it is almost beyond my powers of presentation [*meine Darstellungskunst*], the paper will probably be intelligible to no one outside our immediate circle. How bungled [*Was für Pfuschereien*] our reproductions are, how wretchedly

we dissect [*zerpflücken*] the great art works of psychic nature [*die grosser Kunstwerke der psychischen Natur*] ! Unfortunately this paper in turn is becoming too bulky. It just pours out of me, and even so it's inadequate, incomplete and therefore untrue."[26] —This is the distress of a Flaubert, of a Beckett: Emma, Molloy, or Ernst, it's me, but it's not me.

20. "This voice that speaks, knowing that it lies, indifferent to what it says, too old perhaps and too abased ever to succeed in saying the words that would be its last, knowing itself useless and its uselessness in vain, not listening to itself but to the silence that it breaks [. . .]. It is not mine, I have none, I have no voice and must speak, with this voice that is not mine, but can only be mine, since there is no one but me." "But it's time I gave this solitary a name, nothing doing without proper names. I therefore baptize him Worm. It was high time. Worm. I don't like it, but I haven't much choice, when I needn't be called Mahood any more, if that happy time ever comes. [. . .] Perhaps it's by trying to be Worm that I'll finally succeed in being Mahood, I hadn't thought of that. Then all I'll have to do is be Worm. Which no doubt I shall achieve by trying to be Jones. Then all I'll have to do is be Jones."[27] [. . .] It seems to me besides that I must have already made, contrary to what it seems to me I must have already said, some efforts in this direction. I should have noted them, if only in my head. But Worm cannot note. There at least is a first affirmation, I mean negation, on which to build. Worm cannot note. Can Mahood note? That's it, weave, weave. Yes, it is the characteristic, among others, of Mahood to note, even if he does not always succeed in doing so, certain things, perhaps I should say all things, so as to turn them to account, for his governance."[28] —Hence, with Freud: Mahood, at his desk, in the evening, taking notes on Worm and reproaching himself for not being *wormy* enough, not enough of a worm, and so not truthful enough [*pas assez* wormy, *véreux, vérace*[29]]. Knowing already that in any case what will make the voice of Mahood heard and the voice of Worm heard is the voice of "Jones," speaking before the Salzburg Psycho-Analytical Congress and in the *Jahrbuch*. How wretched!

21. Mahood strives to note the beauty of the representative plots Worm in his creeping along lets pile up in his wake. Not that he hasn't been forewarned by Ernst-Worm himself (or Ernst-Rat). At the beginning of the same session whose notes conclude with the "nodal" importance of the rat stories, Freud noted: "More rat-stories; but as he [Ernst] admitted in the end, he had only collected them in order to evade the transference phantasies which had come up in the meantime."[30] Articulated with such art and beauty, the narrative voice serves well to smother the affectual voice,

the *phōnē*. With his diabolical lucidity, the obsessional neurotic seems to know this better than the analyst: "ah will they never learn sense, there's nothing to be got, there was never anything to be got from those stories, I have mine somewhere, let them tell it to me, they'll see there's nothing to be got from me, it will be the end, of this hell of stories, you'd think I was cursing them."[31] —Freud, during this period, writes of "*a* transference," just as one speaks of a dream, a phantasy, or a memory. Now, during the five or six sessions preceding the notation of the nodal point, Freud has had his share of transferences, he has been berated by a broadside of phantasies in which he, his mother, his wife, his son, and his daughter give themselves to or are given over to copulation, prostitution, coprophagia, fellatio, sodomy, anthropophagia, death by hanging, and murder. Upset, Freud notes: "horrible [*entsetzlichste*]," "most frightful [*grässlichste*] ,"[32] or again "a most wonderful [*herrlichste*] anal phantasy."[33] In the midst of this cacophony, a miracle takes place, the *phōnē* makes itself heard and understood, the affect is addressed, Freud's voice chimes with Ernst's voice, Worm and Mahood scream, quiet down, moan, and murmur, if not together, then at least at the same time: right now. Fear and pity. —In the published case, wretched, "Jones" concedes a page and a half to this transferential storm, in the tone of an obituary ("this school of suffering," "the painful road"[34]). While he spends twenty or thirty pages narrating the pleasures of a safari that sets out in a wholly representational terrain along the carefully scrambled path of a rat.

22. I say fear and pity, *phobos kai eleos,* because the analytical scene is obviously analogical to the tragical scene. Merely analogical, but analogical nonetheless. I would say even more precisely: analogical to the Aeschylean stage. Like the analytical scene, it is a scene with two voices, and these two voices are of a different timbre. Aeschylus invents tragedy out of Dionysian dithyramb by lengthening the time of the recitatives uttered by the hero in-between the songs danced by the chorus and by mounting a speaker of the chorus onto the stage near the hero. The hero remains the tested one, the outcast, the solitary one, deafened by the voice of the god who speaks within his voice even while it is his voice, the victim of *mania*. The speaker of the chorus (who, with Sophocles, will be disseminated into various characters) echoes this dementia comes from elsewhere, sometimes by compassion and wise warnings, sometimes by fright and panicked flight. These two protagonists are not unlike those you know. Between them, there is a combat, and this combat is an unequal one, it pits wisdom against madness, madness against wisdom. In the notes to the Rat Man, Freud

doesn't stop mentioning his *Kampf* with and against Ernst. —But there is more. The tragical genre is, if we believe what remains of Aristotle's *Poetics*, distinguished from all other literary writing inasmuch as it is realized, "performed," if you will, here and now, by protagonists who are *prattontes kai drōntes*, who carry out actions and who put on an act [*qui agissent et qui actent*]. Characters are not what is put on stage, but actions, which develop a plot (the tragical *muthos*) from *nouement* (*desis*) to *dénouement* (*lusis*) through theatrical reversals (*peripeteia*), recognitions (*anagnōrēsis*), and violent effects (*pathos*). The course of tragedy thus entails a moment of caesura, a paroxysm, when the hero's deafness is reversed into a listening to what he was not hearing (this is the *metabolē* also called the *metabasis*).[35] Literarily speaking, this moment is at its best when the recognition (of the *phōnē*) occurs through a theatrical reversal, as if by chance, but by that kind of chance that seems intentional while also plausible, and which entails or fails to entail a violent *pathos*. The perfect model of reversal, according to Aristotle: the good soul, who comes to disculpate Oedipus by revealing to him that he is not who he thinks he is, ends up apprising Oedipus of the fact that he is the criminal.

23. The analytical scene lacks many of the properties needed to be called tragic in the ancient sense. The high social standing and illustrious lineage of the heroes, for example, or the required organization of the actions into a "system," the *sustasis*. Not much of this synthesis is in the situation of analysis. The wretchedness of the published case history must be awaited to see a little bit of it. Even the *katharsis* promised by the tragic spectacle, if we are to believe Aristotle, is certainly something very different from one's purgation through the talking cure.[36] All of this would require some time to be examined. We don't have this time. We would need to confront in the two genres what arises from the stage and what from the hall, from the public and the secret, from aesthetics, from therapeutics, and from ethics, from the teleology of the ancient *phusis* and from the mechanism of modern physics, from the voice of the immortals and from the voice of the Great Pan who is dead, out on Mount Sinai. —You won't be surprised when I observe that if there is tragedy on the stage of the Rat Man's analysis, that tragedy is not the ancient kind, it is the *Trauerspiel*, the modern Baroque drama.[37] The model for Ernst, the obsessional neurotic, is not Oedipus, but Hamlet. With Ernst as with Hamlet, we find the spectral father, the whoring of women and of the sexual, the ontological uncertainty, the accursed force of the mannerist conceit that disjoins and renders ambiguous everything designated by it, thought in the place of action, the inability to act out the voice of the law.[38]

All of these traits are picked up in the *Bemerkungen*. —But after all that, of the old tragedy this remains in the analytical scene: the moment of the reversals which takes effect when the chorus or the characters issued from it (all those who may come to occupy the almost empty place left by the you of the analyst), when that other-there is directly addressed by the hero (the patient) and thrust backstage by him, onto the so-called scene of life. At that moment, that moment of transference (of *a* transference), the *phōnē* issuing from that backstage, where it wasn't heard, is now heard because it is now addressed to you and thus, to me, the hero, the patient. Thanks to this performance, the inflexible now of the affect can be actualized in the now subject to the inflexions (especially temporal inflexions) of the articulated voice. I say, thanks to the performance because it is no longer a question of narrating and of representing, even when one continues to do so—it is a question of acting.

24. Can Ernst, any more than Hamlet, cure his melancholia for having addressed his *phōnē* to Freud and having heard it? Didn't he hear it from the beginning, since he knew that the father's voice told him that the father knew, and that he died from it? Isn't a modern hero modern insofar as he knows himself guilty from the start? And what if it was to his mother, instead, that Ernst addressed his *phōnē*, at the moment of transference? To Freud as being his mother? A mother of whom Freud does not say a word [*ne dit mot*]: *muttum*. —In Act 3, scene 4, the prince visits his mother and fires her way a broadside of transferences. Polonius is hidden behind the curtain. The queen takes fright and calls for help. Polonius, offstage, echoes her. Hamlet pierces the curtain with a sword thrust. Polonius expires. Hamlet says: "How now, a rat? Dead for a ducat, dead!" —Conclusion: it is not because one has killed the rat (and paid for its death) that one is purged of obsessive thoughts and of ontological indecision. Nor because one identifies oneself, and identifies the analyst, with the father, if it is from the mother that it is a matter of hearing the thoughts one has spoken. — What happens to purgation in the *Trauerspiel*, or in the melancholia of the moderns, from which the gods are dead?

25. You might object by saying that in tragedy, the act is that of an actor, which is mimetic, but that it is authentic on the couch. —The question is a metaphysical one. It is one that is raised and that is maintained in the order of representations. In this order, one can answer that every representation (of thing or word) refers to something represented; that as soon as there is articulation, there is a scene, and as soon as there is a scene, there is something behind the scene. I counted three of these, at the beginning of

this essay, just for this single case history. But I said that there are more of them, many more. Whether one imitates or whether one creates the other is not a question on the analytical scene. Freud listens to a phantasm, a dream, or a memory with the same ear. All these bits of narration, these *rushes*,[39] these falls (these *cases*) are important only insofar as their arrival upon the analytical scene allows the affectual voice to make itself heard, *within* the narrative voice, and to make itself heard *by* he, the narrator, who wasn't hearing it. Such ought to be the true force of narrative, its art, its address: to give the *phōnē* the opportunity of address. (I specify that this is not the mystery of the Incarnation.) To deliver the affect from its ellipsis, which resulted in the *Affektentziehung*, the retreat of affect, and the obsessional neurotic's raciocinative phlegm. —To deliver the affect is not to recount it, to describe it as it was, since it is ignorant of passing time, and since it is only what it is: pleasure, pain, jouissance, right now. It is to recount (construction) or let recount (deconstruction, free association) now a story wherein the affect comes to precipitate its own now. —The names of the beasts that title or could title the analyses of children and obsessional neurotics, Freud's wolves, rats, and horses, name the absentmindedness of affects: in fact, they let themselves be gathered. Their intractable inflexibility, which is concomitant, is spoken by the Worms of Beckett,[40] the mice, moles, and cockroaches of Kafka or of Clarisse Lispector, or still the rats of Shakespeare or of Ernst. This is because the animals are the voice. And it is not because that voice lets itself be domesticated that it is any less flexible.

26. I have said nothing (or hardly anything) about Freud's voice in the published case history (the *Bemerkungen*), of the various ways in which he calls on Ernst's voice. I leave that to the narratological scholar, to Gérard Genette, for example, who knows how to distinguish between the way that *narrativizes* the cited voice, the one that *reports* it, and the one that *transposes* it.[41] I would have liked to give you some examples of these procedures in Freud's text, and to assess their various effects of so-called narrative "distance." This would have been a modest but precise means to measure his *Darstellungskunst* and to hear the persuasive voice of the professor in clinical science, his argumentative rhetoric. For there, on the public scene, Freud is Jones [Joe Blow], he must persuade his addressees: that the case is as he says it is, that it is the case of a clinical type, that it needs to be treated as he has done. All this while sealing the patient's identity. Which severely amputates the presentation, as Freud bitterly complains, for the Rat Man as well as for Dora and the Wolf Man. This said, he doesn't do so badly at the tribunal, while he confides to Jung (and this is not coquettishness) that

his talents are exceeded (*übersteigt*), and considerably so, by the talents of psychical nature. —But obviously what exceeds him, what the recension of the case cannot reinstitute, is not so much the immensely beautiful work of composition, the obsessive *Gefüge* (certainly, a whole book would be needed, and Freud was surely thinking along these lines since only for the Rat Man did he break his rule of destroying his notes from psychoanalytical sessions)—no, what cannot be related in the "then" of the *Bericht* (at once, the report and the narrative), is the "right now" of *phōnē*. The relating of one affect can, at best, give rise to another one, right now.

AFTERWORD

"*Nul ne sait écrire*" is the opening to *Lectures d'enfance*. This short statement has a terse, poetic construction that begins to intrigue the reader as to what the book might be. Hiding in the elegant simplicity of the Galilée *débats* series with cream cover and title in a light red serif font, the svelte volume echoes Lyotard's collection published three years previously—*L'Inhumain*, which similarly opened with a seemingly esoteric evocation of its concerns, thereby dovetailing in some ways with *Lectures d'enfance*.

"Nobody knows how to write" is the English translation chosen to render this opening to *Readings in Infancy*. It both opens new possibilities—nobody—and closes—*nul*—simultaneously. This nobody might evoke the desperate cry of the one-eyed Polyphemus, blinded by Odysseus and whose lament is heard yet not listened to by its monocular kind, heard only as the nonsense of "nobody (*outis*) is killing me" that rings out across the island, the victim of cunning. *Nul* does not necessarily connect with persons—no one, or bodies—nobody, not even with mythical creatures, but rather it allows, through its opening, a nothing which is unanchored from the personhood of no one. *Personne ne sait écrire* might properly match the phrase we have chosen, but for Lyotard the personlessness of *nul* and the duality of the negative carries an important timbre, forcing us to acknowledge what we lose in *lexis*. However, judgments must be made—that is the one exigency Lyotard is emphatic about: the demand to link. Linking on to *Lectures d'enfance* is what we have undertaken through this publication of *Readings in Infancy*, linking on to Lyotard's French and the disparate extant English translations to show once more that we do not know how to write, and in doing so we respond to the loss of the anonymous *nul*.

In order to better understand or at least conceptualize where *Readings in Infancy* sits within Lyotard's thought, it is useful to sketch out the intellectual biography to which it belongs. In an attempt to avoid a simplistic model of linear development many areas of study have eschewed straightforward patterns of influence to think rather of multiplicities of contributing factors. In Art History for example, out goes Alfred H. Barr's famous all-explaining history of modern art drawn for MoMA New York in 1936, with its inexorable forward movement of the Western avant-garde to its apogee

Afterword

in the abstract art of its time. This is replaced with models such as the "constellations" offered by Tate in the UK, especially its displays in Liverpool, allowing more diverse sources to coexist in a networked presentation of its collection. While there are limitations to such constellations—not least the comparatively short historic and geographical reach of the references—they do at least refute notions of the lone artist forging ahead in blind disbelief that they do not need the support or succor of others. Considering where *Readings in Infancy* "fits" in the constellation I will sketch out here might compel us to consider overlooked associations.

There are some through lines, some constant points of reference, with which we may begin this task: Immanuel Kant, in particular the third Critique, but also the body of historico-political writings, was a regular if not constant source of study for Lyotard throughout the decade which preceded the publication of *Readings in Infancy* (1991). Lyotard's interpretation of Kant's work played an important role in *The Differend* (1983) which incorporated explorations of judgment from *Just Gaming* (1979), the result of conversations with Jean-Loup Thébaud in 1977–8 prompted by accusations of ethical vacuity evidenced in the notorious 1974 publication, *Libidinal Economy*. This concern with both justice and judgment following Kant, in particular the reflective, indeterminate judgment of the third Critique, was the focus of the 1982 conference at Cerisy-la-Salle, organized by Thébaud and Michel Enaudeau under the title *Comment juger?* (How to Judge?). Including contributions by Jacques Derrida, Jean-Luc Nancy, and Philippe Lacoue-Labarthe, it took place at an important point in the development of what would become *The Differend*, forcing participants who dealt with Lyotard's work to consider recent—though now often overlooked—publications including *Just Gaming*, but also his 1977 book on Marcel Duchamp, *Duchamp's Transformers*. Derrida refers to these texts in the long introduction to his contribution to the conference, *Préjugés: Devant la loi*.[1] Derrida's presentation was an extensive rewriting of an existing paper on Kafka's short story, "Before the Law" (*Vor dem Gesetz* is given as *Devant la loi* in French), which provokes echoes in Lyotard's later paper on Kafka, first delivered at a conference in 1989 under the title *Avant la loi* (also "Before the Law") and included in *Readings in Infancy* as "Prescription."[2]

The encounter with Derrida cannot be downplayed and his prominence for Lyotard as a member of the 1980s constellation is almost unquestioned, in a way that would not necessarily have seemed the case in the previous decade. There had been earlier encounters, but 1982 can be seen as a

Afterword

decisive intellectual meeting point. In addition, there were other more practical spheres of encounter at this time: Corinne Enaudeau writes of their meeting at the Association Jan Hus,[3] the support organization for academics behind the iron curtain in Czechoslovakia, the French branch of which Derrida co-founded in 1981 (and for which he was infamously arrested, temporarily, on his return from Prague while carrying planted drugs). Lyotard also worked alongside Derrida on the foundation of the Collège international de philosophie (CIPh) when he was called on to deputize for his close friend and colleague François Châtelet, due to illness. Lyotard is often overlooked in the account of the official founding figures, given as Derrida, Châtelet, Jean-Pierre Faye and Dominique Lecourt, no doubt due to Lyotard's self-effacement. The Collège was to play a central role for Lyotard during the remainder of his life and several of the contributions which make up *Readings in Infancy*—Kafka, Arendt, and Valéry—were first presented under its auspices. Similarly, many of the figures present at Cerisy were frequent contributors to the symposia, workshops, and conferences organized by the Collège.

What also becomes clear through a brief excursus into the arenas and contexts from which these readings in infancy emerged is the seemingly disparate foci of the events on Joyce, Arendt, and Freud which gave rise to their corresponding chapters. Yet despite this, there is a manifest connection that runs through the work as a coherent whole. Lyotard writes of the preexisting network of names, associations, expectations, and assumptions into which the infant is born, underlining both the myth of individualized subjectivity and the limited contingency of beginnings. It is from a similar preexisting network that *Readings in Infancy* is born. Consequently, I will labor here a while to detail the means by which the constituent elements were arrived at in order to better understand the position of the volume as other than simply a collection. On the one hand, this *is* a collection of recently delivered seminars and conference papers, often already published in conference proceedings, and transformed into chapters with minimal intervention beyond the simplification of the chapter titles to neat single words, accompanied in the table of contents by the name of its subject or interlocutor. On the other, it feels as though the readings, to use our nominated English title, have been born out of subterranean linkages which allow the constituent elements to function together remarkably without repetition and with very limited revisions.

"Return: Joyce" was a contribution to the Eleventh International James Joyce Symposium in Venice, June 1988, under the title "Retour sur

Afterword

le retour" (Return Upon the Return). Derrida had presented at the same symposium four years earlier, with Joyce's multiple yeses as his topic. Such a Joycean "yes, yes, yes, yes" is how Lyotard ended his *Libidinal Economy* in 1974, but by the time of "Return" such confident affirmation had drifted. In 1984, Derrida had played with the French "yes"—*oui, Oui*—and its always possible quotation, slipping on the impossibility of translating either linguistically or graphically.[4] In his "Return," Lyotard asks: "[h]ow can one be sure that what returns is precisely what has disappeared?"[5] It might then be possible to read these two responses to Joyce together, though I am not aware if anyone has made those two paths cross, unlike their respective responses to Kafka.

"Prescription: Kafka" was first presented as *Avant la loi*, as detailed earlier, to a Franco-German conference titled *Morale et Politique* (Politics and Morality) under the auspices of the CIPh, a three-day event in March 1989. It was subsequently published as "La Prescription" in the journal of the Collège, *Rue Descartes*, and in English translation as "Prescription," in the French studies journal of Johns Hopkins University, *L'Esprit créateur*, both in 1991. Lyotard's request or demand: "translate this" made to Christopher Fynsk was the prompt not only for the resulting translation but also a later elegiac essay "Jean-François's Infancy" (2001),[6] itself an insightful consideration of many aspects of *Lectures d'enfance*.

"Survivor: Arendt" was given as "Le Survivant" in April 1988 at a three-day event at the Goethe Institute in Paris, convened jointly with the CIPh and titled *Politique et pensée* (Politics and Thought). Participants included Paul Ricœur and Barbara Cassin among many other distinguished thinkers. Also listed as a participant, but without mention in the subsequent proceedings, is Giorgio Agamben, a figure for whom the theme of infancy plays a different role, but one which I will examine later in this afterword. I am tempted to list all the participants in this event because of the sense of the milieu which is evoked and the centrality of the CIPh to the intellectual life of French thought at this time. Rather than take such a detour, however, I continue to follow the sequence of Lyotard's *Readings in Infancy* and hit the stumbling block that is the chapter on Jean-Paul Sartre.

In contrast to the other chapters which result from spoken contributions to events dating from 1988–90, the chapter "Words: Sartre" originated as a written article, first published in the journal *Critique* in 1983. Ostensibly a book review, it was written as a favor to a friend, Denis Hollier, on the occasion of the publication of his *Politique de la prose: Jean-Paul Sartre et l'an quarante* (*The Politics of Prose: Jean-Paul Sartre and the 1940s*). Published

Afterword

as *Un Succès de Sartre* (A Success of Sartre's), the tone toward its subject is bitter and harsh in a way that contrasts with the other chapters, where there is admiration even in disagreement, and reveals a political difference that is intensely felt. The somewhat sarcastic title was maintained when appended as a foreword to the English translation of Hollier's book published in 1986, but reconfigured simply as "Mots" (Words) in *Lectures d'enfance*. It is an important companion to the previous chapter on Arendt whose distinctly darker post-war narrative casts a shadow over Sartre's valedictory *littérature engagée* (committed writing). The subtitle of Hollier's book in French— *Sartre et l'an quarante*—carries both an implicit reference to the fall of Paris in 1940 and puns on the French expression to not give a shit about something (see note 60, p. 129); while this untranslatable subtitle may have vanished from the title when published in English, its sense remains written throughout Lyotard's account.

The title to Lyotard's chapter, "Words" returns the apparently triumphalist title of Sartre's autobiography, *The Words* with a note of derision. This is particularly apparent in his defense of Claude Lefort, a former member with Lyotard of the anti-authoritarian, anti-PCF (French Communist Party) Marxist group *Socialisme ou barbarie* and with whom Sartre had significant battles in print. Lyotard is clear from the outset: "I did not like the air of capability his writings exuded" and even when he finds areas of agreement with Sartre's pronouncements on writing, he insists that they be divested of his emphasis on the authorial *I*, returning rather to writing itself, that uncertain element which Sartre refused to permit.

The decision to write about Sartre was not entered into altogether willingly it seems. In the essay, there is the suggestion of perhaps being pushed not only by Hollier but also by his son-in-law, Michel Enaudeau. However, the same is not true of the prompt that led to "Disorder: Valéry." Lyotard's turn to the aesthetic work of Paul Valéry came only from the phrase *Ceci est de l'art* (this is art) provided by Thierry de Duve in another cooperation with the CIPh: a small symposium organized by de Duve in the public library of the Centre Georges-Pompidou. Lyotard, Louis Marin, and Jacques Poulain responded to the same phrase, but only Lyotard chose to reference Valéry's aesthetics.[7] It is in the resulting section of *Readings in Infancy* that aspects of the linguistics of pragmatics from *The Differend* are recalled most directly. The deictic "this" of the sentence "this is art" is explored as the missing contents, thereby mimicking the shift from Sartre's confident title *The Words* to Lyotard's more dissolute "Words" in the previous chapter: doubt and hesitancy replace the assumption of capability.

Afterword

Several commentators have made the connection between *Readings in Infancy* and *Discourse, Figure*, published two decades before, with the consideration of Freud's case "A Child Is Being Beaten" being one point of connection; others refer to the matrical aspect of desire at the heart of the figural nominated the *figure-matrice* (matrix-figure) or the important readings of negation, which include Lyotard's own modified translation of Freud's *Verneinung*.[8] In each case, it is the plurality of voices that are being considered, the various roles being played in order to deny, repress, or indicate that which cannot be voiced through discourse yet which inhabits discourse, as that force of incapacity which Sartre of *The Words* denied. It is in the final chapter of *Readings in Infancy*, "Voices: Freud," that this is perhaps most explicitly displayed, yet its concerns are echoed throughout the five previous chapters and its enigmatic preface. "Voices" is an English title that has to compromise the ambiguity of the French, where *Voix* (without article) does not clearly designate either singular or plural, yet whose plurality is implicit in the writings of the chapter. Lyotard's discussion is of the Freud case known as that of the "Rat Man," the account of which exists already in the plural: Freud wrote both a series of journal entries recording the case and a more conventional case history. Lyotard's essay was presented to the Psychoanalytic Association of France in May 1990 as part of a series on case histories organized by Michel Gribinski and published in the *Nouvelle Revue de psychanalyse* in the autumn of the same year, with the longer title *Les voix d'une voix* (Voices of a Voice).

"Voices: Freud" serves as a good example of how the material included in *Readings in Infancy* cuts through both Lyotard's work and theoretical interests in different ways. It is an essay that is key to his work on Freud, which stretches back to the controversial *Figure forclose* (Figure Foreclosed), written in 1968 but not published until 1984, and returned to in *Discourse, Figure*, the libidinal work, and then repeatedly in the late essays such as "Emma," as Robert Harvey highlights in the foreword to this volume. It is a thread through Lyotard's thought that is critically discussed by Élisabeth de Fontenay in her book-length study of Lyotard's consideration of Jewish thought,[9] one that is bound in several ways to Freud. Lyotard's writings on these questions have often been provocative, in particular his adoption of the nomenclature "the jews"—pluralized, lower-case, and in scare quotes— in an attempt to preempt criticisms of lazy categorization and question the forgotten thought that is presented in forgetting. For some, this attempt to mark thought that resists assimilation, without marking it as only or

Afterword

specifically Jewish, provoked an emotive response.[10] Perhaps this was unsurprising given its usage and placement alongside the proper name Heidegger in *Heidegger et "les juifs"* (Heidegger and "the jews"), published in March 1988.

In April 1988 the conference on Hannah Arendt took place against the backdrop of this recent publication, referred to directly by Paul Ricœur in his contribution, and the wider "Heidegger affair" in France. When Victor Farías's *Heidegger et le nazisme* appeared in October 1987 it prompted wider discussions in the mainstream press concerning the acceptance of Heidegger's philosophical thought in France and its absorption into contemporary French philosophy in a seemingly unproblematic way. Several philosophical responses followed, including Derrida, Lacoue-Labarthe, and, subsequently, Lyotard for whom the question was neither the undeniable significance of Heidegger's thought nor the equally unquestionable complicity of his politics during the Nazi era, but his "silence on the extermination of the Jews, a silence observed to the very end by the thinker of Todtnauberg."[11] In his introduction to the English translation, David Carroll notes the wider implications of "the jews" in Lyotard's lexicon, intimating the thought of those writers who strive to resist the tendency to forget, often through their linguistic or geographical displacement. Joyce, Beckett, and Mallarmé are thus described as "non-Irish Irish" and "non-French French," their rejection of a Heideggerian beholding to place echoes Lyotard's own roll call:

> Freud, Benjamin, Adorno, Arendt, and Celan—these great non-German Germans, non-Jewish Jews—who not only question but betray the tradition, the *mimēsis*, the immanence of the unfolding, and its root; whom emigration, dispersion, and the impossibility of integration make despair of any return; exhausted by the dual impotence of not changing and changing, of remaining German and becoming French, American [. . .]. Expelled, doomed to exodus. Thus, their hatred of geophilosophy.[12]

The echoes of infancy are strong. Listening to the resounding sounds extend and reverberate beyond the specificity of the named references redoubles their importance. The term "infancy" itself is used in this publication to evoke the unrecognized *affect* of *Nachträglichkeit*: thought for which "we" are unprepared. A voice to which discourse is deaf yet which exerts a presence in spite of initial unpreparedness.

Afterword

As we are using chronological proximity of publication as a provisional guiding thread to place Lyotard's *Readings in Infancy* within a wider constellation, there is another displaced forgotten which underlies both this passage and the contemporary scene: Algeria. Lyotard's collection of his accounts and analysis of "the Algerians' war," written for *Socialisme ou barbarie* between 1956 and 1963, were published by Galilée in 1989. They were presented without modification but with a new introduction by Lyotard that speaks of the need to recognize the resistance to "the system" that they represent. Lyotard argues that attempts to deny what was driving the fight that *Socialisme ou barbarie* engaged in "perpetuates the very forgetting of what was actually at stake": the intractable [*l'intraitable*]. At stake is "the idea that there is something within that system that it cannot, in principle, *deal with* [*traiter*]. Something that the system must, by virtue of its nature overlook."[13]

Our decision to return "infancy" to the work of Lyotard's reception in English, to turn the focus away from "childhood," makes it necessary to consider Lyotard's infancy in relation to others for whom the term is already associated. Perhaps the most obvious is Giorgio Agamben, whose points of reference and shared philosophical milieu sometimes overlap with Lyotard and yet with whom there is no explicit dialogue.[14] This seeming intellectual proximity makes the following reading a strange one: Agamben's work brings forth aspects of Lyotard's which might less obviously be considered and brings with it a risk of perhaps otherwise unintended associations. Yet this is part of their shared project in allowing writing to suggest, preempt, drive readings elsewhere; as Donna Haraway put it recently in her own generous approach to thinking that she has named tentacular: "an elsewhere and an elsewhen."[15]

Agamben's use of the term "infancy" clusters around *Infancy and History* (1978) and *Literature and Death* (1981) before being absorbed in some ways into considerations of potentiality, for which he has become best known.[16] However, it is the later essay, *Experimentum Linguæ* (1988–9), with which we open this short account and where Agamben's description of all books as mere casts, broken casts or molds for the book that remains unwritten, echoes the refusal of finality or fulfillment throughout Lyotard's writing. For Agamben, the unwritten book engenders other works which are not that unwritten book but are themselves the husks of further unrealized—and it would seem unrealizable—projects. This account brings to mind the promised late work that Lyotard referred to on several occasions: a supplement to *The Differend* that would include those aspects which had been deliberately left out of *The Differend*: art; the body; sexual difference; questions of space, of time, of color. Mentioned in interviews in the early 1990s, it also appeared as a forthcoming volume to be published by Galilée in the bibliography of *Toward the Postmodern* (1993). Usually, the assumption is that other projects, his illness and early death in 1998 cut short this project, though Lyotard's interest in other unfinished works, such as those collected in Merleau-Ponty's *The Visible and the Invisible* could suggest otherwise. It was left to his widow, Dolorès Lyotard to highlight which of the chapters published in the posthumous collection, *Misère de la philosophie*, had been earmarked for this important work to come. The five chapters so indicated present many parallels with those writings in *Reading in Infancy*, in particular "Emma," the reflection on *Nachträglichkeit* (after-effect) that is anticipated or partnered by "Voices," and the short essay which carries a direct reference to the unrealized book in its published title "The Affect-phrase (from a Supplement to *The Differend*)."

"Affect-phrase" is a dense seven-page, sectioned text which opens with the question from §22 of *The Differend* "Is feeling a phrase?" that takes us directly into territory shared with Agamben.[17] Specifically, the essay *Experimentum Linguæ* was written in 1988–9 as the preface to the French edition of *Infancy and History*, published by Payot in 1989 in the series "*Critique de la politique*," directed by Michel Abensour. He had taken over from Lyotard as president of the CIPh in 1985. Both the Lyotard and the Agamben essays reflect and meditate to some extent on the same well-known distinction made by Aristotle in the *Politics* and *De Interpretatione* regarding the particularity of the human as animal endowed with articulated speech and its distinction to voice. In itself this is not remarkable, but it has become one of the most contemplated if controversial considerations of human language: the spoken articulated voice of the human and its relationship or difference to that of the animal. Both writers repeat the importance of *phōnē*, given as the animal voice in Aristotle, as fundamental to considerations of the limitations of language as *logos*. It is in this preface that Agamben gives a clear definition of infancy and, like Lyotard, emphasizes the distinctive etymological roots of *in-fans* (without speech), similarly clarifying that in-fancy is not tied to a particular age or chronological time, nor is it like "a psychosomatic state which a psychology or a paleoanthropology could construct as a human fact independent of language."[18]

For Agamben, it is only through the co-presence of infancy with language that the unsaid or the so-called ineffable is possible; far from indicating the limitations of language, as Wittgenstein would perhaps have us believe in his

Afterword

famous final sentence to the *Tractatus*, which is but the "vulgarly ineffable." In contrast, the concept of infancy for Agamben is an attempt to think through the limits of language "other than that of the vulgarly ineffable."[19] (The naming of infancy as a concept is Agamben's and a point of difference with Lyotard, for whom there is nothing so fixed as a concept in his usage of the term that remains as fluid as that to which it gestures.) Agamben claims in *Infancy and History*, "[t]he ineffable is, in reality, infancy,"[20] not the mystical ineffability of language at its supposed limits but that which denies claims made for language as a totality and which denies experience that is not conceived within its bounds. Hence the subtitle to the English translation of *Infancy and History*: "on the destruction of experience." While taking care not to invoke a nostalgic harking back to a former time, Agamben places the changes in philosophical attitude to experience within a broad historical account, evoking the extent to which the idea of knowledge as separate to experience has been lost. Engendered by modern science and emboldened by a technologically aided empiricism, uncertainty is jettisoned. In contrast, Agamben turns to the celebration of experience as uncertainty in examples from Montaigne and Rousseau. Events where the narrator's separation from the supposed unified self is recounted and the revelation of the threshold Agamben identifies as infancy occurs. It is described as an in-between or gap that extends the separation between the semantic and semiotic as identified in the writings of Émile Benveniste and reasserts divisions: between Aristotle's *noūs* (intellect, reason) and *psychē* (soul) or Kant's distinction between the subject of transcendental apperception and empirical self-consciousness. As Agamben quotes from the *Critique of Pure Reason*, "[t]he subject cannot be cognized." Agamben is not positing infancy as outside the subject constituted in language, the only way in which the subject can be constituted he holds, but that the primary experience he terms "infancy" "coexists in its origins with language" and only through language is it reachable.[21]

The discussion briefly covers some of the same territory as Lyotard's *Discourse, Figure* in its desire to show the paucity of discourse without the necessary figural element that drives its thickness. However, it lacks the fundamental disagreement with Jacques Lacan's acceptance of the necessary dominance of language, in spite of the screen that consciousness places on the unconscious, or the implicit critique of Derrida's excessive textualism, his propensity to put "language everywhere."[22] Agamben's infancy highlights that experience is a knowledge that cannot be spoken of and which is approximated to the *pathēma* of Aristotle's animal voice, the closed-mouth moaning from which mystery and the linguistic root "mu" is derived. The same etymology is used by Lyotard in both "Affect-phrase" and "Voices": the mu—of mute, murmur, mutter, the *muttum* from which comes the French word for word, *mot*. The attempts to play with repetitive phonemes in Lyotard's own writing emphasize the timbre of the voice as carrying with it its infancy, in acknowledgment of the necessary struggle within *lexis* not to disown the *phōnē* that "cannot be broken down into what we call phonemes."[23] Aristotle says the *phōnē* is inarticulate, able only to signal not signify, to signal affect: pain, pleasure, it is tautegorical to and of itself. As Lyotard remarks, it is "supposedly" inarticulate, but it shows,[24] it *affects*, and in so doing has to be referred to by others as if it were outside the narrating, speaking voice. Only within the terms of discourse is it mute. Lyotard is at pains to ensure that it is not understood as an absolute other, an extrinsic transcendental being, but that it "squats"—infancy inhabits writing. As recalled in the roster of animal figures highlighted in "Voices": wolves, rats, worms, and cockroaches of Freud, Beckett, Kafka to which we might add the larvae and the spider of Malraux. These are not experiments operating simply to demonstrate the possibilities of writing but glimpses of the infancy that dwells within discourse and to which discourse itself remains deaf.

Agamben, however, seems to dismiss attempts to manifest such infantile undersides. The interior monologues of Joyce's writings, for example, show nothing of experience but reveal, rather, language itself; neither for Agamben is Freud's unconscious akin to infancy, revealing rather a non-person, a non-subject with no reality but its own. Yet despite this unwillingness to acknowledge a psychic reality, for fear of implying a pre-subjective or pre-linguistic state, the necessary inability to unify experience brought by infancy is what enables potency (knowledge) and history to exist in the difference and discontinuity that is its basis, born into a world of language with voice but without speech. That is the crux of Agamben's infancy: "man is not the 'animal possessing language,' but instead the animal deprived of language and obliged, therefore, to receive it from outside himself."[25]

Lectures d'enfance has less confidence in its own compartmentalization of experience; within these readings dwell a multiplicity of voices that are not simply demonstrations of the "lucidity" of language, that are not simple negations (non-persons, non-subjects), but readings that rub, touch, flex through their own inability to voice. In so doing the readings in infancy embarked on by Lyotard may sometimes seem to correlate with Agamben in his search for experience that is not singular or closed-off. At times their

Afterword

ambitions may seem to overlap; yet the declarations on the predominance of language in Agamben, albeit one acknowledging the infantile, veers toward a control that seems to threaten to find its situation, to place and tether it always to the subject. Such a move might be akin to the inevitable relationship between *phōnē* and *logos* chased in many of Lyotard's writings: how to "link on" without dominating, destroying, and committing an injustice to that which called. But Lyotard warns us: infancy is unable to reply to an articulated sentence. Held hostage, it is unable to put itself into the position of either addressee or addressor, an I/you position, neither does *Infans* speak in the sense that might be translated. But it does affect. That affection might not be able to address but once caught, touched, brushed against, yes . . . felt, then it is given voice by the one who responds and hands over the responsibility in turn to respond. In § 11 of "Voices" Lyotard makes an assertion that renders the connection to the infancy of *Heidegger and "the jews"* perhaps more distinct: *phōnē* "traverses generations," it is "an unheard tradition," a voice that is not mine but holds it hostage. The animal voice of *phōnē*. As Élisabeth de Fontenay asks us: Who, for Lyotard, are the victims par excellence of a wrong (*tort*)—divested of the ability to prove the damage to which they are subjected?[26] —Animals, she replies. And to which we might add the unheard animal voices of infancy.

Kiff Bamford

NOTES

Preface

1. Lyotard, *Le Postmoderne expliqué aux enfants* (1986). The list of sources in the French edition, which make the fictitious construct of these 'letters' clear, is absent in both versions published in English (1992 and 1993).

    All complete bibliographic references to Lyotard works may be found in the Bibliography of Works by Jean-François Lyotard in English Translation located at the end of this volume.

2. "*Infans* properly means *Qui fari non potest*; and he of whom could be predicated, *Fari potest*, was not *Infans*, and was capable of doing certain legal acts. The phrase *Qui fari potest* is itself ambiguous; but the Romans, in a legal sense, did not limit it to the mere capacity of uttering words, which a child of two or three years generally possesses, but they understood by it a certain degree of intellectual development." George Long, "Infans." In William Smith, ed. *A Dictionary of Greek and Roman Antiquities* (London: John Murray, 1875), 636.

3. Lyotard, "La Mainmise." In *Un trait d'union*, 5. Lyotard elaborated this from "Mainmise," a lecture he gave in 1989 [*Autre temps* 25 (1989): 16–26].

4. Lyotard, *The Hyphen* (1999): 2.

5. Miguel Abensour, "L'Intraitable." In Dolorès Lyotard, Jean-Claude Milner, Gérald Sfez, eds. *Jean-François Lyotard: L'Exercice du différend* (Paris: La Librairie du Collège International de philosophie, 2001), 257.

6. The term for the condition, as I am calling it here, came to the fore a bit before *The Inhuman*, during a colloquium held on May 29, 1987 at the Centre Sèvres, near Paris, on Lyotard's work to that point. See François Guibal and Jacob Rogozinski, eds. *Témoigner du différend: Quand phraser ne se peut* (Paris: Osiris, 1989), 93. See also Emine Sarıkartal's dissertation, "Enfances chez Jean-François Lyotard: Sur les traces d'une notion plurielle" (Université Paris-Nanterre, 2017), 7–8.

7. "Return" in this volume, 11. I've changed Lyotard's syntax to fit my sentence.

8. Lyotard, *The Hyphen*.

9. Originally published in the *Nouvelle revue de psychanalyse* 39 (1989): 43–70, "Emma" reappears in the posthumous *Misère de la philosophie* (2000), parts of which were to become a second volume of *The Differend*. The importance of the Emma case for Lyotard lies in its presentation of *Nachträglichkeit*— the sole phenomenon through which a link between the "human" and the "inhumanity" of infancy is preserved. Between 1989 and 2000 stands "Voices," published in this volume, which resonates uncannily with the iterations of

Notes

"Emma." Two essential studies in these areas are Claire Nouvet, "For 'Emma'" and Anne Tomiche, "Anamnesis," both found in Julie Gaillard, Claire Nouvet, and Mark Stoholski, eds. *Traversals of Affect: On Jean-François Lyotard* (London and New York: Bloomsbury Academic, 2016).

10. "Postmodernism [...] is not modernism at its conclusion, but in its nascent state. And that state is constant." Jean-François Lyotard, "Answering the Question: What Is Postmodernism?" in *The Postmodern Condition*. Translation modified.
11. Julia Kristeva, *Dostoïevski* (Paris: Buchet/Chastel, 2019), 56.
12. Published in Lyotard, *Des dispositifs pulsionnels* (1973): 304–19.
13. *Revue philosophique de la France et de l'étranger* 180, no. 2 (April–June 1990).
14. Jean-François Lyotard, ed., *La Faculté de juger* with Jacques Derrida et al. (Paris: Éditions de Minuit, 1985), 97. See also Gérald Sfez, "Mélancolies kafkaïennes." *Les Cahiers philosophiques de Strasbourg* 33, no. 1 (2003): 149–78.
15. See Jacques Derrida, "Préjugés, devant la loi." In *La Faculté de juger*, 107ff. See also Élisabeth de Fontenay, *Une tout autre histoire: Questions à Jean-François Lyotard* (Paris: Fayard, 2006).
16. Jacques Derrida, "Lyotard et *nous*." In *Jean-François Lyotard: L'Exercice du différend*, 169–96. Tr. as "Lyotard and Us," by Boris Belay, *Parallax* 6, no. 4 (2000): 28–48.
17. For a sustained, well-documented history of *Les Immatériaux*, see Kiff Bamford, *Jean-François Lyotard* (London: Reaktion Books, 2017).
18. *Illusio* no. 18 (2018) (L'Enfance au temps de l'humanité superflue, 1: Émancipation, éducation, aliénation).
19. *Illusio* no. 19 (2020) (L'Enfance au temps de l'humanité superflue, 2: Subjectifications, réification, anéantissement).
20. For some reason Bennington and Bowlby decided to translate *causeries* as "reflections," which they are, but . . . .
21. In this, and despite our admiration for her doctoral work on this topic in Lyotard, we disagree with Emine Sarıkartal's choice of "Childhood Lectures" in "Childhood and Education in Jean-François Lyotard's Philosophy." *Educational Philosophy and Theory* (2009), doi:10.1080/00131857.2019.1605899.
22. "Voices" in this volume, 100.

Return

1. [James Joyce, *Ulysses* (Paris: Shakespeare and Company, 1922), 606, modified here by the editors. In English in the original, with no reference given.]
2. [The usual proper noun for Odysseus in French is *Ulysse*—a convenient homonym in this case for the title Joyce lent to his novel of 1922.—Eds.]

Notes

3. [In English in the original.—Eds.]
4. Joyce, *Ulysses*, 162.
5. Erich Auerbach, *Mimesis: The Representation of Reality in Western Literature*, tr. Willard R. Trask (Princeton, NJ: Princeton University Press, 1953). [The chapter on the *Odyssey* is entitled "Odysseus' Scar," 3–23.—Eds.]
6. Ibid., 7, 13.
7. Ibid., 17.
8. [Lyotard uses this word to designate *chansons de geste*, medieval biblical chronicles in verse. The genre is akin to the passion play.—Tr.]
9. [Note 1 on page 407 in Paul Claudel, *Œuvres en prose* (Paris: Gallimard [Bibliothèque de la Pléiade], 1965) indicates that Claudel's "Lecture de *l'Odyssée*" was first published in *Le Figaro* on September 27, 1947. It served as preface to Victor Bérard's translation of the Odyssey (Paris: Gallimard, 1949) and was collected in Claudel's *Accompagnements* (1949).—Eds.]
10. Auerbach, *Mimesis*, 22. [To alleviate any ambiguity between Lyotard's use of this quote and Auerbach's meaning, we have decided to furnish more of the sentence than appeared in the original French.—Tr.]
11. [See Jean-Luc Nancy, *The Inoperative Community*, tr. Peter Connor, Lisa Garbus, Michael Holland, and Simona Sawhney (Minneapolis: University of Minnesota Press, 1990).—Eds.]
12. Joyce, *Ulysses*, 110.
13. Ibid., 117.
14. Ibid., 118.
15. Ibid., 137.
16. [In English in the original.—Eds.]
17. [Lyotard uses the phrase "*il se couchera tête-bêche*," which is a description used by Samuel Beckett in *Malone meurt* (Paris: Minuit, 1951), 146; when translated by the author as *Malone Dies* (1956), the phrase is rendered as "tetty-beshy." See Samuel Beckett, *Malloy, Malone Dies, The Unnamable* (London, Montreuil and New York: Calder, 1959), 263. The expression *tête-bêche* occurs in literature as early as François Rabelais' *Gargantua* (1534) where *teste à teste beschevel* refers to a game where children would guess whether hidden objects were in "tetty-beshy" position or not. The adverb is also used in philately when two stamps are printed upside down one with respect to the other. In *Ulysses* the same sleeping position is favored by Bloom, though Molly sees it as an anal or dorsal sexual proclivity, rather than the likely connotations of mutual oral sex in Beckett. For Lyotard, however, "*tête-bêche*" would seem to indicate the opposite—an absence of sexual fulfilment.—Eds.]
18. [See Joyce, *Ulysses*, 1021. The reference described in the Ithaca episode is as follows "Lighted Candle in Stick bone by / BLOOM / Diaconal Hat on Ashplant borne by / STEPHEN."—Eds.]
19. Joyce, *Ulysses*, 40.

Notes

20. Ibid., 537.
21. [The reference to the Torah here is not to the Pentateuch, but to the Tanakh, or Hebrew Bible.—Eds.]
22. [*The Jewish Study Bible, featuring the Jewish Publishing Society Tanekh translation* (Oxford: Oxford University Press, 2013), 1411.—Eds.]
23. Ibid., 453.
24. Ibid., 164.
25. Ibid., 170.
26. Ibid., 175.
27. Ibid., 170–1.
28. Ibid., 170.
29. [Lyotard uses a neologism here: *paternation* which we have rendered as "paternization."—Eds.]
30. Ibid., 172.
31. Ibid., 173.
32. Ibid., 550.
33. Ibid., 176.
34. Ibid., 573.
35. Ibid., 161.
36. Ibid., 162.
37. Ibid.
38. Ibid.
39. Ibid.

Prescription

1. [As set out in the Civil Code, *prescription* in French law refers to the legal effects of a lapse of time on a right or obligation. The rules of prescription (or statute of limitations) provide for two distinct situations: either the prescription is "*extinctive*," meaning that after a certain period it extinguishes a right or obligation or the prescription is "*acquisitive*" when, after a certain time, its effect is to acquire or consolidate a right. From a legal perspective, the French Civil Code's prescription rules should not be confused with penal prescription, to which "In the Penal Colony" is more closely related as Lyotard shows. In criminal matters, the rules of prescription cover a different reality: prescription is a period (a time limit) after which it is no longer legal for judicial authority either to pursue proceedings with respect to an offense or a crime or to carry out a sentence pronounced against the perpetrator of an offense or a crime.—Eds.]

Notes

2. [We have chosen to translate "*la morale*" as "moral law" rather than "morality" in order to avoid the ambiguity of the term, whilst maintaining Lyotard's decision not to use the term "ethics," and to highlight the connection to Kant's *Critique of Practical Reason*. "*Morale et politique*" was the title of a Franco-German conference organized by the Collège international de philosophie where Lyotard first delivered this lecture. According to an account given by Geoffrey Bennington, this lecture was given under the title "Avant la loi," which Jacques Derrida understood as referring to his own contribution to "Comment juger? à partir du travail de Jean-François Lyotard," the 1982 conference on Lyotard's work at Cerisy-la-Salle. Titled "Devant la loi," Derrida's subject was Kafka's parable "Before the Law" (*Vor dem Gesetz*), contained within his unfinished novel, *The Trial*. The title of Lyotard's 1993 publication, *Moralités postmodernes*, might also be noted; these morality tales or fables are published in English translation as *Postmodern Fables* (1997).—Eds.]

3. [Although Kafka's term, *Urteil*, can be translated in several ways, we have opted for "judgment" in accordance with Corngold and in agreement with his observation that this aligns with Kafka's story of 1912, *The Judgment* (*Das Urteil*). See Franz Kafka, "In the Penal Colony" in *Kafka's Selected Stories*, tr. Stanley Corngold (New York: W.W. Norton & Co., 2007), 39 n. 3.—Eds.]

4. [Lyotard has "acting out" in English in the original: *l'acting-out*.—Eds.]

5. Franz Kafka, "In der Strafkolonie." In *Erzählungen*, hrsg. Max Brod (Frankfurt am Main: Fischer Taschenbuch Verlag, 1976), 155; "In the Penal Colony," tr. Stanley Corngold, 40. [Since Lyotard reproduces generous portions of Kafka's original text, we are exceptionally providing the reader with those references first, followed by those to Corngold's translation.—Eds.]

6. Ibid. 155; 40.

7. Ibid. 156; 40.

8. Ibid.

9. Ibid.

10. Ibid.

11. Ibid. 157; 41.

12. Ibid. 159; 43.

13. Ibid.

14. Ibid.

15. Ibid. 155; 39.

16. Ibid. 160; 44–5.

17. [*Sûppot*, is notoriously difficult to translate. "Instrument" had been the choice made in *Toward the Postmodern* (1993), where the term appeared notably in "False Flights in Literature" which discusses works by Michel Butor, Pierre Klossowski, and an obscure *Cut Confession* by an eighteenth-century Franciscan. Lyotard gets *suppôt* from Klossowski. Here is how Daniel

Notes

W. Smith, the translator of Klossowski's *Nietzsche et le cercle vicieux* (Paris: Mercure de France, 1969), justifies his choice of "agent": "We have translated the unusual but important term *suppôt* as 'agent'. The word is derived from the Latin *suppositum*, 'that which is placed under'. In contemporary usage, it refers to a subordinate who acts on behalf of someone else [...] and usually implies that the subordinate is carrying out the designs of a wicked superior." Finding this explanation quite convincing, we have followed Smith's lead. Pierre Klossowski, *Nietzsche and the Vicious Circle*, tr. Daniel W. Smith (London: The Athlone Press, 1997), xii–xiii.—Eds.]

18. "In the Penal Colony," 171; 54.
19. Sigmund Freud, "The Unconscious" (1915): *SE* 14, 187.
20. "In the Penal Colony," 164; 48.
21. Ibid., 164; 48.
22. [*bifrons*: "with double forehead or countenance, epithet of Janus, Vergil," *Cassell's New Latin Dictionary* (New York: Funk and Wagnalls, 1959).—Eds.]
23. Kafka, "In the Penal Colony," 176–7; 58–9.
24. Ibid., 166; 52.

Survivor

1. [Time (t) is dependent on the infinitesimal quantity (dt), hence the instant written as t.dt. But given this dependence, some mathematicians might argue that t_{dt} is the most appropriate notation to represent that t depends on the change in t.—Eds.]
2. Elias Canetti, *Crowds and Power*, tr. Carol Stewart (New York: Farrar, Straus, Giroux, 1973).
3. Hannah Arendt, *The Human Condition* (Chicago: University of Chicago Press, 1958), 246–7.
4. Ibid., 246–7.
5. Hannah Arendt, "Die Verborgene Tradition." In *Sechs Essays* (Heidelberg: Lambert Schneider, 1948), 81–111; "The Jew as Pariah: A Hidden Tradition." In Ron H. Feldman, ed. *The Jew as Pariah: Jewish Identity and Politics in the Modern Age* (New York: Grove Press, 1978), 67–90.
6. Hannah Arendt, *The Origins of Totalitarianism* (New York: Schocken, 1951).
7. Arendt, "The Jew as Pariah," 85.
8. Ibid., 71.
9. Hannah Arendt, "We Refugees." In *The Jew as Pariah*, 55–66.
10. Rolf Hochhuth, *Der Stellvertreter* (Reinbek bei Hamburg: Rowohlt, 1963); *The Deputy*, tr. Richard and Clara Winston (New York: Grove Press, 1964).

Notes

11. Hannah Arendt, *Eichmann in Jerusalem: A Report on the Banality of Evil* (New York: Viking Press, 1963).
12. Arendt, "The Jew as Pariah," 66.
13. Ibid., 64.
14. Hannah Arendt, *Rahel Varnhagen: The Life of a Jewess*, tr. Richard and Clara Winston (London: Published for the Institute by the East and West Library, 1958).
15. [Arendt gave a series of lectures on Kant at the New School for Social Research, New York, Fall 1970. See Hannah Arendt, *Lectures on Kant's Political Philosophy*, ed. Ronald Beiner (Chicago: University of Chicago Press, 1989)—Eds.]
16. Arendt, *Eichmann in Jerusalem*, 256.
17. Ibid., 305.
18. See "What is Authority?" in Hannah Arendt, *Between Past and Future: Eight Exercises in Political Thought* (New York: Viking Press, 1968), 91–141.
19. Arendt, *Origins of Totalitarianism*, second enlarged edition (New York: Harcourt Brace, 1973), 413.
20. Arendt, *Between Past and Future*, 100.
21. ["*pare-excitation*," given in *Lectures d'enfance*, corresponds to "*Reizschutz*" in German and "shield" (against stimuli) in the Standard Edition of Freud. See Sigmund Freud, "Beyond the Pleasure Principle," tr. James Strachey, *The Standard Edition of the Complete Works of Sigmund Freud*, vol. 18 (London: Hogarth Press, 1955), 28–9—Eds.]
22. Arendt, *Between Past and Future*, 264.
23. ["short story" in English in the original.—Eds.]
24. Arendt, *Origins of Totalitarianism*, second enlarged edition, 473. [Lyotard's emphasis.—Eds.]
25. Ibid., 337, 338.
26. Ibid., 463, 465, 465.
27. [It is currently believed that the death of the sun will result in its expansion into a red giant, followed by its implosion into a white dwarf. It is unclear what Lyotard is referring to here as "Nova noir."—Eds.]
28. Arendt, *Between Past and Future*, 1968 edition, 188.
29. [The Gallicized "squatte" is in italics in the original to indicate the foreign origin.—Eds.]
30. Ibid., 7.
31. Arendt, *Origins of Totalitarianism*, 474ff.

Words

1. Jean-Paul Sartre, *The Words* [*Les Mots* (1963)], tr. Bernard Frechtman (New York: George Brazillier, 1964).

Notes

2. Jean-Paul Sartre, *The Communists and Peace, with A Reply to Claude Lefort* ["Les Communistes et la paix" in *Situations, VI: Problèmes du marxisme, 1*; "Réponse à Claude Lefort" in *Situations, VII: Problèmes du marxisme, 2*], tr. Philip R. Berk, Martha H. Fletcher, John R. Kleinschmidt (New York: George Brazillier, 1968).

3. [Claude Lefort (1924–2010), political philosopher and co-founder in 1949, with Cornelius Castoriadis, of the leftist, anti-authoritarian group and journal *Socialisme ou barbarie*. Lefort left the group following disagreements in 1958. Lyotard, having joined the group in 1954, remained until 1963. Lefort clashed with Sartre over the role of the USSR and the French Communist Party in a series of articles written for *Les Temps modernes* 1952–54, and their animosity was repeated in several subsequent publications.—Eds.]

4. Jean-Paul Sartre, *Being and Nothingness: An Essay on Phenomenological Ontology* [*L'Être et le Néant: Essai d'ontologie phénoménologique* (1943), tr. Hazel E. Barnes (New York: Philosophical Library, 1948).

5. Sartre, *The Communists and Peace* [etc.], 95.

6. Jean-Paul Sartre, *Transcendence of the Ego: A Sketch for a Phenomenological Description* [*La Transcendance de l'ego: Esquisse d'une description phénoménologique* (1936–7)], tr. Forrest Williams and Robert Kirkpatrick (New York: Noonday Press, 1962).

7. Jean-Paul Sartre, *Dirty Hands* [*Les Mains sales*, 1948], tr. Lionel Abel in *No Exit, and Three Other Plays* (New York: Vintage, 1989); *The Condemned of Altona* [*Les Séquestrés d'Altona* (1959)], tr. Sylvia and George Leeson (New York: Alfred A. Knopf, 1969).

8. [*Les Chemins de la liberté* (*The Roads to Freedom*) is Sartre's trilogy comprising *L'Âge de raison* (*The Age of Reason*), *Le Sursis* (*The Reprieve*), and *La Mort dans l'âme* (*Troubled Sleep*).—Eds.]

9. [André Malraux, *La Condition humaine* (1933) (*Man's Fate*), Antoine de Saint-Exupéry, *Terre des hommes* (1939) (*Wind, Sand, and Stars*) and, of course, Victor Hugo, *Les Misérables* (1862).—Eds.]

10. Sartre, *The Words*, 252–3.

11. Ibid., 254. [Translator adjusted translation.—Eds.]

12. See note 8.

13. Sartre, *The Words*, 255.

14. [Poulou, we learn in *The Words*, was Sartre's childhood nickname.—Eds.]

15. Sartre, *The Words*, 92.

16. Sartre, *The Communists and Peace* [etc.], 254.

17. Ibid., 282. [In *Lectures d'enfance* this citation mistakenly refers to the Komintern not the Kominform; we have corrected this in line with Sartre's French original, and the English translation. Both terms are also rendered as Comintern (The Communist International, 1919–43) and Cominform (Information Bureau of the Communist Parties, 1947–56), referring to

Notes

organizations that promote international communism under the aegis of the Soviet Union.—Eds.]

18. [Lyotard's reference is rendered as Komintern in the original, we have altered this to Kominform in line with the previous revised quotation from Sartre. See note 17.—Eds.]
19. Ibid., 253.
20. Ibid., 239. [Translation modified.—Eds.]
21. [Michel Contat (1938—) is a writer, filmmaker, and literary critic who was very close to Sartre. He conducted *Autoportrait à soixante-dix ans*—the extended interview with Sartre first published in the June–July issue of *Le Nouvel Observateur*, then in *Situations, X*. Contat also co-directed (with Alexandre Astruc and Guy Séligmann) the 1976 film, *Sartre par lui-même*.—Eds.]
22. Jean-Paul Sartre, "Self Portrait at Seventy." In *Life/Situations: Essays Written and Spoken* [*Situations X: Politique et autobiographie* (1976)], tr. Paul Aster and Lydia Davis (New York: Pantheon Books, 1977), 51.
23. Denis Hollier, *Politics of Prose: Essay on Sartre* [*Politique de la prose: Jean-Paul Sartre et l'an quarante*], tr. Jeffrey Mehlman (Minneapolis: University of Minnesota Press, 1986), 203.
24. Sartre, "Justice and the State." In *Life/Situations*, 190.
25. Sartre, "Self Portrait at Seventy," 51.
26. Hollier, *Politics*, 71.
27. [Pierre Guyotat (1940–2020) was a writer whose first books—*Tombeau pour cinq cent mille soldats* (1967) and *Éden, Éden, Éden* (1970)—both scandalized institutions and drew the admiration of the likes of Philippe Sollers, Michel Foucault, and Roland Barthes. Guyotat wrote of extreme violence and sexuality in a language blending French, Arabic, and onomatopoeia.—Eds.]
28. Jean-Paul Sartre, *The Imagination: A Psychological Critique* [1936], tr. Forrest Williams (Ann Arbor: The University of Michigan Press, 1962), 1, 2.
29. Hollier, *Politics*, 58.
30. Internal quotation from Jean-Paul Sartre, *What is Literature?* [*Situations II*, (1948)], tr. Bernard Frechtman (New York: Philosophical Library, 1949), 158.
31. Ibid., 85–6.
32. Ibid., 86–7.
33. ["Présentation des *Temps modernes*" was republished in Sartre's *Situations, II*. This is J. Mehlman's translation in Hollier, *Politics*, 71.—Eds.]
34. Ibid., 81.
35. Ibid.
36. Philippe Gavi, Jean-Paul Sartre, and Pierre Victor, *It Is Right to Rebel* [*On a raison de se révolter*, 1974], tr. Adrian van den Hoven and Basil Kingstone (New York: Routledge, 2018), 53.

Notes

37. Jean-Paul Sartre, *Saint Genet: Actor and Martyr* [*Saint Genet: Comédien et martyr* (1952)], tr. Bernard Frechtman (New York: 1963), 324.

38. Jean-Paul Sartre, "Man and Things" ["L'Homme et les choses," collected in *Situations, I* (1947) translated as *Critical Essays*], *Critical Essays*, tr. Chris Turner (Kolkata: Seagull Press, 2017), 422.

39. Jean-Paul Sartre, *Sketch for a Theory of the Emotions* [*Esquisse d'une théorie des émotions* (1939)], tr. Philip Mairet (London: Methuen, 1962), 10ff.

40. Sartre, *Saint Genet*, 246.

41. [Michel Enaudeau (1943–), journalist, critic, and Lyotard's son-in-law, wrote his master's dissertation in 1968 on the aesthetics of Sartre, which Lyotard read and discussed with him in the early 1970s. The specific reference here is to Sartre's lesser-known obsession with poetry. As he wrote in his *Carnets* in 1940 "[I]t makes me furious not to be a poet—to be so ponderously tethered to prose," which complicates the seeming opposition between poetry and prose found elsewhere in his writings and which Lyotard challenges here. See Jean-Paul Sartre, *War Diaries: Notebooks from a Phoney War, 1939–40* [*Les Carnets de la drôle de guerre: novembre 1939–mars 1940* (1983)], tr. Quintin Hoare, (London: Verso, 1984): 314. Personal correspondence with Corinne Enaudeau 1 August 2020.—Eds.]

42. Henri Meschonnic, "Situation de Sartre dans le langage." *Obliques*, 163.

43. Sartre, *Saint Genet*, 304.

44. Ibid., 309.

45. Sartre, *What is Literature?*, 284.

46. Sartre, *Saint Genet*, 304.

47. Jean-Paul Sartre, *Situations IX: Mélanges* (1972), 47. [J. Mehlman's translation.—Eds.]

48. Sartre, *What is Literature?*, 20.

49. Meschonnic, 165. [J. Mehlman's translation.—Eds.]

50. [This is an allusion to *L'Idiot de la famille* (*The Family Idiot*), Sartre's monumental unfinished study of Gustave Flaubert, published in three volumes (1971–72) in the Bibliothèque de philosophie collection at Éditions Gallimard.—Eds.]

51. Meschonnic, 166. [J. Mehlman's translation.—Eds.]

52. Sartre, *Saint Genet*, 304.

53. [Pierre Verstraeten (1933–2013) was a Belgian philosopher. As a student at the École normale supérieure, he was close to Louis Althusser and Alain Badiou. He served with Sartre as co-editor at Éditions Gallimard of the series "Bibliothèque de philosophie."—Eds.]

54. Sartre, *Situations IX*, 60. [J. Mehlman's translation.—Eds.]

55. Ibid., 59.

56. Ibid., 61.
57. Sartre, *What is Literature?*, 19.
58. Sartre, *Situations IX*, 61–3. [J. Mehlman's translation.—Eds.]
59. Ibid.
60. [With his original subtitle, Hollier's referenced the 1940s as follows: *Politique de la prose: Jean-Paul Sartre et l'an quarante,* thereby punning on French expression *se foutre* or *se moquer (de quelque chose) comme de l'an quarante,* or to not give a fig (a shit, a fuck, etc.) about something.—Eds.]
61. ["L'Homme et les choses" ("Man and Things") is the title of Sartre's review article of Francis Ponge's *Le Parti pris des choses* (1942). It was collected in *Situations, I* (1947) as *Critical Essays,* tr. Chris Turner (Kolkata: Seagull Press, 2017).—Eds.]
62. Sartre, *Critical Essays*, 193. [Sartre used the term in reference to Maurice Blanchot's *Aminidab* (1942).—Eds.]
63. Cf. Sartre, *What is Literature?*, 36.
64. Sartre, *What is Literature?*, 14.
65. Sartre, *Situations I,* 140.
66. Sartre, *What is Literature?*, 14.
67. Sartre, *Saint Genet,* 429.
68. Sartre, *What is Literature?*, 37.
69. Ibid.
70. [See Lyotard, *Discourse, Figure,* 3–19, "the bias of the figural" [*le parti pris du figural*] for Lyotard's discussion of "the thickness of words" in reference to Stéphane Mallarmé and, by inference, Ponge's *Le Parti pris des choses.*—Eds.]
71. [Chapter 8 of Hollier's *The Politics of Prose* is titled "Insinuations (Questions of Method)."—Eds.]

Disorder

1. [This paper was first presented at a workshop, titled "Ceci est de l'art," organized by Thierry de Duve as program director, Belgium, for the Collège internationale de philosophie. Lyotard had acted as a member of the jury for de Duve's PhD in 1981, which was directed by Louis Marin.—Eds.]
2. ["noun-phrases" and "verb-phrase" are rendered in English in the original.—Eds.]
3. [See Lyotard, *Le Différend* (1983).—Trans.]
4. [February 2, 1989, is the date of the first presentation of the paper at a workshop organized by the Bibliothèque Populaire at the Centre Georges-Pompidou and the Collège international de philosophie.—Eds.]

Notes

5. [See Saul Kripke, *Naming and Necessity* (Cambridge, MA: Harvard University Press, 1972).—Eds.]

6. "Première Leçon" in Paul Valéry, *Introduction à la poétique* (Paris: Gallimard, 1938), tr. Ralph Manheim as "The Opening Lecture of the Course in *Poetics*" in Paul Valéry, *Aesthetics* (Collected Works of Paul Valéry, v. 13) (New York: Pantheon Books [Bollingen Series XLV], 1964), 98–9; italics in original.

7. Ibid., 100; italics in original.

8. Ibid., 104.

9. Ibid., 111.

10. Ibid., 104. [Lyotard's italics.—Eds.]

11. Ibid., 105. [italics in original.—Eds.]

12. Ibid., 102–3 and 104.

13. Ibid., 105–6.

14. Ibid., 109. [Lyotard's italics. Translation modified.—Eds.]

15. Paul Valéry, *Cahiers* (Paris: Gallimard, 1987).

16. Paul Valéry, *La Soirée de Monsieur Teste* (Paris: Nouvelle Revue française, 1927).

17. Valéry, "Opening Lecture," 100; italics in original.

18. Ibid., 101; italics in original.

Voices

1. [Freud discussed the Rat Man case in April 1908 at the First International Psycho-Analytical Congress, held in Salzburg, Austria. The published version of the case history first appeared in the *Jahrbuch für psychoanalytische und psychopathologische Forschungen* 1 (1909): 357–421. The "Original Record of the Case" has been partially translated into English and published in the *Standard Edition* (Vol. 10, 153–318) as an "addendum" to the published version. Lyotard also refers to Elza Rebeiro Hawelka's edition of the complete German text accompanied by its translation into French: *"L'Homme aux rats." Journal d'une analyse* (Paris: PUF, 1974). Page references to this edition will be given for those portions of the "Original Record" not already included in the *Standard Edition*. —Trans.]

2. Sigmund Freud, "Notes upon a Case of Obsessional Neurosis." In *Collected Papers of Sigmund Freud. Volume 3*, tr. Alix and James Strachey. (London: Hogarth, 1924–5): 293–383.

3. [Lyotard is distinguishing here between the case notes, written by Freud in his notebook in the evening following the sessions (referred to by Lyotard as "le *Journal*" see n.1), and the case history published in the *Jahrbuch*.—Eds.]

Notes

4. For further clarifications, I refer to Jean-Louis Labarrière, "Imagination humaine et imagination animale chez Aristote." *Phronesis* 29, no. 1 (1984): 17–49.
5. [In English in the original. —Trans.]
6. [See Sigmund Freud, "A Child is Being Beaten: A Contribution to the Study of the Origin of Sexual Perversions." *The Standard Edition of the Complete Psychological Works of Sigmund Freud*, tr. and ed. James Strachey. Vol. 17 (London: Hogarth, 1955), 179–203. For Lyotard's detailed commentary on the phantasy, see Lyotard, *Discours, figure* (1971): 325–54. —Eds.]
7. Sigmund Freud, "Psycho-Analytic Notes upon an Autobiographical Account of a Case of Paranoia (Dementia Paranoides)." *SE*. Vol. 12. 9–82, 63–5.
8. Cf. Labarrière.
9. Aristotle, *De interpretatione*. Lines 16–28; *The Complete Works of Aristotle*, ed. Jonathan Barnes, tr. J. L. Ackrill, Vol. 1. (Princeton: Princeton University Press, 1984), 25.
10. *SE* 14: 187.
11. Aristotle, *Nichomachean Ethics*. Book X, §4. [The translation used by Lyotard differs from the standard English translation, which we have thus modified, but which runs as follows: "for it does not lack anything which coming into being later will complete its form. [. . .] that which takes place in a moment is a whole." *The Complete Works of Aristotle*, ed. Jonathan Barnes, tr. W. D. Ross, revised J. O. Urmson, Vol. 2, 1729–1867 (Princeton: Princeton University Press, 1984), 1856. —Eds.]
12. [*Vorstellungsrepräsentanz* is translated as "ideational representation" in the Standard Edition; see Sigmund Freud, "Repression." *SE* Vol. 14. 141–58— Eds.]
13. [A conflation of the words allegory and tautology, "tautégorie" appears in contemporary French thought as an expression designating a mode of signification that points only to itself, unlike the workings of allegory where every meaning points to another. —Trans.]
14. Freud, "Obsessional Neurosis," 177; translation modified.
15. [In English in the original. —Trans.]
16. [*Macbeth* 3.4.78. —Eds.]
17. Freud, "Obsessional Neurosis," 157.
18. Ibid., 164 and 232.
19. Ibid., 228.
20. Ibid., 162.
21. Freud, *"L'Homme aux rats." Journal d'une analyse* (Paris: PUF, 1974), 10.
22. Freud, "Obsessional Neurosis," 292.
23. Ibid., 245, 226–7.

Notes

24. Maurice Blanchot, *De Kafka à Kafka* (Paris: Gallimard, 1981). The text was initially published as "La voix narrative" in *L'entretien infini* (Paris: Gallimard, 1969), 556–67.
25. Freud, "*L'Homme aux rats*," 17.
26. Sigmund Freud, *The Freud/Jung Letters: The Correspondence between Sigmund Freud and C.G. Jung*, ed. William McGuire, tr. Ralph Manheim and R. F. C. Hull (Princeton: Princeton UP, 1974), 238.
27. [Beckett uses "Jones" to represent any male person, such as "Joe Blow" in the US or "Joe Bloggs" in the UK; in French, this was *Tartempion*, also used by Lyotard in §26, there rendered as "Jones [Joe Blow]." —Eds.]
28. Samuel Beckett, *The Unnamable*, tr. Samuel Beckett (New York: Grove, 1958), 26, 69, 72–3.
29. [Lyotard has *wormy* in English in the original. —Eds.]
30. Freud, "Obsessional Neurosis," 289.
31. Beckett, *The Unnamable*, 130.
32. Freud, "Obsessional Neurosis," 284.
33. Ibid., 287.
34. Ibid., 209.
35. I follow here the French translation and edition of Aristotle's *Poetics* by Roselyne Dupont-Roc and Jean Lallot (Paris: Seuil, 1980).
36. ["talking cure" in English in the original. —Eds.]
37. [The *Trauerspiel*, or mourning play, was the subject of Walter Benjamin's dissertation which drew attention to this minor genre, as commented on by Christine Buci-Gluckmann in her works on the Baroque. See note 32. —Eds.]
38. Cf. Christine Buci-Glucksmann, *Tragique de l'ombre: Shakespeare et le maniérisme* (Paris: Galilée, 1990).
39. [In English in the original. —Trans.]
40. ["Worms" in English in the original. —Eds.]
41. Gérard Genette, *Narrative Discourse: An Essay in Method*, tr. Jane E. Lewin (Ithaca, NY: Cornell University Press, 1980), 171–3.

Afterword

1. Jacques Derrida, *Before the Law: The Complete Text of Préjugés*, tr. Sandra Van Reenen and Jacques de Ville (Minneapolis: University of Minnesota Press, 2018).
2. See Geoffrey Bennington, "Before." In Robert Harvey, ed. *Afterwords: Essays in Memory of Jean-François Lyotard* (New York: Stony Brook, 2000): 7.

3. Corinne Enaudeau, "La Politique entre nihilism et histoire." *Cités* no. 45 (2001): 104 [103–15].
4. Jacques Derrida, "Ulysses Gramophone: Hear Say Yes in Joyce." In Bernard Benstock, ed. *James Joyce: The Augmented Ninth. Proceedings of the Ninth International James Joyce Symposium* (Syracuse, NY: Syracuse University Press, 1988), 27–75.
5. "Return" in this volume, 3.
6. Christopher Fynsk, "Jean-François's Infancy." *Yale French Studies* no. 99 (2001): 44–61.
7. Personal correspondence with Thierry de Duve.
8. See Mary Lydon, "Veduta on *Discours, figure*." *Yale French Studies* no. 99 (2001): 10–26; Christopher Fynsk, "Jean-François's Infancy." In Emine Sarıkartal, ed. *Enfances chez Jean-François Lyotard: Sur les traces d'une notion plurielle* (Paris: Université Paris-Nanterre, 2017).
9. Élisabeth de Fontenay, *Une tout autre historie. Questions à Jean-François Lyotard* (Paris: Fayard, 2006).
10. For a critical consideration and evaluation of the reception of *Heidegger and "the jews,"* see Sarah Hammerschlag, "Troping the Jew: Jean-François Lyotard's *Heidegger and 'the jews'*." *Jewish Studies Quarterly* 12, no. 4 (2005): 371–98. For a wide-ranging discussion of both this text and "Prescription: Kafka," see Jean-François Lyotard, "Before the Law, After the Law, interview with Elisabeth Weber" (1991).
11. Jean-François Lyotard, *Heidegger and 'the jews'*, (1990): 4.
12. Ibid., 92–3.
13. Jean-François Lyotard, *Political Writings* (1991): 166.
14. Agamben makes direct reference to *The Differed* in *Remnants of Auschwitz: The Witness and the Archive* [1998] (New York: Zone, 1999), 34–5, though his presence throughout is more significant as argued by Nicholas Chare, "The Gap in Context: Giorgio Agamben's 'Remnants of Auschwitz.'" *Cultural Critique* no. 64 (Autumn 2006): 40–68. See also Robert Harvey, *Witnessness: Beckett, Dante, Levi and the Foundations of Responsibility* (New York and London: Continuum, 2010), 28–9.
15. Donna J. Haraway, *Staying with the Trouble: Making Kin in the Chthulucene* (Durham, NC and London: Duke University Press, 2016): 32.
16. For a detailed account of the occurrence and usage of the term "infancy" by Agamben, including reference to untranslated writings in Italian, see Leland de la Durantaye, *Giorgio Agamben: A Critical Introduction* (Stanford, CA: Stanford University Press, 2009).
17. Jean-François Lyotard, "The Affect-phrase (from a Supplement to *The Differend*)." *The Lyotard Reader and Guide* (2006): 104 [104–10]; *Lyotard and Critical Practice* (2022): 67 [67–73].
18. Giorgio Agamben, *Infancy and History: On the Destruction of Experience*, tr. Liz Heron (London: Verso, 2007), 4.

Notes

19. Ibid., 4.
20. Ibid., 58.
21. Ibid., 55.
22. Jean-François Lyotard, *Discourse, Figure* (2011): 9.
23. "Voices" §7 in this volume, 92.
24. "Voices" §6 in this volume, 92.
25. Agamben, *Infancy and History*, 65.
26. "Entretien avec Élisabeth de Fontenay" with Michèle Cohen-Halimi and Gérald Sfez, *Cahiers philosophiques* no. 117 (April 2009): 106 [99–109].

BIBLIOGRAPHY

Works by Jean-François Lyotard available in English translation

1948

"La Culpabilité allemande." *L'Âge Nouveau* no. 28: 90–4. [See *Political Writings* (1993): 127–34.]

"Nés en 1925." *Les Temps modernes* 3, no. 32 (May): 2052–7. [See *Political Writings* (1993): 85–9.]

1954

La Phénoménologie. Paris: Presses Universitaires de France. *Phenomenology* (tr. Brian Beakley) with foreword by Gayle L. Ormiston, 1–25. New York: State University of New York Press, 1991.

1956

"La Situation en Afrique du Nord" (as F. Laborde). *Socialisme ou barbarie* 3, no. 18 (January–March): 87–94. [See *Political Writings* (1993): 171–8.]

1957

"La Bourgeoisie nord-africaine" (as F. Laborde). *Socialisme ou barbarie* 3, no. 20 (January–March): 188–94. [See *Political Writings* (1993): 179–86.]

"Nouvelle Phase dans la question algérienne" (as F. Laborde). *Socialisme ou barbarie* 4, no. 21 (March–May): 162–8. [See *Political Writings* (1993): 187–96.]

1958

"La Guerre 'contre-révolutionnaire,' la société coloniale et de Gaulle" (as F. Laborde). *Socialisme ou barbarie* 5, no. 25 (July–August): 20–7. [See *Political Writings* (1993): 214–20.]

"Mise à nu des contradictions algériennes" (as F. Laborde). *Socialisme ou barbarie* 4, no. 24 (May–June): 17–34. [See *Political Writings* (1993): 197–213.]

Bibliography

1960

"Le Contenu social de la lutte algérienne." *Socialisme ou barbarie* 5, no. 29 (December 1959–February 1960): 1–38. [See *Political Writings* (1993): 221–51.]
"L'État et la politique dans la France de 1960." *Socialisme ou barbarie* 5, no. 30 (April–May): 45–72. [See *Political Writings* (1993): 252–76.]

1961

"Le Gaullisme et l'Algérie." *Socialisme ou barbarie* 6, no. 31 (December 1960–February 1961): 24–32. [See *Political Writings* (1993): 277–85.]

1962

"L'Algérie, sept ans après." *Socialisme ou barbarie* 6, no. 33 (December 1961–February 1962): 10–6. [See *Political Writings* (1993): 286–92.]

1963

"L'Algérie évacuée." *Socialisme ou barbarie* 6, no. 34 (March–May): 1–43. [See *Political Writings* (1993): 293–326.]

1971

Discours, figure. Paris: Klincksieck. *Discourse, Figure* (tr. Antony Hudek and Mary Lydon) with introduction by John Mowitt, xi–xxiii. Minneapolis: University of Minnesota Press, 2011.

1972

"En finir avec l'illusion de la politique," with Gilbert Lascault. *La Quinzaine littéraire* no. 140 (1–15 May): 18–9. [See *The Interviews and Debates* (2020): 29–31.]

1973

Dérive à partir de Marx et Freud. Paris: Union Générale d'Éditions.
  Dérives, 5–21. [See *Driftworks* (1984): 9–17.]
  Préambule à une charte, 22–9. [See *Political Writings* (1993): 41–5.]
  Désirévolution, 30–5. "Desirevolution" (tr. Iain Hamilton Grant) In Robin Mackay and Armen Avanessian, eds., *The Accelerationist Reader*: 241–9. Falmouth: Urbanomic, 2014.

Bibliography

Un Marx non marxiste, 36–46.
Cadeau d'organes, 47–52. [See *Driftworks* (1984): 85–9.]
Principales tendances actuelles de l'étude psychanalytique des expressions artistiques et littéraires, 53–77. [See *Toward the Postmodern* (1993): 2–11.]
La place de l'aliénation dans le retournement marxiste, 78–166.
Œdipe juif, 167–88. [See *Driftworks* (1984): 35–55.]
Nanterre: ici, maintenant, 189–210. [See *Political Writings* (1993): 46–59.]
Sur la théorie, 210–29. [See *Driftworks* (1984): 19–33; *The Interviews and Debates* (2020): 17–27.]
Notes sur la fonction critique de l'œuvre, 230–47. [See *Driftworks* (1984): 69–83.]
"A few words to sing" Sequenza III, 248–71. [See *Toward the Postmodern* (1993): 41–59; *Textes dispersés II / Miscellaneous Texts II*, 56–93].
Leçon d'impouvoir, 272–5.
Espace plastique et espace politique, 276–304. "Plastic Space and Political Space" (tr. Mark S. Roberts), *boundary 2* 14, no. 1–2 (Autumn 1985–Winter 1986): 211–23.
Le 23 mars, 305–16. [See *Political Writings* (1993): 60–7.]

Des dispositifs pulsionnels. Paris: Union Générale d'Éditions.

Capitalisme énergumène, 7–52. "Energumen Capitalism" (tr. Robin Mackay) in Robin Mackay and Armen Avanessian, eds., *The Accelerationist Reader*: 163–208. Falmouth: Urbanomic, 2014.
L'Acinéma, 53–69. [See *The Lyotard Reader* (1989): 169–80.]
Freud selon Cézanne, 71–94. "Freud according to Cézanne" (tr. Ashley Woodward and Jon Roffe), *Parrhesia* no. 23 (2015): 26–42.
La Dent, la paume, 95–104. "The Tooth, the Palm" (tr. Anne Knap and Michel Benamou), *SubStance* 5, no. 15 (1976): 105–10.
Esquisse d'une économie de l'hyperréalisme, 105–13. [See *Textes dispersés I/ Miscellaneous Texts I* (2012): 103–15.]
Adorno come diavolo, 115–33. "Adorno as the Devil" (tr. Robert Hurley), *Telos* no. 19 (Spring 1974): 127–37.
Sur une figure de discours, 135–56. [See *Toward the Postmodern* (1993): 12–26.]
"L'Eau prend le ciel": Proposition de collage pour figurer le désir bachelardien, 157–78.
Petite économie libidinale d'un dispositif narratif: La Régie Renault raconte le meurtre de P. Overney, 179–224. [See *The Lyotard Reader and Guide* (2006): 200–30.]
En attendant Guiffrey (Quatre pièces pour un abstrait), 225–36. [See *Textes dispersés II/Miscellaneous Texts II* (2012): 103–21.]
La Peinture comme dispositif libidinal, 237–80. [See *The Lyotard Reader and Guide* (2006): 302–29.]
Plusieurs silences, 281–303. [See *Driftworks* (1984): 91–110.]
Notes sur le retour et le capital, 304–19. "Notes on a Return and Kapital" (tr. Roger McKeon), *Semiotext(e)* 3, no. 1 (1978): 44–53.

Bibliography

"Esquisse d'une économique de l'hyperréalisme." *L'Art Vivant* no. 36 (February): 9–12. [See *Textes dispersés I/ Miscellaneous Texts* I (2012): 103–15.]

"Les Filles machines folles de Lindner." *L'Art vivant* no. 41 (July): 8–9. [See *Textes dispersés I/ Miscellaneous Texts* I (2012): 103–15.]

1974

Économie libidinale. Paris: Galilée. *Libidinal Economy* (tr. Iain Hamilton Grant). London: Athlone; Bloomington: Indiana University Press, 1993; re-issued London: Continuum, 2004; re-issued London: Bloomsbury, 2015.

"Par-delà la representation," preface to French translation of *The Hidden Order of Art* by Anton Ehrenzweig. *L'Ordre caché de l'art: Essai sur la psychologie de l'imagination artistique*. Paris: Gallimard. [See *The Lyotard Reader* (1989): 155–68.]

1975

"À propos du département de psychanalyse à Vincennes" (with Gilles Deleuze). *Les Temps modernes* no. 342 (January): 862–3. [See *Political Writings* (1993): 68–9; *The Interviews and Debates* (2020): 39–40.]

"L'Important, ce sont les 'intensités,' pas le sens" (interview with Christian Descamps). *La Quinzaine littéraire* no. 201 (1–15 January): 5–6. [See *The Interviews and Debates* (2020): 35–8.]

Le Mur du Pacifique, published with *Toil* by Michel Vachey, preceded by an introduction and *"Le Mur du Pacifique"* by Jean-François Lyotard, 9–56. Paris: Christian Bourgois. Re-edited as *Le Mur du Pacifique*, Paris: Galilée, 1979. *The Pacific Wall* (tr. Bruce Boone), Venice, CA: Lapis Press, 1990.

1976

"Un Barbare parle du socialisme" (with Bernard-Henri Lévy). *Le Nouvel Observateur* no. 584 (19 January): 52–3. [See *The Interviews and Debates* (2020): 41–3.]

"Petite mise en perspective de la décadence et de quelques combats minoritaires à y mener" in Dominique Grisoni, ed., *Politiques de la philosophie*, 121–53. Paris: Grasset. "A Brief Putting into Perspective of Decadence and of Several Minoritarian Battles to be Waged" (tr. Taylor Adkins), *Vast Abrupt* (March 12, 2018): 1–20, https://vastabrupt.com/2018/03/12/lyotard-brief-putting-perspective-decadence [accessed July 14, 2020.]

"Sur cinq peintures de René Guiffrey" [exhibition catalogue] Paris: Galerie Stevenson et Palluel, 5–10. [See *Textes dispersés II/ Miscellaneous Texts II* (2012): 122–35.]

"Sur la force des faibles." *L'Arc* no. 64: 4–12. Republished in *Jean-François Lyotard*, 19–36. Paris: Éditions Inculte, 2009. [See *Toward the Postmodern* (1993): 62–72.] A spoken version of this text was published in *Semiotext(e)* 3, no. 2 (1978): 204–14. (tr. Roger McKeon).

1977

Instructions païennes. Paris: Galilée. "Lessons in Paganism" (tr. David Macey). [See *The Lyotard Reader* (1989): 122–54.]

"Narrations incommensurables" (interview with Patrick de Haas). *Art Press International* no. 13 (December): 19. [See *The Interviews and Debates* (2020): 45–7.]

Rudiments païens: genre dissertif. Paris: Union Générale d'Editions. [See *Rudiments païens* (2011).]

    Apathie dans la théorie, 9–31. [See *Lyotard and Critical Practice* (2022): 141–50].

    Humour en sémiothéologie, 32–59. [See *Toward the Postmodern* (1993): 73–86.]

    Rétorsion en théopolitique, 60–80. [See *Toward the Postmodern* (1993): 115–24.]

    Faux-fuyant dans la littérature, 81–114. [See *Toward the Postmodern* (1993): 125–42.]

    Expédient dans la décadence, 115–56 [See "Petite mise en perspective de la décadence et de quelques combats minoritaires à y mener" (1976).]

    Futilité en révolution, 157–212. [See *Toward the Postmodern* (1993): 87–114.]

    Féminité dans la métalangue, 213–32. [See *The Lyotard Reader* (1989): 111–21.]

    Dissertation sur une inconvenance, 233–44. "Theory as Art: A Pragmatic Point of View" (tr. Robert Vollrath) in Wendy Steiner, ed. *Image and Code*, 71–7, Ann Arbor: University of Michigan Press, 1981.

Les Transformateurs Duchamp. Paris: Galilée. *Duchamp's Trans/formers* (tr. Ian Macleod), Venice, CA: Lapis Press, 1990; Re-edited as bi-lingual edition with preface by Herman Parret, 32–45 and epilogue by Dalia Judowitz, 239–55. Leuven: Leuven University Press, 2010.

"The Unconscious as Mise-en-scène" (tr. Joseph Maier), In Michel Benamou and Charles Caramello, eds., *Performance in Postmodern Culture*, 87–98. Madison, WI: Coda Press, 1977. Reprinted in Graham Jones and Ashley Woodward, eds., *Acinemas: Lyotard's Philosophy of Film*, 43–54. Edinburgh: Edinburgh University Press, 2017.

1978

"Endurance et la profession." *Critique* 34, no. 369 (February): 198–205. [See *Political Writings* (1993): 70–6.]

1979

Au Juste, with Jean-Loup Thébaud. Paris: Christian Bourgois. *Just Gaming* (tr. Wlad Godzich) with afterword by Samuel Weber, 101–20. Minneapolis: University of Minnesota Press, 1985. [See *Au Juste* (2006).]

Bibliography

"Entretien entre Jean-François Lyotard et Alain Pomarède." *Art Présent* no.8 (Spring): 3–11. [See *Lyotard and Critical Practice* (2022): 151–63.]

"Pour faire de ton fils un baruchello." In Gianfranco Baruchello, ed. *L'Altra casa: planches*, 9–15, Paris: Galilée. [See *Textes dispersés II/ Miscellaneous Texts II* (2012): 164–171.]

Rapport sur les problèmes du savoir dans les sociétés industrielles les plus développées. Québec: Conseil des universités. Published as *La Condition postmoderne: Rapport sur le savoir*. Paris: Les Éditions de Minuit. *The Postmodern Condition: A Report on Knowledge* (tr. Geoff Bennington and Brian Massumi) with additional appendix: "Answering the Question: What is Postmodernism?" (tr. Régis Durand), 71–82, and a foreword by Fredric Jameson, vii–xxi. Minneapolis: University of Minnesota Press, 1984. [See "Réponse à la question: qu'est-ce que le postmoderne?" (1982).]

1980

Des dispositifs pulsionnels. Paris: Christian Bourgois; second edition with "avertissement," i–iii. [See *Des dispositifs pulsionnels* (1973).]

"Deux Métamorphoses du séduisant au cinema." In Maurice Oleander and Jacques Sojcher, eds. *La Séduction*, 93–100. Paris: Aubier Montaigne. "Two Metamorphoses of the Seductive in Cinema" (tr. Peter W. Milne and Ashley Woodward) in Graham Jones and Ashley Woodward, eds., *Acinemas: Lyotard's Philosophy of Film*, 55–61. Edinburgh: Edinburgh University Press, 2017.

La Partie de peinture, with illustrations by Henri Maccheroni, Cannes: Maryse Candela. [See *Textes dispersés II/ Miscellaneous Texts II* (2012): 274–99.]

"Plusieurs manières, un seul enjeu." In *Tromeur: extraits, collages, répétitifs, documentations, collections* [Exhibition catalogue] Paris: Galerie Stadler. [See *Textes dispersés II/ Miscellaneous Texts II* (2012): 304–11.]

Sur la constitution du temps par la couleur dans les œuvres récentes d'Albert Ayme. Paris: Traversière. [See *Textes dispersés II/ Miscellaneous Texts II* (2012): 312–61.]

"Vincennes survivra-t-elle?" (with Christian Descamps). *La Quinzaine littéraire* no. 322 (1–15 April): 20. [See *The Interviews and Debates* (2020): 49–51.]

1981

"Discussions, ou: Phraser 'après Auschwitz.'" In Jean-Luc Nancy and Philippe Lacoue-Labarthe, eds., *Les fins de l'homme: à partir du travail de Jacques Derrida*, 283–315. Paris: Galilée. [See *The Lyotard Reader* (1989): 360–92, also *The Interviews and Debates* (2020): 53–8.]

"'The Works and Writings of Daniel Buren: An Introduction to the Philosophy of Contemporary Art." (tr. Lisa Liebmann), *Artforum* 19, no. 6 (February): 56–64. [Modified version, see *Que peindre?* (1987): 89–98.]

Bibliography

1982

"Monogrammes /Loin du doux" [exhibition catalogue Gianfranco Baruchello] Paris: Galerie Le Dessin. [See *Textes dispersés II/ Miscellaneous Texts II* (2012): 206-9.]

"Pierre Souyri: Le marxisme qui n'a pas fini." *Esprit* 61, no. 1 (January): 11-31. "A Memorial for Marxism" (tr. Cecile Lindsay) in *Peregrinations: Law, Form, Event*. 45-75. New York: Columbia University Press, 1988. [See *Peregrinations* (1988).]

"Presenting the Unpresentable. The Sublime" (tr. Lisa Liebmann), *Artforum* 20, no. 8 (April): 64-69. [See revised version *L'Inhumain* (1988): 131-40; *The Inhuman* (1991): 119-28.]

"Réponse à la question: Qu'est-ce que le postmoderne?" *Critique* no. 419 (April): 377-67. "Answering the Question: What is Postmodernism?" (tr. Régis Durand). [See *Rapport sur les problèmes du savoir dans les sociétés industrielles les plus développées* (1979).] Also "An Answer to the Question, What Is the Postmodern?" (tr. Julian Pefanis and Morgan Thomas et al.). [See *The Postmodern Explained to Children* (1992): 11-25.]

1983

Le Différend. Paris: Les Éditions de Minuit. *The Differend: Phrases in Dispute* (tr. Georges Van Den Abbeele). Minneapolis: University of Minnesota Press, 1988.

L'Histoire de Ruth, with Ruth Francken. Paris: Le Castor Astral. "The Story of Ruth" (tr. Timothy Murray). [See *The Lyotard Reader* (1989): 250-64; *Textes dispersés II/ Miscellaneous Texts II* (2012): 370-99.]

"On dirait qu'une ligne . . . " in Adami [Special Issue] *Repères*, Paris: Galerie Maeght. "It's as if a line . . . " (tr. Mary Lydon). *Contemporary Literature* 29, no. 3 (1988): 457-82. [Modified version, see *Que peindre?*: 37-48.]

1984

L'Assassinat de l'expérience par la peinture: Monory. Paris: Le Castor Astral. *The Assassination of Experience by Painting, Monory* (tr. Rachel Bowlby) with preface by Herman Parret, 28-47 and epilogue by Sarah Wilson, 226-53, bilingual edition. Leuven: Leuven University Press, 2013.

Driftworks, ed. Roger McKeon, with introduction by Roger McKeon, 1-7. New York: Semiotext(e).

Adrift (tr. Roger McKeon), 9-17. [See *Dérive* (1973): 5-21.]

On Theory: An Interview (edited and tr. Roger McKeon), 19-33. [See *Dérive* (1973): 210-95.]

Jewish Oedipus (tr. Susan Hanson), 35-55. [See *Dérive* (1973): 167-88.]

The Connivances of Desire with the Figural (tr. Anne Knab), 57-68. [See *Discours, figure* (1971): 271-9.]

Bibliography

Notes on the Critical Function of the Work of Art (tr. Susan Hanson), 69–83. [See *Dérive* (1973): 230–47.]
Gift of Organs (tr. Richard Lockwood), 85–9. [See *Dérive* (1973): 47–52.]
Several Silences (tr. Joseph Maier), 91–110. [See *Des dispositifs* (1973): 281–303.]
Appendice svelte à la question postmoderne, 77–87. [See *Political Writings* (1993): 25–9.]
"Figure forclose." *Écrit du temps* no. 5 (Winter): 65–105. [See *The Lyotard Reader* (1989): 69–110.]
"L'Instant, Newman." In Michel Baudson, ed. *L'Art et le temps. Regards sur la quatrième dimension* [exhibition catalogue]. Brussels: Palais des Beaux-Arts, 99–105. [See *L'Inhumain* (1988): 89–99; *The Lyotard Reader* (1989): 240–9; *The Inhuman* (1991): 78–88; *Textes dispersés II/ Miscellaneous Texts II* (2012): 424–43.]
"Interview: Jean-François Lyotard" (with Georges Van Den Abbeele). *diacritics* 14, no. 3 (Autumn): 15–21. [See *The Interviews and Debates* (2020): 59–66.]
"Plaidoyer pour la métaphysique: 'Passage du témoin' de Jacques Derrida à Jean-François Lyotard" (with Jacques Derrida). *Le Monde* [*Aujourd'hui*] no. 12366 (October 28–29, 1984): xi. [See *The Interviews and Debates* (2020): 67–70.]
"The Sublime and the Avant-Garde" (tr. Lisa Liebmann), *Artforum* 22, no. 8 (April): 64–9. [See revised version *L'Inhumain* (1988): 101–18; *The Lyotard Reader* (1989): 196–211; *The Inhuman* (1991): 89–107.]
Tombeau de l'intellectuel et autres papiers. Paris: Galilée.
   Tombeau de l'intellectuel, 11–22. [See *Political Writings* (1993): 3–7.]
   Le Différend, 23–31. [See *Political Writings* (1993): 8–10.]
   Pour une non-politique culturelle, 35–40. [See *Political Writings* (1993): 11–13.]
   Nouvelles technologies, 43–56. [See *Political Writings* (1993): 14–18.]
   Wittgenstein, "après," 59–66. [See *Political Writings* (1993): 19–22.]
   Les modes intellectuelles, 69–73. [See *Political Writings* (1993): 23–4.]

1985

"Anamnèse du visible, ou: la franchise." In *Adami* [exhibition catalogue]: 50–60. Paris: Centre Georges Pompidou, 1985. [See *The Lyotard Reader* (1989): 220–39; re-edited with additions as "La Franchise" and "L'Anamnèse" in *Que Peindre?* (1987), vol. I: 49–66.]
"L'Attraction." In *Jean-Luc Parant. Cent mille et une boules* [exhibition catalogue]. Paris: Castor Astral. [See *Textes dispersés II/ Miscellaneous Texts II* (2012): 444–9.]
"Histoire universelle et différences culturelles." *Critique* 41, no. 456 (May): 559–68. [See *The Lyotard Reader* (1989): 314–23.]
"*Les Immatériaux*: A Conversation" with Bernard Blistène, *Flash Art* no. 121 (March): 32–9. [See *The Interviews and Debates* (2020): 77–85.]

"*Les Immatériaux*: un entretien avec Jean-François Lyotard" with Jacques Saur and Philippe Bidaine, *CNAC magazine* (March): 13–16. [See *The Interviews and Debates* (2020): 71–5.]
"Judicieux dans le différend." In Jean-François Lyotard, ed. *La Faculté de juger*, 195–236. Paris: Minuit. [See *The Lyotard Reader* (1989): 324–59.]
"Les Petits Récits de Chrysalide" with Élie Théofilakis, in Élie Théofilakis, ed. *Modernes et après: Les Immatériaux*: 4–14. Paris: Autrement. [See *The Interviews and Debates* (2020): 87–93.]
"La Philosophie et la peinture à l'ère de leur experimentation," in *L'Art des confins. Mélanges offerts à Maurice de Gandillac*, 465–77. Paris: Presses Universitaires de France, 1985. [See *The Lyotard Reader* (1989): 155–68.]

1986

L'Enthousiasme: La Critique kantienne de l'histoire. Paris: Galilée. *Enthusiasm: The Kantian Critique of History* (tr. Georges Van Den Abbeele), with translator's preface, ix–xiv. Stanford, CA: Stanford University Press, 2009.
Le Postmoderne expliqué aux enfants: Correspondance 1982–5. Paris: Galilée. *The Postmodern Explained to Children: Correspondance 1982–5* (tr. Julian Pefanis, Morgan Thomas et al.) London: Turnaround, 1992. Also published as *The Postmodern Explained: Correspondance 1982–5*, with an afterword by Wlad Godzich. Minneapolis: University of Minnesota Press, 1993.

1987

Que Peindre? Adami, Arakawa, Buren. 2 vols. Paris: Éditions de la Différence. Republished with preface by Bruno Cany and Postface by Gérald Sfez. Hermann: Paris, 2008. [See *Que peindre? /What to Paint?* (2012).]
"Sensus communis." *Le Cahier* (*Collège international de philosophie*) no. 3 (March): 67–87. "Sensus communis" (tr. Geoffrey Bennington and Marian Hobson) in Andrew Benjamin, ed. *Judging Lyotard.* 1–25. London: Routledge, 1992.

1988

"Débat general," in Guy Petitdemange and Jacques Rolland, eds., *Autrement que savoir: Emmanuel Levinas*, 67–95. Paris: Éditions Osiris; extract reprinted in Paul Audi, ed. *Logique de Levinas*, 75–90. Paris: Éditions Verdier, 2015. [See *The Interviews and Debates* (2020): 95–103.]
Heidegger et "les juifs". Paris: Galilée. *Heidegger and "the jews"* (tr. Andreas Michel and Mark S. Roberts) with foreword by David Carroll, vii–xxix. Minneapolis: University of Minnesota Press, 1990.
L'Inhumain: Causeries sur le temps. Paris: Galilée. *The Inhuman: Reflections on Time* (tr. Geoffrey Bennington and Rachel Bowlby), Stanford, CA: Stanford University Press, 1991.

Bibliography

"L'Intérêt du sublime," in Jean-François Courtine et al. *Du sublime*, 149–77. Paris: Belin. "The Interest of the Sublime" (tr. Jeffrey S. Librett) in *Of the Sublime: Presence in Question*: 109–32. Albany: State University of New York Press, 1993.

"Les Lumières, le sublime" (interview with Willem van Reijen and Dick Veerman). *Les Cahiers de Philosophie* no. 5 (Spring), 63–98. [See *The Interviews and Debates* (2020): 105–27.]

Peregrinations: Law, Form, Event, including the afterword "A Memorial for Marxism" (tr. Cecile Lindsay), 45–75. New York: Columbia University Press, 1988. [See *Pérégrinations* (1990) and "Pierre Souyri: Le Marxisme qui n'a pas fini." (1982).]

"Réécrire la modernité." *Les Cahiers de Philosophie* no. 5 (Spring): 193–203. [See *L'Inhumain* (1988): 33–44; *The Inhuman* (1991): 24–35.]

"Scapeland." *Revue des sciences humaines* 80, no. 209 (January–March), 39–48. [See *L'Inhumain* (1988): 193–201; *The Lyotard Reader* (1989): 212–9; *The Inhuman* (1991): 182–90.]

1989

"Argumentation et presentation: La Crise des fondements." In André Jacob, ed. *Encyclopédie philosophique universelle*, vol. 1, *L'Univers philosophique*. Paris: Presses Universitaires de France, 738–50. [See "Argumentation and Presentation: The Foundation Crisis" (2013).]

"Cher François Lapouge. Je ne vous connais pas . . . ," in *Francis Lapouge* [exhibition catalogue] Le Havre: Théâtre de l'Hôtel de Ville, 2–3. [See *Textes dispersés II/ Miscellaneous Texts II* (2012): 450–5.]

"Fûts." In Michel Nuridsany, ed. *Daniel Buren au Palais-Royal*. Lyon: Art Edition. [See *Que peindre?/What to paint?* (2012)].

La Guerre des Algériens: Écrits 1956–63, with introduction by Mohammed Ramdani, 9–31. Paris: Galilée.

Note: Le Nom d'Algérie [1989], 33–8. [See *Political Writings* (1993): 165–70.]

La Situation en Afrique du Nord [1956], 41–50. [See *Political Writings* (1993): 171–8.]

La Bourgeoisie nord-africaine [1957], 53–62. [See *Political Writings* (1993): 179–86.]

Nouvelle Phase dans la question algérienne [1957], 65–76. [See *Political Writings* (1993): 187–96.]

Les Comptes du "gérant loyal" [1957], 79–86.

Mise à nu des contradictions algériennes [1958], 89–108. [See *Political Writings* (1993): 197–213.]

La Guerre "contre-révolutionnaire," la société coloniale et de Gaulle [1958], 111–9. [See *Political Writings* (1993): 214–20.]

Le Contenu social de la lutte algérienne [1959–60], 121–63. [See *Political Writings* (1993): 221–51.]

L'État et la politique dans la France de 1960 [1959], 165–96. [See *Political Writings* (1993): 252–76.]

Le Gaullisme et l'Algérie [1961], 199–209. [See *Political Writings* (1993): 277–85.]

En Algérie, une vague nouvelle [1961], 211–23.

L'Algérie, sept ans après [1962], 225–32. [See *Political Writings* (1993): 286–92.]

L'Algérie évacuée [1963], 235–83. [See *Political Writings* (1993): 293–326.]

"Lyotard et Vidal-Naquet: parler encore de la guerre d'Algérie" (with Pierre Vidal-Naquet, interview by Antoine de Gaudemar). *Libération* (9 November): 30–1. [See *The Interviews and Debates* (2020): 129–34.]

The Lyotard Reader, ed. Andrew Benjamin. Oxford: Blackwell.

Foreword (tr. David Macey), vi–xiv. [See *Moralités Postmodernes* (1993): 131–41; *Postmodern Fables* (1997): 149–62.]

The Tensor (tr. Sean Hand), 1–18. [See *Economie Libidinale* (1974): 57–115.]

The Dream-Work Does Not Think (tr. Mary Lydon), 19–55. [See *Discours, figure* (1971): 239–70.]

Passages from *Le Mur du Pacifique* (tr. Pierre Brochet, Nick Royle, and Kathleen Woodward), 56–68. [See *Le Mur du Pacifique* (1979).]

Figure Foreclosed (tr. David Macey), 69–110. [See "Figure forclose" (1984).]

One of the Things at Stake in Women's Struggles (tr. Deborah J. Clarke with Winifred Woodhull and John Mowitt), 111–21. [See *Rudiments païens* (1977): 213–32.]

Lessons in Paganism (tr. David Macey), 122–54. [See *Instructions païennes* (1977).]

Beyond Representation (tr. Jonathan Culler), 155–68. [See "Par-delà la représentation" (1974).]

Acinema (tr. Paisley N. Livingston), 169–80. [See *Des dispositifs pulsionnels* (1973): 53–69.]

Philosophy and Painting in the Age of Their Experimentation. Contribution to an Idea of Postmodernity (tr. Mária Minich Brewer and Daniel Brewer), 181–95. [See "La philosophie et la peinture à l'ère de leur expérimentation" (1985).]

The Sublime and the Avant-Garde (tr. Lisa Liebmann, Geoff Bennington and Marian Hobson), 196–211. [See *The Inhuman* (1991): 89–107.]

Scapeland (tr. David Macey), 212–9. [See *The Inhuman* (1991): 182–90.]

Anamnesis of the Visible, or Candour (tr. David Macey), 220–39. [See "Anamnèse du visible, ou: la franchise" (1985).]

Newman: The Instant (tr. David Macey), 240–9. [See *The Inhuman* (1991): 78–88.]

The Story of Ruth (tr. Timothy Murray), 250–64. [See *L'Histoire de Ruth* (1983).]

Analysing Speculative Discourse as Language-Game [1981] (tr. Geoff Bennington), 265–74.

Levinas' Logic [1978] (tr. Ian McLeod), 275–313. [See *Logique de Levinas* (2015): 19–74.]

Universal History and Cultural Differences (tr. David Macey), 314–23. [See "Histoire universelle et différences culturelles" (1985)].

Bibliography

Judiciousness in Dispute, or Kant after Marx (tr. Cecile Lindsay), 324–59. [See "Judicieux dans la différend" (1985).]
Discussions, or Phrasing "after Auschwitz" (tr. Georges Van Den Abbeele), 360–92. [See "Discussions, ou: Phraser 'après Auschwitz'" (1981).]
The Sign of History [1982] (tr. Geoff Bennington), 393–411.

1990

"Notes du traducteur." *Revue philosophique de la France et de l'étranger* 180, no. 2 (April–June): 285–92. "Translator's Notes" (tr. Roland-François Lack), *Pli: Warwick Journal of Philosophy* no. 6 (Summer 1997): 51–7.
"Painting Right on It" (tr. Geoffrey Bennington). *Blank Page* no. 4 (June), n.p. [See *Textes dispersés II/ Miscellaneous Texts II* (2012): 508–15.]
Pérégrinations: Loi, forme, événement, transcribed from the American by Jean-François Lyotard, including the afterword "Pierre Souyri: Le marxisme qui n'a pas fini." Paris: Galilée, 1990. [See *Peregrinations* (1988).]

1991

"Before the Law, After the Law," interview with Elisabeth Weber [1991], in Elisabeth Weber, *Questioning Judaism: Interviews by Elisabeth Weber* (tr. Rachel Bowlby): 104–21. Stanford: Stanford University Press, 2004. [See *The Interviews and Debates* (2020): 135–47.]
"La Brûlure du silence," in *Ruth Francken: Mirrorical Returns, Hostages and Wittgenstein Variations* [exhibition catalogue] Metz: Musée du Metz, 11–36. [See *Textes dispersés II/ Miscellaneous Texts II* (2012): 400–23.]
"La Face des choses," in *François Lapouge* [exhibition catalogue] Le Havre: Théatre de l'Hôtel de Ville. [See *Textes dispersés II/ Miscellaneous Texts II* (2012): 456–69.]
"Foreword after the Words," in Joseph Kosuth, *Art after Philosophy and After: Collected Writings 1966-90*. Cambridge MA: MIT Press, xv–xviii. [See *Textes dispersés II/ Miscellaneous Texts II* (2012): 418–27.]
The Inhuman: Reflections on Time (tr. Geoffrey Bennington and Rachel Bowlby), Stanford, CA: Stanford University Press. [See *L'Inhumain* (1988).]
Leçons sur l'Analytique du sublime. Paris: Galilée. *Lessons on the Analytic of the Sublime* (tr. Elizabeth Rottenberg), Stanford, CA: Stanford University Press, 1994.
Lectures d'enfance. Paris: Galilée. *Readings in Infancy* (tr. Robert Harvey et al.) with foreword by Robert Harvey and afterword by Kiff Bamford, eds. London and New York: Bloomsbury Academic, 2023.

1992

"Probes: Lino Centi's "Timbres" (tr. the journal). *Art & Design* (December): 73–80. [*See Textes dispersés II/ Miscellaneous Texts II* (2012): 532–41.]

"That Which Resists After All (an interview with Gilbert Larochelle)." *Philosophy Today* 36, no. 4 (Winter): 402–17.

1993

"Généalogie de la touche." In *Henri Martin* [exhibition catalogue], 13–38. Cahors: Musée Henri Martin / Toulouse: Capitole. [See *Textes dispersés II/ Miscellaneous Texts II* (2012): 594–611.]

Libidinal Economy (tr. Iain Hamilton Grant), London: Athlone; re-issued London: Continuum, 2004; re-issued London: Bloomsbury, 2015. [See *Économie libidinale* (1974).]

Moralités postmodernes. Paris: Galilée. *Postmodern Fables* (tr. Georges Van Den Abbeele). Minneapolis: University of Minnesota Press, 1997.

"The Other's Rights" (tr. Chris Miller and Robert Smith), in Stephen Shute and Susan Hurley, eds., *On Human Rights: The Oxford Amnesty Lectures 1993*, 135–47. New York: Basic Books. [See *Lyotard and Critical Practice* (2022): 75–81.]

Political Writings, foreword by Bill Readings (tr. Bill Readings and Kevin Paul Geiman). Minneapolis: University of Minnesota Press.
 Tomb of the Intellectual, 3–7. [See *Tombeau de l'intellectuel* (1984): 11–22.]
 The Differend, 8–10. [See *Tombeau de l'intellectuel* (1984): 23–31.]
 For a Cultural Nonpolicy, 11–13. [See *Tombeau de l'intellectuel* (1984): 35–40.]
 New Technologies, 14–18. [See *Tombeau de l'intellectuel* (1984): 43–56.]
 Wittgenstein "After," 19–22. [See *Tombeau de l'intellectuel* (1984): 59–66.]
 Intellectual Fashions, 23–4. [See *Tombeau de l'intellectuel* (1984): 69–73.]
 A Svelte Appendix to the Postmodern Question, 25–9. [See *Tombeau de l'intellectuel* (1984): 77–87.]
 Dead Letter [1962], 33–40.
 Preamble to a Charter, 41–5. [See *Dérive* (1973): 22–9.]
 Nanterre, Here, Now, 46–59. [See *Dérive* (1973): 189–210.]
 March 23, 60–7. [See *Dérive* (1973): 305–16.]
 Concerning the Vincennes Psychoanalysis Department, 68–9. [See "À propos du département de psychanalyse à Vincennes," (1975).]
 Endurance and the Profession, 70–6. [See "Endurance et la profession" (1978).]
 Ersiegerungen [1989], 77–82.
 Born in 1925, 85–9. [See "Nés en 1925" (1948).]
 A Podium without a Podium: Television According to J.-F. Lyotard [1978], 90–5.
 Oikos [1988], 96–107.
 The General Line (for Gilles Deleuze) [1990], 108–11. [See *Moralités postmodernes* (1993): 105–10; *Postmodern Fables* (1997): 115–22.]
 The Wall, the Gulf, and the Sun [1990], 112–23. [See *Moralités postmodernes* (1993): 65–77; *Postmodern Fables* (1997): 67–83.]
 German Guilt, 127–34. [See "La Culpabilité Allemande" (1948).]
 Heidegger and "the jews": A Conference in Vienna and Freiburg [1989], 135–47.

Bibliography

The Grip (*Mainmise*), 148–58. [See *Un trait d'union* (1993): 5–19; *Misère de la Philosophie* (2000): 119–32.]

Europe, the Jews, and the Book [1990], 159–62.

The Name of Algeria, 165–70. [See *La Guerre des Algériens* (1989): 33–8.]

The Situation in North Africa, 171–81. [See *La Guerre des Algériens* (1989): 41–50.]

The North African Bourgeoisie, 179–86. [See *La Guerre des Algériens* (1989): 53–62.]

A New Phase in the Algerian Question, 187–96. [See *La Guerre des Algériens* (1989): 65–76.]

Algerian Contradictions Exposed, 197–213. [See *La Guerre des Algériens* (1989): 89–108.]

The "Counterrevolutionary" War, Colonial Society, and de Gaulle, 214–20. [See *La Guerre des Algériens* (1989): 111–19.]

The Social Content of the Algerian Struggle, 221–51. [See *La Guerre des Algériens* (1989): 121–63.]

The State and Politics in the France of 1960, 252–76. [See *La Guerre des Algériens* (1989): 165–96.]

Gaullism and Algeria, 277–85. [See *La Guerre des Algériens* (1989): 199–209.]

Algeria: Seven Years After, 286–92. [See *La Guerre des Algériens* (1989): 225–32.]

Algeria Evacuated, 293–326. [See *La Guerre des Algériens* (1989): 235–83.]

Sam Francis: Lessons of Darkness – Like the Paintings of a Blind Man (tr. Geoffrey Bennington). Los Angeles: Lapis Press. [See *Sam Francis. Leçon de Ténèbres / Sam Francis. Lesson of Darkness* (2010)].

Toward the Postmodern. Robert Harvey and Mark S. Roberts, eds. Atlantic Highlands NJ: Humanities Press.

The Psychoanalytic Approach to Artistic and Literary Expression (tr. Anonymous), 2–11. [See *Dérive* (1973): 53–77.]

On a Figure of Discourse (tr. Mark S. Roberts), 12–26. [See *Des dispositifs pulsionnels* (1973): 135–56.]

Jewish Oedipus (tr. Susan Hanson), 27–40. [See *Dérive* (1973): 167–88.]

"A Few Words to Sing" (tr. Leonard R. Lawlor), 41–59. [See *Dérive* (1973): 248–71.]

On the Strength of the Weak (tr. Fred J. Evans), 62–72. [See "Sur la force des faibles" (1976).]

Humor in Semiotheology (tr. Mira Kamdar), 73–86. [See *Rudiments païens* (1977): 32–59.]

Futility in Revolution (tr. Kenneth Berri), 87–114. [See *Rudiments païens* (1977): 157–212.]

Retortion in Theopolitics (tr. Mira Kamdar), 115–24. [See *Rudiments païens* (1977): 60–80.]

False Flights in Literature (tr. Robert Harvey), 125–42. [See *Rudiments païens* (1977): 81–114.]

The Survivor (tr. Robert Harvey and Mark S. Roberts), 144–63. [See *Lectures d'enfance* (1991): 59–87.]

On What Is "Art" (tr. Robert Harvey), 164–75. [See *Lectures d'enfance* (1991): 109–26.]
Prescription (tr. Christopher Fynsk), 176–91. [See *Lectures d'enfance* (1991): 35–56.]
Return Upon Return (tr. Robert Harvey and Mark S. Roberts), 192–206. [See *Lectures d'enfance* (1991): 11–33.]
Un trait d'union. with Eberhard Gruber. Saint-Foy, Québec: Éditions le Griffon d'Argile. [See *The Hyphen* (1999), with additional "Responding Questions."]

1994

Dérive à partir de Marx et Freud. Paris: Galilée, re-edited with new introduction, seven chapters removed. [See *Dérive* (1973).]
[Introduction] 9–10.
Dérives, 11–23. [See *Driftworks* (1984): 9–17.]
Un Marx non marxiste, 25–33.
La place de l'aliénation dans le retournement marxiste, 35–105.
Le 23 mars, 107–15. [See *Political Writings* (1993): 60–7.]
Principales tendances actuelles de l'étude psychanalytique des expressions artistiques et littéraires, 117–37. [See *Toward the Postmodern* (1993): 2–11.]
Espace plastique et espace politique, 139–61. "Plastic Space and Political Space" (tr. Mark S. Roberts), *boundary 2* 14, no. 1–2 (Autumn 1985–Winter 1986): 211–23.
"A Few Words to Sing" Sequenza III, 163–82. [See *Toward the Postmodern* (1993): 41–59].
Œdipe juif, 183–99. [See *Driftworks* (1984): 35–55.]
Des dispositifs pulsionnels. Paris: Galilée, re-edited edition with "Avis de déluge" [1993], 9–15; and "avertissement" [1979], 17–19; two chapters removed: "Esquisse d'une économie de l'hyperréalisme" and "La Peinture comme dispositif libidinal." [See *Des dispositifs pulsionnels* (1973).]
"Nietzsche and the Inhuman" (with Richard Beardsworth). *Journal of Nietzsche Studies* 7 (1994): 67–130.
"Resistances: A Conversation of Sergio Benvenuto with Jean-François Lyotard." [1994] *JEP: European Journal of Psychoanalysis* 2 (1995–1996): n.p. http://www.psychomedia.it/jep/number24/lyotard.htm [accessed July 14, 2020.]
"Le Vœu." In *Gigliola Fazzini*. [exhibition catalogue] Paris: Galerie J. & J. Donguy. [See *Textes dispersés II/ Miscellaneous Texts II* (2012): 542–9.]

1995

"L'Extrême réel" with Gérald Sfez. *Rue Descartes* no. 12–13 (May), 200–4. [See *The Interviews and Debates* (2020): 169–72.]
"Nécessité de Lazare," in *Albert Ayme, Les nuicts: un exercise de style et six interventions sur trois couleurs*, Paris: Éditions Traversière, 58–69.

Bibliography

"Resisting a Discourse of Mastery: A Conversation with Jean-François Lyotard" with Gary A. Olson, *JAC* 15, no. 3, 391–410.

"Les Traces diffractées / Diffracted Traces," in Bracha Lichtenberg Ettinger. *Halala-Autistwork* [exhibition catalogue], bi-lingual edition, 22–31. Aix en Provence: Cité du livre / Jerusalem: The Israel Museum. [See *Textes dispersés II/ Miscellaneous Texts II* (2012): 550–61.]

"What is Just?" (*Ou Justesse*) with Richard Kearney, in Richard Kearney, *States of Mind: Dialogues with Contemporary Thinkers on the European Mind*. Manchester: Manchester University Press, 1995. 209–304. [See *The Interviews and Debates* (2020): 149–58.]

1996

"La male oreille," preface to Philippe Bonnefis, *Céline. Le Rappel des oiseaux*, iii–xiv. Paris: Galilée. "Foreword" (tr. Kristine Butler) in Philippe Bonnefis, *Céline. The Recall of the Birds* (tr. Paul Weidmann), ix–xx. Minneapolis: University of Minnesota Press, 1997.

"Musique et postmodernité." *Surfaces* 6, no. 203 (1996), 4–16. "Music and Postmodernity" (tr. David Bennett), *New Formations* no. 66 (2009): 37–45. [See *Textes dispersés I/ Miscellaneous Texts* (2012): 200–23.]

"Nécessité de Lazare." In Albert Ayme, *Les Nuicts. Un exercise de style*. Paris: Traversière, 57–69. [See *Textes dispersés II/ Miscellaneous Texts II* (2012): 350–61.]

Signé Malraux, Paris: Grasset. *Signed, Malraux* (tr. Robert Harvey), Minneapolis: University of Minnesota Press, 1999.

"La Vie de Malraux doit être lue comme recueil de legends," with Philippe Bonnefis. *Magazine littéraire* no. 347 (October): 26–8, 30. Reprinted in Martine Boyer-Weinmann and Jean-Louis Jeannelle, eds., *Signés Malraux: André Malraux et la question biographique*, 241–52. Paris: Garnier, 2015. [See *The Interviews and Debates* (2020): 173–8.]

1997

Flora Danica: La Secession du geste dans la peinture de Stig Brøgger. Paris: Galilée. [See *Textes dispersés II: /Miscellaneous Texts II* (2012): 627–43.]

"Mirótopos," in *François Rouan* [exhibition catalogue]. Paris: Galerie Daniel Templon. [See *Textes dispersés II: / Miscellaneous Texts II* (2012): 644–53.]

Postmodern Fables (tr. Georges Van Den Abbeele). Minneapolis: University of Minnesota Press, 1997. [See *Moralités postmodernes* (1993).]

1998

Chambre sourde: L'Antiesthétique de Malraux. Paris: Galilée. *Soundproof Room: Malraux's Anti-aesthetics* (tr. Robert Harvey), bi-lingual edition. Stanford, CA: Stanford University Press, 2001.

La Confession d'Augustin, with introduction by Dolorès Lyotard. Paris: Galilée.
The Confession of Augustine (tr. Richard Beardsworth). Stanford, CA: Stanford University Press, 2000.
Karel Appel: Ein Farbgestus, Essays zur Kunst Karel Appel mit einer Bildauswahl des Authors. Bern/Berlin: Gaschnang & Springer. [See *Karel Appel. Un geste de couleur / Karel Appel. A Gesture of Colour* (2009)].

1999

"Freud, Energy and Chance: A Conversation with Jean-François Lyotard" (with Richard Beardsworth). *Teknema: Journal of Philosophy and Technology* 5 (Fall): u.p. http://tekhnema.free.fr/5Beardsworth.html [accessed July 14, 2020.]
The Hyphen: Between Judaism and Christianity, with Eberhard Gruber (tr. Pascale-Anne Brault and Michael Naas), with "Responding questions" [1995], 73–83, and translator's foreword. Amherst, NY: Humanity Books. [See *Un trait d'union* (1993); *The Interviews and Debates* (2020): 159–67.]

2000

Misère de la philosophie, Dolorès Lyotard ed. Paris: Galilée.
Avant-propos by Dolorès Lyotard, 9–12.
Sensus communis, le sujet à l'état naissant, 15–41. [See "Sensus communis" (1987).]
La Phrase-affect (D'un supplement au *Différend*), 45–54. [See *The Lyotard Reader and Guide* (2006): 104–10; *Lyotard and Critical Practice* (2022): 67–73.]
Emma, 57–95. "Emma: Between Philosophy and Psychoanalysis" (tr. Michael Sanders with Richard Brons and Norah Martin), in Hugh J. Silverman, ed. *Lyotard: Philosophy, Politics, and the Sublime*: 23–45. New York: Routledge, 2002.
La Peinture, anamnèse du visible, 99–115. [modified version See "Anamnesis: Of the Visible" (2004); *Textes dispersés II: / Miscellaneous Texts II* (2012): 563–93.]
La Mainmise, 119–32. [See *The Hyphen* (1999): 1–12; *Political Writings* (1993): 148–58.]
D'un trait d'union, 135–51. [See *The Hyphen* (1999): 13–27.]
À l'écrit bâté, 155–74. "To Burdened Writing" (tr. Stephen Barker), in Rob Shields and Heidi Bickis, eds., *Rereading Jean-François Lyotard: Essays on His Later Works*: 73–80. Farnham: Ashgate, 2013.
François Châtelet, une philosophie en acte, 177–90.
Gilles Deleuze (*post-scriptum*), 193–6.
Conventus, 199–208.
Idée d'un film souverain, 211–21. "The Idea of a Sovereign Film" (tr. Peter W. Milne and Ashley Woodward), in Graham Jones and Ashley Woodward, eds., *Acinemas: Lyotard's Philosophy of Film*: 62–70, Edinburgh: Edinburgh University Press, 2017.

Bibliography

Au regard du réel, 225-35. [See *Textes dispersés II/Miscellaneous Texts II* (2012): 471-87.]
D'un chat (Malraux et la gloire), 237-56.
C'est-à-dire le supplice (Une glose de *L'Expérience intérieure*), 259-72.
Formule charnelle, 275-83.
Donec transeam, 287-98.
Parce que la couleur est un cas de la poussière, 301-7. [See *Textes dispersés II/ Miscellaneous Texts II* (2012): 655-67.]
"Pharaonne." *Obliques* [Special Issue] *Henri Maccheroni: 2000 photographies du sexe d'une femme*, Nyons, France: Le Magasin Universel, 17. [See *Textes dispersés II: / Miscellaneous Texts II* (2012): 302-3.]

2004

"Anamnesis of the Visible" (tr. Couze Venn and Roy Boyne). *Theory, Culture and Society* 21, no. 1 107-19. [See *Textes dispersés II / Miscellaneous Texts II* (2012): 562-93; modified version, see *Misère de la philosophie* (2000): 99-115.]

2006

Au Juste, with Jean-Loup Thébaud, re-issued with preface by Jean-Loup Thébaud [2006], 9-22. Paris: Christian Bourgois. [See *Au Juste* (1979).]
The Lyotard Reader and Guide. Keith Crome and James Williams, eds. Edinburgh: Edinburgh University Press.
Introduction by Keith Crome and James Williams, 1-20.
Introduction: Philosophy, by Keith Crome and James Williams, 23-33.
Taking the Side of the Figural (tr. Mark Sinclair), 34-48. [See *Discours, figure* (1971): 9-23.]
The Great Ephemeral Skin, 49-65. [See *Economie Libidinale* (1974): 9-30.]
Presentation [edited extracts], 66-82. [See *Le Différend* (1983): §94-151.]
The Postmodern Condition, chapters 10-12, 83-103. [See "*Rapport sur les problèmes du savoir* ... " (1979).]
The Affect-phrase (tr. Keith Crome), 104-10. [See *Misère de la philosophie* (2000): 45-54.]
Answering the Question: What is Postmodernism?, 123-32. [See "Réponse à la question: Qu'est-ce que le postmoderne?" (1982).]
Return upon the Return, 133-47. [See *Toward the Postmodern* (1993): 192-206.]
Soundproof Room, chapters 4-6, 148-64. [See *Chambre sourde: L'Antiesthétique de Malraux* (1998).]
Sendings (from *The Confession of Augustine*), 159-64. [See *La Confession d'Augustin* (1998): 91-103.]
Introduction: Politics and the Political, by Keith Crome and James Williams, 167-75.
The State and Politics in the France of 1960, 176-99. [See "L'État et la politique dans la France de 1960" (1960).]

Bibliography

A Short Libidinal Economy of a Narrative Set-up: The Renault Corporation Relates the Death of Pierre Overney (tr. Keith Crome and Mark Sinclair), 200–30. [See *Des dispositifs pulsionnels* (1973): 179–224.]

A Memorial of Marxism: For Pierre Souyri, 231–53. [See "Pierre Souyri: Le marxisme qui n'a pas fini" (1982).]

The Communication of Sublime Feeling, 254–65. [See *Leçons sur l'Analytique du sublime* (1991): 269–86.]

Time Today, 266–80. [See *L'Inhumain: Causeries sur le temps* (1988): 69–88.]

Introduction: Art-events by Keith Crome and James Williams, 283–92.

The Connivances of Desire with the Figural (tr. Anne Knab), 293–301. [See *Discours, figure* (1971): 271–9.]

Painting as a Libidinal Set-up (Genre: Improvised Speech), 302–29. [See *Des dispositifs pulsionnels* (1973): 237–80.]

Newman: The Instant, 330–8. [See "L'Instant, Newman." (1984).]

On What is "Art," 339–50. [See *Toward the Postmodern* (1993): 164–75.]

2009

Karel Appel: Un geste de couleur / Karel Appel: A Gesture of Colour, bi-lingual edition (tr. Vlad Ionescu and Peter W. Milne) with preface by Herman Parret, 15–21, and epilogue by Christine Buci-Glucksmann, 237–49. Leuven: Leuven University Press. [See *Karel Appel: Ein Farbgestus* (1998)].

2010

Sam Francis. Leçon de Ténèbres / Sam Francis. Lesson of Darkness, bi-lingual edition (tr. Geoffrey Bennington) with preface by Herman Parret, 20–31, and epilogue by Geoffrey Bennington, 216–223. Leuven: Leuven University Press. [See *Sam Francis: Lessons of Darkness* (1993)].

2011

Rudiments païens: genre dissertif. Republished with preface by Élisabeth de Fontenay, 7–16, and glossary by Gaëlle Bernard, 167–85. Paris: Klincksieck. [See *Rudiments païens* (1977).]

2012

Pourquoi philosopher? [1964] with présentation by Corinne Enaudeau, Paris: Presses Universitaires de France. *Why Philosophize?* (tr. Andrew Brown), Cambridge: Polity, 2013.

Que peindre? Adami, Arakawa, Buren / What to Paint? Adami, Arakawa, Buren. bi-lingual edition (tr. Antony Hudek) with preface by Herman Parret, 46–81,

Bibliography

epilogue by Gérald Sfez, 449–79, and two supplements. Leuven: Leuven University Press, 2012. [See *Que peindre?* (1987).]

Supplement I "Arakawa. Reserves of Spatial Events" (tr. Anne Boyman), 384–407, in *Constructing the Perceiver – Arakawa Experimental Works* [exhibition catalogue]. Tokyo: The National Museum of Modern Art, 1991.

Supplement II "Daniel Buren. Shafts" (tr. Antony Hudek), 408–17. [See "Fûts," (1989)].

Textes dispersés I: Esthétique et théorie de l'art / Miscellaneous Texts I: Aesthetics and Theory of Art, bi-lingual edition, with preface by Herman Parret, 18–29, epilogue by Jean-Michel Durafour, 252–64. Leuven: Leuven University Press.

Painting and Desire [1972] (tr. Vlad Ionescu and Peter W. Milne), 53–75.

Painting as a Libidinal Set-Up [partial], 77–101. [See *Des dispositifs pulsionnels* (1973), 237–52; full translation See *The Lyotard Reader and Guide* (2006): 302–29.]

Sketch of an Economy of Hyperrealism (tr. Vlad Ionescu and Peter W. Milne), 103–15. [See "Esquisse d'une économie de l'hyperréalisme" (1973).]

Beyond Representation [1974] (tr. Jonathan Culler), 117–45. [See *The Lyotard Reader* (1989): 155–68.]

Philosophy and Painting in the Age of Their Experimentation [1981] (tr. Mária Minich Brewer and Daniel Brewer), 147–75. [See *The Lyotard Reader* (1989): 181–95.]

Enframing of Art, *Epokhe* of Communication [1985] (tr. Vlad Ionescu and Peter W. Milne), 177–93.

On Two Kinds of Abstraction [1988] (tr. Vlad Ionescu and Peter W. Milne), 195–9.

The Inaudible. Music and Postmodernity [1991] (tr. David Bennett), 201–23. [See "Musique et postmodernité" (1996).]

The Pictorial Event of Today [1993] (tr. Vlad Ionescu and Erica Harris), 225–39.

Textes dispersés II: artistes contemporains/ Miscellaneous Texts II: Contemporary Artists, bi-lingual edition (tr. Vlad Ionescu, Peter W. Milne and Erica Harris), edited and introduced by Herman Parret, 32–52, epilogue by Dolorès Lyotard, 687–95. Leuven: Leuven University Press.

Luciano Berio: "A Few Words to Sing," Sequenza III, 56–93 [See *Dérive* (1973): 248–71.]

Richard Lindner: Lindner's Crazy Girls (tr. Vlad Ionescu and Peter W. Milne), 94–101. [See "Les Filles folles de Lindner" (1973).]

Waiting for Guiffrey (Four Pieces for an Abstract) (tr. Vlad Ionescu and Erica Harris), 102–21. [See *Des dispositifs pulsionnels* (1973): 225–36.]

On Five Paintings by René Guiffrey (tr. Vlad Ionescu and Erica Harris), 122–35. [See "Sur cinq peintures de René Guiffrey" (1975).]

Discussion with René Guiffrey about the Colour White, the Line and the Unpresentable (Fragments) [1982] (tr. Vlad Ionescu and Erica Harris), 135–63.

To Make a Baruchello of Your Son" (tr. Vlad Ionescu and Peter W. Milne), 165–71. [See "Pour faire de ton fils un baruchello" (1979): 17–18.]

Bibliography

Commentary to Baruchello's *Notebooks* [1980] (tr. Vlad Ionescu and Erica Harris), 172–206.
Far from Sweet (tr. Vlad Ionescu and Erica Harris), 206–9.
Essay on the Secret in Baruchello's Work [1984] (tr. Vlad Ionescu and Erica Harris), 210–49.
Discussion with Gianfranco Baruchello on Sweetness (excerpts) [1984] (tr. Vlad Ionescu and Erica Harris), 250–73.
Henri Maccheroni: A Game of Painting (tr. Vlad Ionescu and Erica Harris), 274–99. [See *La Partie de peinture* (1980).]
The Last Time (New York) [1981] (tr. Vlad Ionescu and Peter W. Milne), 300–1.
She-Pharaoh (tr. Vlad Ionescu and Peter W. Milne), 302–3. [See "Pharaonne" (2000).]
Riwan Tomeu: Several Ways, a Single Stake (tr. Vlad Ionescu and Peter W. Milne), 305–11. [See "Plusieurs manières, un seul enjeu" (1980).]
On the Constitution of Time through Colour in the Recent Works of Albert Ayme (tr. Vlad Ionescu and Erica Harris), 312–49. [See *Sur la constitution du temps par la couleur dans les œuvres récentes d'Albert Ayme* (1980).]
Fait pictural: Necessity of Lazarus (tr. Vlad Ionescu and Peter W. Milne), 350–61. [See "Nécessité de Lazare" (1995).]
Manuel Casimiro: Beyond Pathos [1985] (tr. Vlad Ionescu and Peter W. Milne), 362–9.
Ruth Francken: The Story of Ruth (tr. Timothy Murray), 370–99. [See *L'Histoire de Ruth* (1983).]
Sear of Silence (tr. Ronnie Halligan), 400–23. [See "La Brûlure du silence" (1991).]
Newman: The Instant (tr. David Macey), 424–43. [See "L'Instant, Newman" (1984).]
Jean-Luc Parant: Attraction (tr. Vlad Ionescu and Peter W. Milne), 444–9. [See "L'Attraction" (1985).]
"Dear François Lapouge ... " (tr. Hege Smith and Marc Gaudry), 450–5. [See "Cher François Lapouge ... " (1989).]
The Face of Things (tr. Vlad Ionescu and Erica Harris), 456–69. [See "La Face des choses" (1991).]
Looking at the Real (tr. Vlad Ionescu and Erica Harris), 470–87. [See *Misère de la philosophie* (2000): 225–35.]
Paradox on the Graphic Artist, 488–507. [See *Moralités postmodernes* (1993), 37–48; *Postmodern Fables* (1997): 33–47.]
Sam Francis: Painting Right on It (tr. Geoffrey Bennington), 508–15. [See "Painting Right on It (1990).]
"On André Dubreuil's Commode" [1991] (tr. Vlad Ionescu and Erica Harris), 516–17.
Joseph Kosuth: Foreword. After the Words, 518–31. [See "Foreword. After the Words" (1991).]
Sarah Flohr [No title, 1992] (tr. Vlad Ionescu and Peter W. Milne), 528–31.
Probes: Lino Centi's "Timbres," 532–41. [See "Probes" (1992).]

Bibliography

Gigliola Fazzini: The Vow (tr. Saverio Campione and Matteo Spender). [See "Le Vœu" (1994).]
Bracha Lichtenberg Ettinger: Diffracted Traces (tr. Elodie Picquet and Joseph Simas), 550–61. [See "Les Traces diffractées" (1994).]
Anamnesis of the Visible, 562–93. [See "Anamnesis of the Visible" (2004).]
Henri Martin: Genealogy of Touch (tr. Vlad Ionescu and Erica Harris), 594–611. [See "Généalogie de la touche" (1993).]
Michel Bouvet: The Announcement [1995] (tr. Unknown), 612–9.
Corinne Filippi: Syncopes, paysages / Syncopes, Landscapes [1997] (tr. Unknown), 620–5.
Flora Danica: The Secession of the Gesture in the Painting of Stig Brøgger (tr. Vlad Ionescu and Erica Harris), 626–43. [See *Flora danica: La Sécession du geste dans la peinture de Stig Brøgger* (1997).]
François Rouan: Mirótopos (tr. Vlad Ionescu and Peter W. Milne), 644–53. [See "Mirótopos" (1997).]
Pierre Skira: Because Colour is a Case of Dust (tr. Vlad Ionescu and Erica Harris), 654–67. [See *Misère de la philosophie* (2000): 301–7.]
Béatrice Casadesus: "Livre unique" [1997] (tr. Vlad Ionescu and Erica Harris), 668–78.

2013

"Argumentation and Presentation: The Foundation Crisis" (tr. Chris Turner), *Cultural Politics* 9, no. 2 (July): 117–43. [See "Argumentation et presentation: La Crise des fondements" (1989).]

2015

"After Six Months of Work . . . (1984)" (tr. Robin Mackay) In Yuk Hui and Andreas Broeckmann, eds., *30 Years after Les Immatériaux*: 29–66, Luphana, Germany: Meson Press.
Logique de Levinas. Paul Audi, ed. Paris: Verdier. [See *The Lyotard Reader* (1989): 275–313; *The Interviews and Debates* (2020): 95–103.]

2020

Jean-François Lyotard: *The Interviews and Debates,* edited and introduced by Kiff Bamford, 1–11. London: Bloomsbury Academic.
Letter to Jean-François Lyotard from Gilles Deleuze [c. 1975-6] (tr. Roger McKeon), 15.
On Theory: An Interview, with Brigitte Devismes [1970] (tr. Roger McKeon), 17–27. [See *Dérive* (1973): 210–29.]
"Doing Away with the Illusion of Politics" with Gilbert Lascault (tr. Kiff Bamford and Roger McKeon), 29–31. [See "En finir avec l'illusion de la politique" (1972).]

Bibliography

"The 'Intensities' are What Imports, Not the Meaning" with Christian Descamps (tr. Roger McKeon), 35–8. [See "L'important, ce sont les 'intensités,' pas le sens" (1975).]

Concerning the Vincennes Psychoanalysis Department, with Gilles Deleuze (tr. Bill Readings and Kevin Paul Geiman), 39–40. [See "À propos du département de psychanalyse à Vincennes" (1975).]

A "Barbarian" Speaks about Socialism, interview with Bernard-Henri Lévy (tr. Roger McKeon), 41–3. [See "Un barbare parle du socialisme" (1976).]

"Incommensurable Narrations," interview with Patrick de Haas (tr. Roger McKeon), 45–7. [See "Narrations incommensurables" (1977).]

Will Vincennes Survive? With Christian Descamps (tr. Roger McKeon), 49–51. [See "Vincennes survivra-t-elle?" (1980).]

Debate on "Discussions, or: Phrasing 'after Auschwitz'" [1980] with Jacques Derrida et al. (tr. Georges Van Den Abbeele), 53–8. [See "Discussions, ou: Phraser 'après Auschwitz'" (1981).]

"In reading your work . . . " interview with George Van Den Abbeele; including the short text "Decor" (tr. Georges Van Den Abbeele), 59–66. [See "Interview: Jean-François Lyotard" (1984).]

Philosophy: The Case for the Defence, interview with Jacques Derrida (tr. Roger McKeon), 67–70. [See "Plaidoyer pour la métaphysique" (1984).]

Les Immatériaux. "A Staging" with Jacques Saur and Philippe Bidaine (tr. Roger McKeon), 71–5. [See "*Les Immatériaux*: un entretien" (1985).]

Les Immatériaux. A Conversation with Bernard Blistène (tr. Unknown), 77–85. [See "*Les Immatériaux*: A conversation" (1985).]

Chrysalide's Little Narratives with Elie Théofilakis (tr. Roger McKeon), 87–93. [See "Les petits récits de Chrysalide" (1985).]

Otherwise than Knowing, debate with Emmanuel Levinas [1986], 95–103. [See *Logique de Levinas* (2016): 75–90.]

The Enlightenment, the Sublime, Philosophy and Aesthetics, interview with Willem van Reijen and Dick Veerman (tr. Roy Boyne), 105–27. [See "Les Lumières, le sublime" (1987).]

Lyotard and Vidal-Naquet. Talking about the Algerian War Still, with Pierre Vidal-Naquet (tr. Roger McKeon), 129–34. [See "Lyotard et Vidal-Naquet: parler encore de la guerre d'Algérie" (1989).]

Before the Law, After the Law, interview with Elisabeth Weber [1991], 135–47. [See "Before the Law" (1991).]

"What is Just?" (*Ou Justesse*) with Richard Kearney [1994], 149–58. [See "What is Just?" (1995).]

Responding Questions, with Eberhard Gruber (tr. Pascale-Anne Brault and Michael Naas), 159–67. [See *The Hyphen* (1999): 73–83.]

The Real Extreme, with Gérald Sfez (tr. Roger McKeon), 169–72. [See "L'extrême réel" (1995).]

"La Vie de Malraux (Malraux's life) must be read as a collection of legends," interview with Philippe Bonnefis (tr. Roger McKeon), 173–8. [See "La Vie de Malraux . . . " (1996).]

Bibliography

2022

Lyotard and Critical Practice. Kiff Bamford and Margret Grebowicz, eds. with introduction by Kiff Bamford and Margret Grebowicz, 1–11, afterword by Peter Gratton, 219–23. London: Bloomsbury Academic, 2022.

The Affect-phrase (from a Supplement to *The Differend*) (tr. Keith Crome), 67–73. [See *Misère de la philosophie* (2000): 45–54.]

The Other's Rights (tr. Chris Miller and Robert Smith), 75–81. [See "The Other's Rights" (1993)].

Apathy in Theory (tr. Roger McKeon), 140–51. [See *Rudiments païens* (1977): 9–31.]

"What we cannot reach flying we must reach limping . . . " *Art Présent*, interview with Jean-François Lyotard, Alain Pomarède (tr. Kiff Bamford and Roger McKeon), 151–63. [See "Entretien entre Jean François Lyotard et Alain Pomarède" (1979)].

INDEX

Abensour, Michel 115, 119 n.5
addressedness 22, 24, 92, 97–9, 104
Adorno, Theodor 37, 55, 113
Aesthetics/*aesthesis* 24–5, 27, 29–31, 33–4, 37, 103, 111, 128 n.41.
    See also Kant, Immanuel
    an-aesthetic 9
    negative aesthetics 24
affect 87, 92–9, 113, 117–18. *See also phōnē*
    address 94–5
    "The Affect-phrase" 115, 117
    debt of affect 100
    the time of now 104–6 (*see also* time)
Agamben, Georgio 110, 114–17, 133 n.14, 133 n.16
    "*Experimentum Linguæ*" 114–15
    Infancy and History 114–16
agent (*suppôt*) 31, 123 n.17, 123 n.17
aisthesis 29–31, 33–4, 37
Algeria 114
anamnesis 11, 16, 119–20 n.9. *See also* forgetting
animals 3, 93, 105, 117–18
Antigone 44
Arendt, Hannah 1, 33, 39–60, 109–11, 113
    Between Past and Future 52–3, 57
    "The Crisis in Education" 56
    Eichmann in Jerusalem 49, 51, 53
    The Human Condition 45–8
    The Jew as Pariah 48–9
    "The Hidden Tradition" 48
    The Jewish War 51
    natality 46–8, 54
    The Origins of Totalitarianism 52, 54, 58
    Rahel Varnhagen 50
Aristotle 62, 76, 90–4, 103, 115
    animal voice 115–16
    Poetics 103
    soul (*psychē*) 103, 116

Auerbach, Erich
    Mimesis 6, 8

Beckett, Samuel 61–2, 101, 105, 113, 117
    The Unnamable 11, 121 n.7
    Waiting for Godot 8
being and non-being 39, 42, 45, 51–2, 58, 60
Benjamin, Walter 10, 41, 48, 113
    Ursprung des deutschen Trauerspiels 160 n.37
betrayal 40–2
birth
    debt 44–5, 55
    infancy 1, 24, 33, 44, 59
    and the law 30
    ontology of (Arendt) 41–9
Blanchot, Maurice 1, 66
    De Kafka à Kafka 100, 132 n.24
blood 21–2, 25–7, 31
Blücher, Heinrich 59

Canetti, Elias 44
cat (pussycat…) 16
Celan, Paul 49, 113
Chalier, Catherine 55
Chomsky, Noam 76
Christianity 7
cognitive phrase 75–7, 80
Collège International de Philosophie (CIPh) 109–11, 115, 123 n.2, 129 n.4
consistency/inconsistency 5, 75, 80–6
Contat, Michel 64, 127 n.21

debt 13–14, 16, 25, 30, 48, 50. *See also* birth, infancy
deconstruction 5, 105
deictics 76, 78–9, 81, 93. *See also* Kripke, Saul
Derrida, Jacques 108–10, 113, 123 n.2
development 55–8

Index

differend   26–7
Duve, Thierry de   75, 111, 129 n.1

Eichmann, Adolf   51, 58
Enaudeau, Michel   70, 74, 108, 111, 128 n.41
entropy   42, 45–6, 49, 56
  neg-entropy   42

father, fatherhood   3–5, 7, 11–17, 98, 103–4
feminine, the   69
Fontenay, Élisabeth de   112, 118
forgetting   11, 16, 37, 41, 49, 54, 59, 112–14. *See also* anamnesis
Francken, Ruth (*Mirrorical Return*)   66
French Communist Party   69, 111, 126 n.3
Freud, Sigmund   1, 23, 33, 39, 42–3, 53, 56, 89–106, 109, 112–13
  Beyond the Pleasure Principle   42, 125 n.21
  the case study of Dora   99
  dissiezure   33, 83
  free association   83, 99, 105
  hysteria   89, 96
  Nachträglichkeit (after-effect)   94, 113, 115, 119 n.9
  "Notes upon a Case of Obsessional Neurosis [The Rat Man]"   90, 96, 99–100, 102–3, 105, 130 n.1, 130 n.3
    Ernst's [the Rat Man] voice   90, 99, 101–2
  "On Narcissism"   95
  unconscious, the   17, 23–4, 89, 93–6, 99, 116–17

Genette, Gérard   105
Guyotat Pierre   67, 127 n.27

Hegel, G.W.F.   39, 41, 44, 63
  Phenomenology of Spirit   7, 41
  sublation (*Aufhebung*)   39–40
Heidegger, Martin   40, 41, 113, 118. *See also* Lyotard, Jean-François, *Heidegger and "the jews"*
Heine, Heinrich   48–9
Himmler, Heinrich   54
Hitler, Adolf   53, 55
Hochhuth, Rolf (*The Deputy*)   49

Hollier, Denis
  The Politics of Prose   61, 63, 65–7, 74, 110–11, 129 n.60
home   1, 3, 5, 11–12, 48
Hungarian Councils   59
Husserl, Edmund   40, 69, 93. *See also* phenomenology

ideology   53, 56, 59, 90
infans   1, 118, 119 n.2
  in-fans   95, 115
inoperative   5, 10. *See also* Nancy, Jean-Luc
inscription   13, 21, 23, 25, 27, 30–4, 49, 89
intractable   21, 31–2, 34, 37, 105, 114
  the body of *aisthesis* 37 (*see also* Aesthetics/*aesthesis*)

Jesus Christ   8, 26, 29, 47–8, 95
Josephus (*The Jewish War*)   51
Joyce, James   1, 3–19, 62, 109–10, 113, 120 n.2
  Ulysses   3–19, 97
    Bloom, Leopold   4–6, 8, 10–16, 121 n.17
    Bloom, Molly   8, 11, 14, 97, 121 n.7
    Dedalus, Stephen   4, 12–15, 17–19
    displacements and correspondences with *Odyssey*   4
    Homeric motifs in   4–6
    wanderer [*métèque*]   5, 6, 10
Judaism
  Jewish theme (*Ulysses*)   6–11
  Jewish tradition   48, 50
  Jews   17, 49–50
  Torah   12, 122 n.21
Jung, Carl   100, 105
Junger, Ernst   55–6

Kafka, Franz   1, 21–37, 105, 108–10, 117, 123 n.3
  "Before the Law"   108, 123 n.2, 133 n.10
  The Castle   48, 57
  In the Penal Colony   21–37, 122 n.1
Kant, Immanuel   33, 40–1, 46, 75–6, 95, 108
  Critique of Practical Reason   46
  Critique of Pure Reason   24, 32, 86, 116, 123 n.2
    antinomy of reason   32

Index

Critique of the Power of Judgment 46, 50, 59, 85–6, 108
   "*as if*" clause 44–6
   sensus communis 59
   sublime feeling 87
Kripke, Saul 77

Lacan, Jacques 72, 85, 94, 116
Lacoue-Labarthe, Philippe 108, 113
Lanzer, Ernst (the "Rat Man"). *See* Freud, Sigmund
law
   and the body 24–6, 29, 34, 36–7
   of development 56
   former law (Kafka) 22, 25, 29, 35
   French law 29–30, 122 n.1
   Justice 29, 31–7
   Law, the 10
   moral law 21, 32
   of mortality 45–6
   statute of limitations 21, 29–30, 122 n.1
Lefort, Claude 61, 63–5, 111, 129 n.3. *See also* Sartre, Jean-Paul, "Reply to Claude Lefort"
Les Temps modernes 67. *See also* Sartre, Jean-Paul
Levinas, Emmanuel 95
listening 29, 44, 97, 101, 103, 113
   to listen 9, 16, 105
Longinus (*Peri hypsous*) 9
Lyotard, Jean-François
   "Affect-phrase (from a supplement to *The Differend*)" 115, 117
   The Differend 76, 82
   Discourse, Figure 112, 116, 129 n.70
   "Emma" 112, 115, 119–20 n.9
   Heidegger and "the jews" 110, 112–13, 133 n.10
   The Inhuman 119 n.6
   Toward the Postmodern 115

Malraux, André 62, 118
melancholia 24, 36, 41–2, 44–5, 51, 60, 104
   as loss of presence 41–2
memory. *See* forgetting
Merleau-Ponty, Maurice 64–5, 115
Meschonnic, Henri 70–1
modernity 7, 73

modern literature, art 9–10, 24, 70, 75, 107. *See also* Joyce, James; Sartre, Jean-Paul; Valéry, Paul
mourning 39, 41

Nancy, Jean-Luc 10, 108, 121 n.11. *See also* inoperative

Odyssey (Homer) 3–7, 10, 12, 17

paralogism 79, 95
Pascal, Blaise 43, 60
passibility 9, 30, 33, 83
phenomenology 39, 41, 67. *See also* Husserl, Heidegger
phōnē 92–100, 102–6, 117
politics 21, 31, 35, 37, 53, 113. *See also* Socialisme ou barbarie
   totalitarianism 52–6, 59
   postmodern 13
   Sartre's 62–4, 73
Ponge, Francis 73, 129 n.61, 129 n.70

resistance 21, 24, 29, 31, 36, 41, 51, 59–60, 87, 114
Rousset, David 59

Sartre, Jean-Paul 1, 61–74, 110–12. *See also* writing, Sartre's; time, of writing
   Bariona 68
   Being and Nothingness 61
   "The Communists and the Peace" 61, 62
   The Condemned of Altona 61–2
   Dirty Hands 61
   The Family Idiot 128 n.50
   The Imagination 66–7
   Nausea 69
      Roquentin, Antoine 66–8
   on poetry and prose 70–4
   politics of populism 65–6, 69
   "Reply to Claude Lefort" 62–5, 126 n.3
   The Roads to Freedom 62, 68, 126 n.8
      Troubled Sleep 62
   Saint Genet 70, 71
   Sketch for a Theory of the Emotions 69
   The Transcendence of the Ego 61
   What Is Literature? 70–1
   The Words 61–3, 65

Index

Schreber, Daniel Paul   91–2
sexual difference   16–18, 43, 53, 85, 115
Shakespeare
   Hamlet   5, 14, 18–19, 103–4
   Macbeth   96
Shoah   49–51
Socialisme ou barbarie   64, 111, 114, 126 n.3
soul, the   6, 10, 17–18, 42–4, 50, 57–8, 60. *See also* Aristotle
space-time   24, 77
Spartacus movement   59
Stalin   64
sublime (aesthetic of the)   9, 50–1, 85, 87. *See also* Kant, Immanuel

temporality   27, 47, 58, 93–4. *See also* time
   instant   40–1
   "now"   77–8
Thing, the (Lacan)   53–4, 94
time. *See also* temporality
   administered (Kafka)   57
   backward   5, 6, 18
   displaced   1–2, 6
   immemorial   17
   intemporal   33
   of judgment   27, 57

torsion   32
of writing   67–9
touch, touching   24–5, 69. *See also* inscription
   being touched   24, 33(*see also* a possibility)
   of the law   25
   re-touching   26, 34

Valéry, Paul   1, 75–87, 109, 111
   Introduction à la poétique   79–80
   La Soirée de Monsieur Teste   85
Verstraeten, Pierre   72, 128 n.53

"we"   22, 39–40, 49, 51, 113
Wiesel, Elie   50
witness, the   41, 45, 48, 73, 90, 94
   to bear witness   9–11, 18, 44, 57, 74, 100
   witnessing   10, 57, 75
writing   1, 11, 21. *See also* inscription
   as artistic operation   24, 75, 80
   commentary   21, 84
   Freud's   100–1
   Joyce's   4–5, 9–11
   in the penal colony (Kafka)   36
   Sartre's   68, 70, 72–4
   as witness   15, 18